It's Going VIRL Guide

Your personal

Cisco Virtual Internet Routing Lab Simulator

Configuration Guide

Physical routers…you don't need 'em…we've got 'em!

Physical switches…you don't need 'em…we've got 'em!

Physical firewalls…you don't need 'em…we've got 'em!

LT IT Services, LLC

Content available at LTITSERVICES.COM

It's Going VIRL Guide

Published by:
LT IT Services, LLC

Printed in the United States of America

ISBN-13: 978-0-692-10588-7

Warning and Disclaimer

All efforts have been made in the preparation of this book to ensure the accuracy of the information presented. However, the information contained within this book is sold without warranty, either express or implied. Neither the author nor LT IT Services, LLC and its dealers and distributors will be held liable for any damages caused or alleged to be caused directly or indirectly by this guide.

The information contained herein is based on the software releases, network topologies at the time of being written; as well as the author's experience. Due to technologies constantly changing, the configuration examples presented here may change. We hope you find the information provided here very helpful; however, we cannot be held responsible for any changes that may affect the applicability of the information provided.

The opinions expressed in this guide are those of the author and are not necessarily those of Cisco Systems, Inc. The author is not affiliated with Cisco Systems, Inc.

Trademark Acknowledgments

Trademarks that are used are without any consent and the publication of the trademark is without permission or backing by the trademark owner. All trademarks and brands within this guide are for clarifying purposes only and are the property of the owners themselves and are not affiliated with this document.

About the Author

Lyndon Tynes is the founder of LT IT Services, LLC. and a Senior Network/Security Engineer for a privately held IT firm. He has worked in the IT field since 1987 as a publications editor; as well as in desktop support, server administration, network and cyber engineer while along the way obtaining industry recognized accredited certifications:

- Cisco: CCNP/CCDA
- Cyber Security: EndPoint Security and Network Access Control, Vulnerability Assessment and Defending the Perimeter from Cyber Attacks
- Wireless: CWSP/CWNA
- Microsoft: MSCE
- Palo Alto: ACE8
- Novell: CNE
- ITILv3 Foundations

Besides writing this guide Lyndon is currently...and finally...pursuing the completion of his Cisco CCIE certification. His passion for the various aspects of IT has afforded him the ability to not only share his knowledge with many others – in varying capacities – but to demonstrate his competencies as an IT consultant and engineer in designing networks for small and large private firms as well as several government agencies. He has been blessed in being afforded the opportunity to lead installation teams in the design and installation of low- and high-side networks in US Embassies around the world.

Dedication

- To my beautiful wife, Karen, who encouraged me to keep this project going and who kept me company all the while.
- To my lovely daughter, Brianna, in designing the cover's graphic image. Thank you for showing me there's more to a guide than just words.
- Lastly, many thanks to my technical contributor, Samir Sarwary, who painstakingly verified the guide's content and flow. He made certain that each of you would be able to follow along just as easily.

CONTENTS

CHAPTER 1: Guide Overview

I decided to write this guide for three reasons: 1) there is a very limited number of books written on this subject, 2) the online material written by Cisco can be confusing to follow and 3) I believe in getting right to it – step-by-step - in allowing users of this software the ability to "get-to-using" the application. I knew I could write this material more precisely since I'm focusing on specific hardware, a specific OS, a specific VM platform, and a specific Virtual Internet Routing Lab Personal Edition v1.5.145 software (known as VIRL from herein forward) - rather than trying to cover the gamut of multiple hardware platforms, multiple OSes, multiple VM platforms, and multiple VIRL versions. That is why I call this a "guide" rather than a "book". I will guide you from start to finish in downloading, installing and configuring your software so that you can get to designing networks.

I've gone through the problems encountered with installing and configuring VIRL – and some of the accompanying add-ons that I'll be mentioning – even after purchasing previous VIRL reference material and looking over Cisco's various website links. I was frustrated because details were left out with both resources and I had to keep searching the Internet for answers. I was troubleshooting the installation and configuration more than I was using the application. You will not have to go through what I went through. You made the right choice. I've gone through all the pain points so that you will not have to. Every aspect of downloading, installing and configuring a single VIRL server installation WILL BE COVERED in this guide…and more.

What WILL NOT BE COVERED here is setting up a VIRL cluster configuration, but I will reference online resources to this and other features that you may want to learn more about.

Please keep in mind that each simplified lab created in this guide is to demonstrate a single particular feature that can be used in building your simulated topology; thus there is no need for me to create a single, all-encompassing, topology. I will though reflect on best practices when building a simulation. I feel that "piecemealing" you the different features or add-ons helps you to best retain the knowledge of using that feature at a later time. You can also simply revisit the section pertaining to a particular feature without having to read through pages of documentation that does not pertain to what you're trying to achieve.

When I first heard of Cisco releasing this software (for a considerable time they kept it in-house only) I knew I had to have it. Don't get me wrong, nothing beats having physical hardware to learn about switching and routing, along with the various services they provide. So if you can get your hands on a physical, managed switch or router, do it. You will have a better appreciation for how this software works and then realize that you can do nearly everything you need to in enhancing your CCNA through CCIE skills.

I could go on further about the benefits of this training platform software, but you're not here for that. You're here because:

- You've never used switching and routing simulation/emulation software and you want to experience what VIRL can do.
- You've used GNS3 in the past but now want to see if VIRL is better. Believe me…it is!
- You've been in the switching and routing field for some time but you can't keep buying the latest and greatest hardware in order to keep your skills sharp.

CHAPTER 2: Why is it Going VIRL?

Since its release in December 2014, VIRL's audience has exploded in transitioning to this training platform rather than continuing to use the well-established Dynamics GNS3 software. Why? Because Cisco engineers have been using this software since its inception, continue to use it and are at the forefront in recommending the upgrades so important in keeping the software's features in line with "true" production equipment features. Let's make another point perfectly clear about VIRL: although it supports many (and I do mean many) features exhibited in the "true" hardware platforms; it does NOT support all features.

With VIRL You Can

- Create models and what-if scenarios of real-world and future networks
- Automatically generate configurations
- Visualize protocols
- Use Cisco IOS network operating systems, with routers and switches
- Connect virtual and physical environments
- Study for Cisco and other 3rd party certifications

What Features Does VIRL Support?

Cisco's Virtual Product Features

Source: https://learningnetworkstore.cisco.com/virlfaq/features

Source: https://www.cisco.com/c/en/us/products/collateral/routers/asr-9000-series-aggregation-services-routers/datasheet-c78-734034.html

Here's a listing of features supported per Cisco virtualized platform:

List of Supported Features for IOSv

802.1Q, AAA, ACL, BGP, DHCP, DNS, EEM, EIGRP, EoMPLS, Flex Netflow + TNF, GRE, ICMP, IGMP, IP SLA, IPSec, IPv6, ISIS, L2TPv3, MPLS, MPLS L2VPN, MPLS L3VPN, MPLS TE, Multicast, NAT, NTP, OSPF, PfR, PIM, PPPoE, RADIUS, RIP, SNMP, SSH, SYSLOG, TACACS, TFTP, VRF-LITE

Features Likely to Work for IOSv

HSRP, VRRP, GLBP, EZVPN, QoS, LISP, ZBFW, Performance Monitor

List of Supported Features for IOSvL2

Layer-2 forwarding (auto-config'd), Switchport (auto-config'd), 802.1q trunk, 802.1q VLANs (auto-config'd), Spanning Tree (auto-config'd), Port-Channel (Pagp and Lacp), 802.1x passthrough, Port-ACLs, Dynamic Arp Inspection, DHCP Snooping, IP device tracking, Switched Virtual Interfaces, Layer-3 forwarding over SVIs, Routing protocol support, VTP v1-3, PVST, QoS, Inter-VLAN routing, VLAN Access Maps (VACLs / access control lists for VLANs), ACL functionality for both layer2 and layer3 protocol packets, Dynamic Trunking Protocol support, Switchport protected mode

List of Supported Features for IOS-XRv

IPv4, IPv6, BGP, MP-BGP, EIGRP, ICMP, OSPF, NTP, TFTP, MPLS, MPLS L3VPN, MPLS TE, ISIS, mVPN GRE / mLDP / P2MP TE, AAA, RADIUS, TACACS, SNMP, FLEX CLI, Multicast (PIM, MSDP, IPv6), Syslog, VLANs / QinQ (.1Q, .1AD), RPL, ACLs, SSH, VRF-LITE

List of Supported Features for NX-OSv

802.1x, AAA, AMT, BGP, CDP/LLDP, EIGRP, FHRP-HSRP, GLBP, VRRP, ICMP, IGMP, IPv4, IPv4/6, IPv6, ISIS, L3 Routing Protocols, LDAP, LISP, MLD, MSDP, NTP, OSPF, PIM/PIM6, Radius, RIP, SNMP, Syslog, TACACS+, VRF, XML/Netconf, NX-API

List of Supported Features for CSR1000v

802.1Q, AAA, ACL, BGP, DHCP, DNS, EEM, EIGRP, EoMPLS, Flex Netflow + TNF, GRE, ICMP, IGMP, IP SLA, IPSec, IPv6, ISIS, L2TPv3, MPLS, MPLS L2VPN, MPLS L3VPN, MPLS TE, Multicast, NAT, NTP, OSPF, PfR, PIM, PPPoE, RADIUS, RIP, SNMP, SSH, SYSLOG, TACACS, TFTP, VRF-LITE

Features Likely to Work for CSR1000v

HSRP, VRRP, GLBP, EZVPN, QoS, LISP, ZBFW, Performance Monitor

List of Supported Features for ASAv

Supported in single context mode only. Does not support multiple context mode.

Features Not Supported for ASAv

Clustering, Multiple context mode, Active/Active failover, EtherChannels, Shared AnyConnect Premium Licenses

List of Supported Features for NX-OS 9000v

Bash Shell, Guest Shell, SSH, RPM Installation, POAP, NXAPI, Puppet Integration (Native), Puppet Integration (Guest Shell), Chef Integration (Native), Chef Integration (Guest Shell), CDP, LLDP, BGPv4, BGPv6, OSPFv2, OSPFv3, EIGRP, RIP, L2 Switching Unicast, L2 Switching Broadcast, L2 Switching Multicast, MAC Learning, Static/Router MAC, Switchport, 802.1q Trunking, 802.1q Access, STP, L3 SVI, Subinterfaces, VXLAN, vPC, Port Channel

Features Not Supported (Not Tested) for **NX-OS 9000v**

QoS, BFD, ACL, Policy maps, ARP Suppression, SPAN, IGMP Snooping, AMT, LISP, OTV

List of Supported Features for IOS XRv 9000

NFV: virtual PE (vPE) and virtual RR (vRR)

Routing: BGP, OSPF, IS-IS, Static Routing, MPLS, and Label Distribution Protocol (LDP), RFC 3107

Encapsulations: IEEE802.1q VLAN, IEEE 802.1ad (QinQHigh Availability: Process-Restart, SMU, Bidirectional Forwarding Detection (BFD), BGP Prefix-Independent Convergence (PIC)

Data plane features: Hierarchical QoS (H-QoS), ACL, Lawful Intercept, and Unicast Reverse Path Forwarding (uRPF)

3rd Party Virtual Appliances

Source: **https://learningnetwork.cisco.com/docs/DOC-30476**

The above referenced URL provides guidance in implementing 3rd party VMs with VIRL. I have personally found that some of the parameters set (i.e., hw_ram) do not work as advertised. Experimenting with these parameters may/will be needed.

Importing 3rd party VMs into VIRL is a cookie cutter process. The process is performed the exact same way with the only difference being the parameters set in the cut-and-paste "import dynamic subtypes" information. To demonstrate, we'll be importing a Palo Alto firewall into VIRL.

CHAPTER 3: Software Downloads

As referenced on the cover of this guide I chose to work with:

- Microsoft Windows 10 (Home or Pro version)
- VMware Workstation 14 and later
- VIRL Personal Edition v1.5.145

Why? Simple:

- These two Windows versions are more widely used in homes and labs due to their cost.
- VMware Workstation is very affordable as well and easy to use.
- As for VIRL PE, well…it's more readily available to everyone than the VIRL Academic Edition. Even my wife didn't complain about the $199/yr price □

Microsoft Windows 10

Okay let's be honest here. Your system should already have Windows 10 installed. Hopefully you're also up-to-date in regards to its Windows updates and antivirus software, but I digress. The next screenshot shows you the version I'm using and a bit about the hardware it's running on.

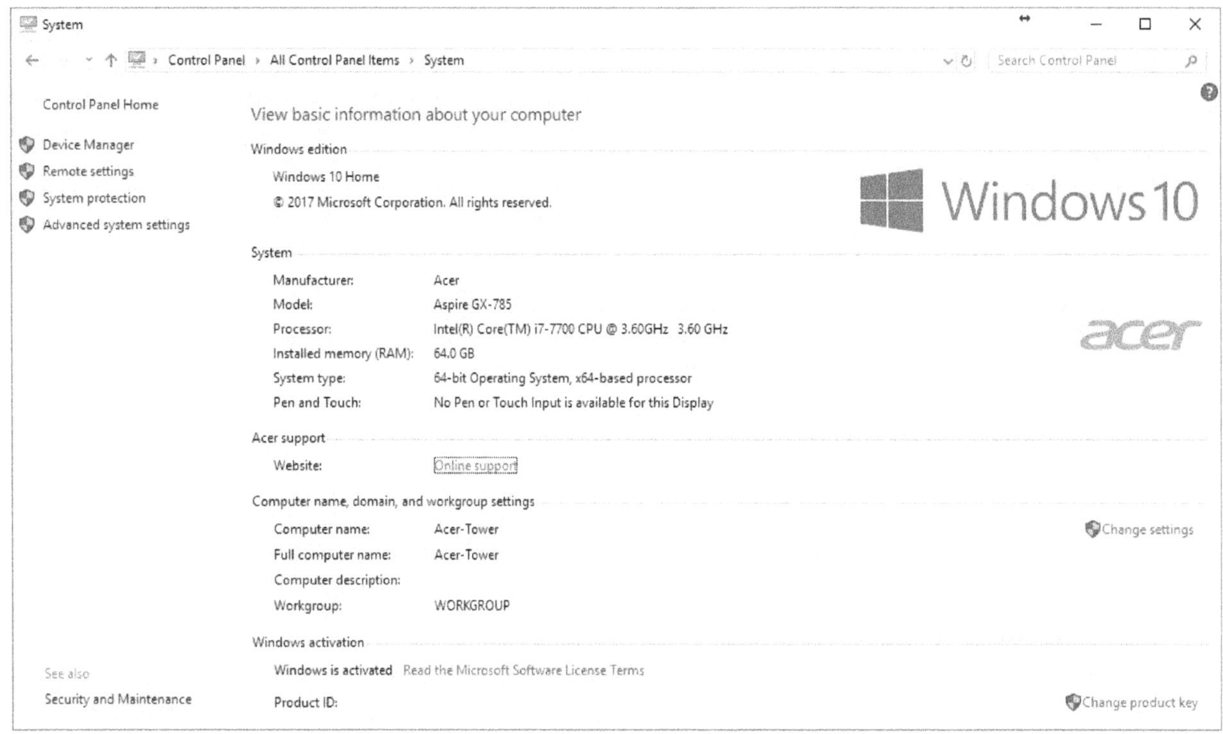

VMware Workstation 14

Now you could go directly to VMware's store at: https://www.vmware.com , click on Store, click on Products, and finally click on Workstation Pro **OR** go to Amazon.com and buy it for a fraction of that cost. I chose the latter. No I'm not getting kickbacks from Amazon for recommending them, but that would be nice.

If you purchased it from Amazon.com (my instructions are based on this) you'll receive an email with the download link as well as the license key. They'll also mail this information to you - not sure why but they do. Put this software and the license key in a directory somewhere for now. We'll come back to it later.

Cisco VIRL v1.5.145

Go to https://learningnetworkstore.cisco.com/virtual-internet-routing-lab-virl and click ***Add to Cart*** (as shown below).

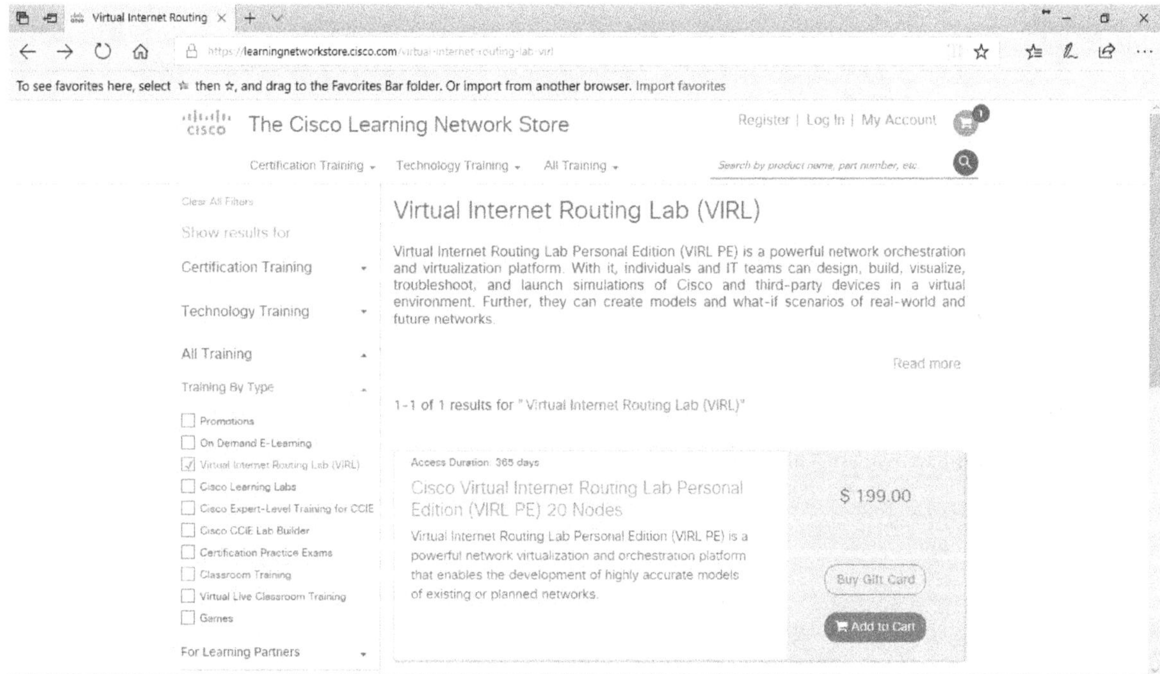

1. Now when you click the cart icon, shown above, unless you already have a Cisco account (which you can simply use to login and continue) you will have to create an account in order to continue (shown next). Go ahead and do that by clicking ***Register Now***.

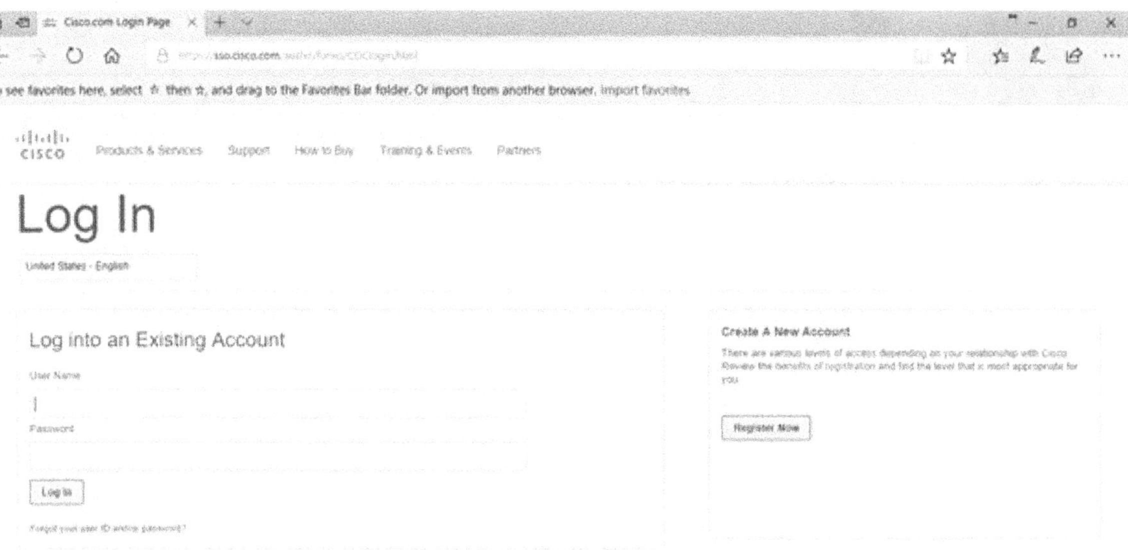

2. To keep this simple, leave ***Guest*** in the first field and fill in all the remainder fields respectively – making sure that you use a legitimate email address because you will receive an email for verification purposes.

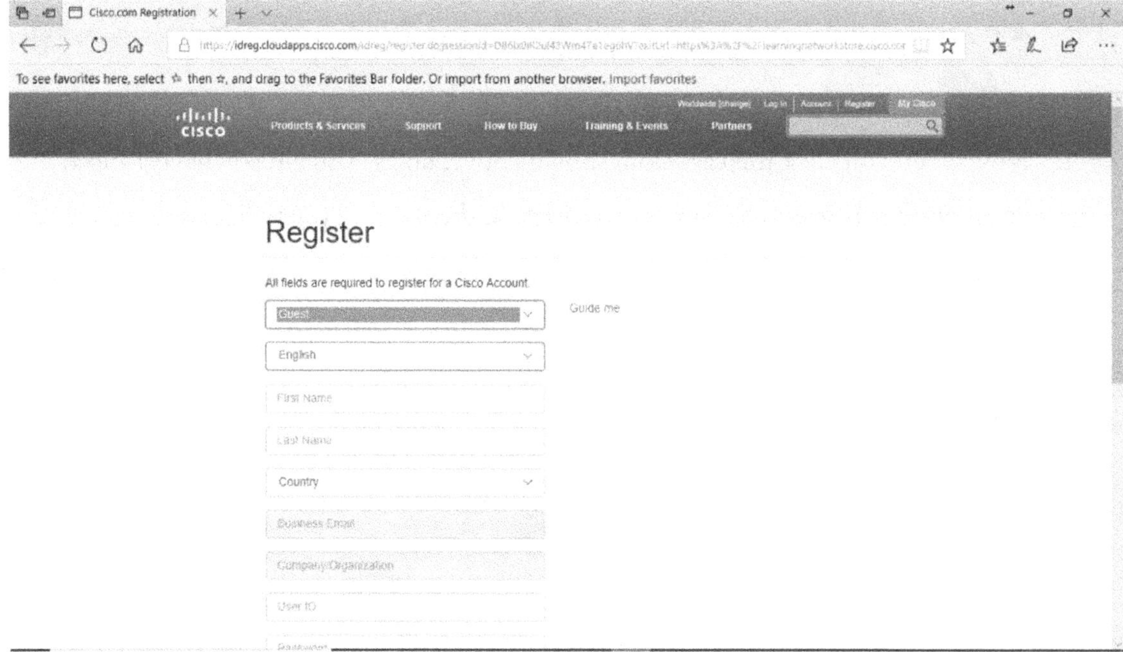

3. After responding to the verification email from adminsupport@cisco.com you should be able to login and see your shopping cart item. Click ***Proceed to Checkout*** to complete the purchase.

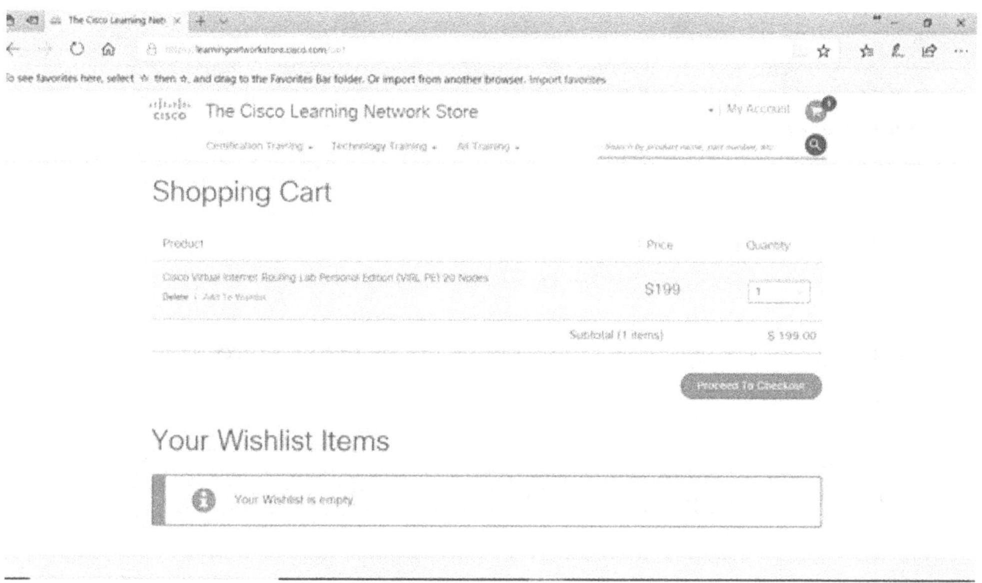

4. Once the payment goes through you should see something similar to this (next screenshot). As you see I actually ordered mine last year, but still entitles me to future

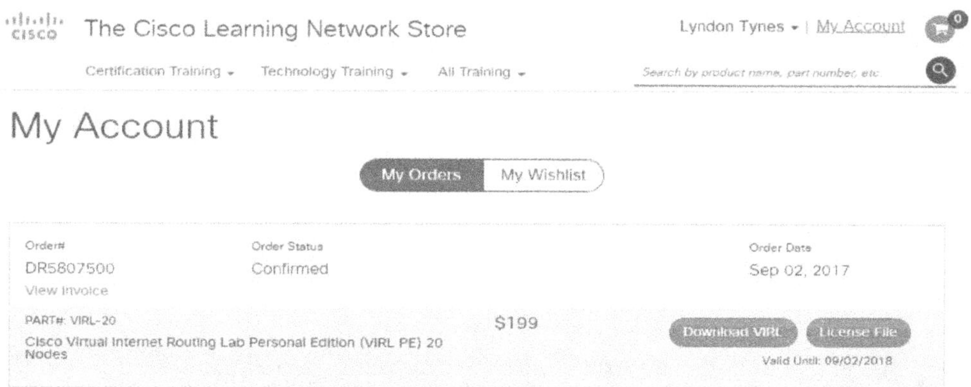

(more current) VIRL images, when available.

5. Click ***License File*** to download the license. This file has a .PEM extension.

6. Click ***Download VIRL*** and then download the image shown next.

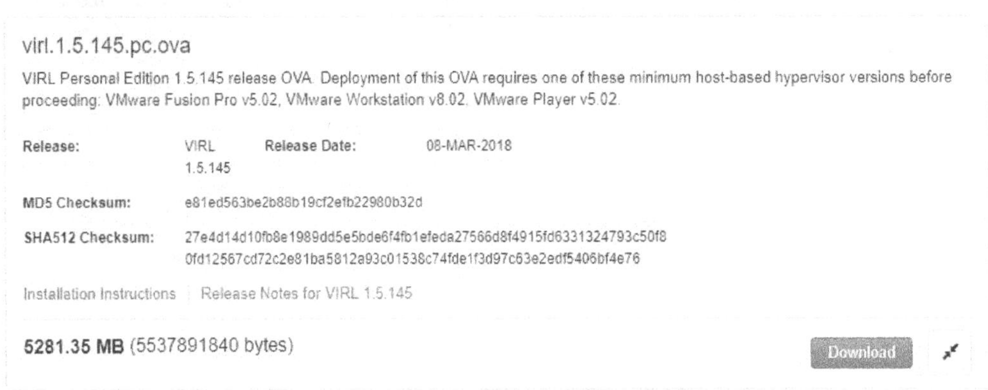

7. Now you have your VIRL image and license file stored in a directory. We'll come back to them later.

We're done with the software. Let's now get to the hardware.

CHAPTER 4: Hardware Requirements

Since we're focused on using Microsoft Windows 10, undoubtedly you'll be using either an Intel- or AMD-based system. Now although Intel first released virtualization technology (VT-x/EPT) in their x86 platform in 2005 and AMD (AMD-V/RVI) did likewise in 2006, I hope that the system you'll be using is a lot more recent. As of 2015, almost all server, desktop and mobile Intel processors support VT-x. With some motherboards, users must enable Intel's VT-x or AMD's AMD-V feature in the BIOS before applications can make use of it. These features allow for hardware acceleration of virtualization for near native performance of virtual machines. So, if your hardware supports this, definitely enable it. Check your system's BIOS settings (examples shown below), review your system's manual or go to your vendor's website to learn more about enabling virtualization in your system's BIOS.

The next screenshots display Intel- and AMD-based systems with VT-x or AMD-V virtualization enabled.

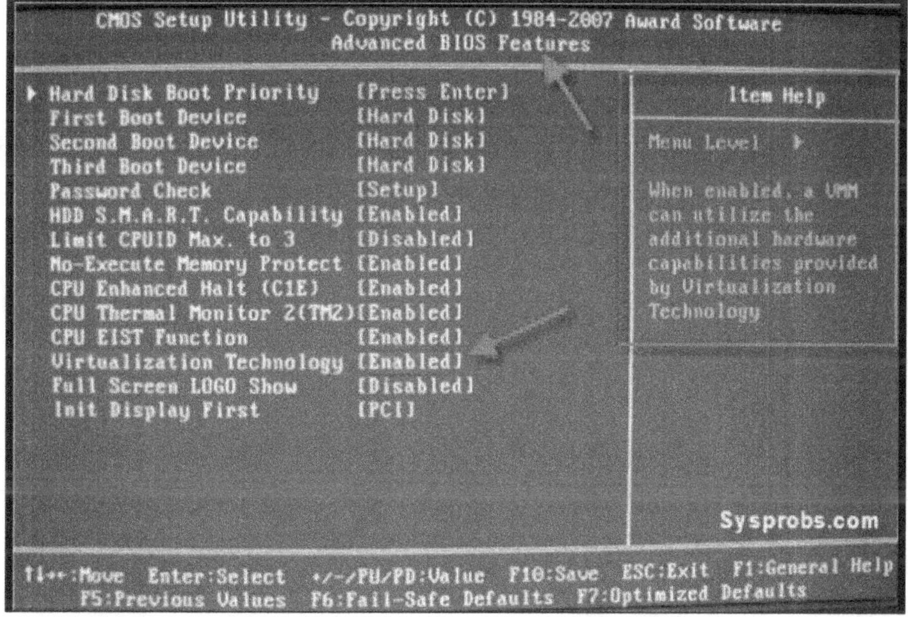

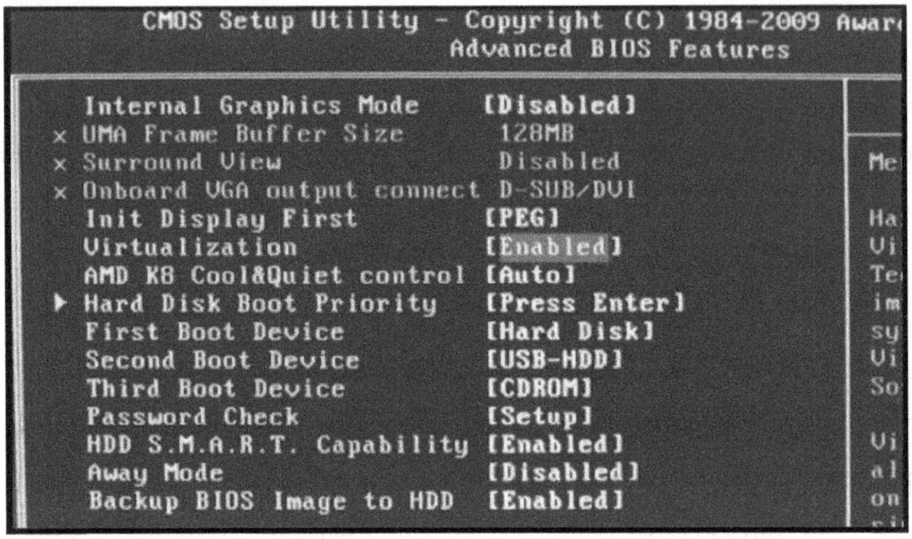

```
CMOS Setup Utility - Copyright (C) 1984-2009 Awar
                    Advanced BIOS Features

  Internal Graphics Mode      [Disabled]
x UMA Frame Buffer Size        128MB
x Surround View                Disabled
x Onboard VGA output connect  D-SUB/DVI
  Init Display First          [PEG]
  Virtualization              [Enabled]
  AMD K8 Cool&Quiet control   [Auto]
▶ Hard Disk Boot Priority     [Press Enter]
  First Boot Device           [Hard Disk]
  Second Boot Device          [USB-HDD]
  Third Boot Device           [CDROM]
  Password Check              [Setup]
  HDD S.M.A.R.T. Capability   [Enabled]
  Away Mode                   [Disabled]
  Backup BIOS Image to HDD    [Enabled]
```

The minimum amount of system resources needed for our specific configuration are as follows:

- 4+ CPU Cores
- 16 GB RAM
- 300GB disk space (recommended)

In case you were wondering, my system consists of:

- 4 CPU Cores
- 64GB DDR4 RAM
- Dual 1TB SSD drives
- 3 Network Adapters (1 for day-to-day traffic, 1 used for L2 FLAT1 and 1 used for L3 (SNAT)).

My own experience dictates that the responsiveness I get from SSD drives far surpasses what older SATA drives can do; especially with virtualization – but yes you can still use these older drives if you're more concerned with just functionality rather than functionality <u>and</u> responsiveness.

Please keep in mind that although VIRL supports many software features, there are hardware limitations. Of those:

- VIRL does not emulate ASICs in hardware because particular features are difficult to emulate in software.
- VIRL cannot and should not be used for performance testing. Rather it should be seen as a functional, proof of concept, environment.
- VIRL currently supports a maximum of 20 nodes per simulation.

Let me briefly step away from the actual hardware needed to run your virtualized system to talk about another piece of hardware in your environment: your firewall. Whether you're using a software-based firewall and/or a hardware-based firewall or proxy server, you must allow the following ports outbound to the Internet in order to allow VIRL to function properly:

- NTP (UDP port 123) since your system needs to sync with a "true" time source
- TCP ports 4505 – 4506 which are used to talk to Cisco's SALT servers. I'll explain what this is later in the installation section.

Now that your hardware is ready, are you ready for some hands-on work? Me too. Let's get to installing some software.

CHAPTER 5: Software Installation

As mentioned back in Chapter 3, I'm certain that your system already has Microsoft Windows 10 running on it, but if not, please stop at this point and upgrade...upgrade…upgrade before proceeding. Also being that we're all seasoned network guys here – at least I play one at work – it's not my intent to insult your intelligence with the verbose inclusion of so many software installation screenshots; but keep in mind, this is a step-by-step guide and I'm a man of my word - so let's continue.

Installing VMware Workstation 14

1. Go to the directory where you downloaded your VMware Workstation software, right-click the executable and *Run as Administrator* (if needed).
2. Click *Next.*

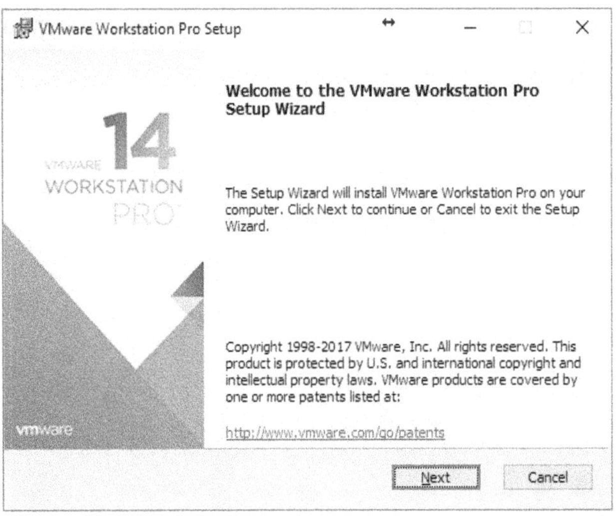

3. Check: I accept the terms in the License Agreement and click Next.

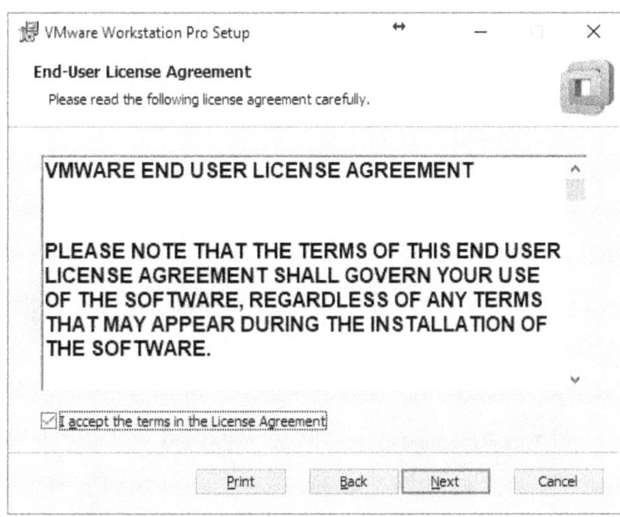

4. Choose the location for your installation and check the installation of the *Enhanced Keyboard Driver*, then click *Next.*

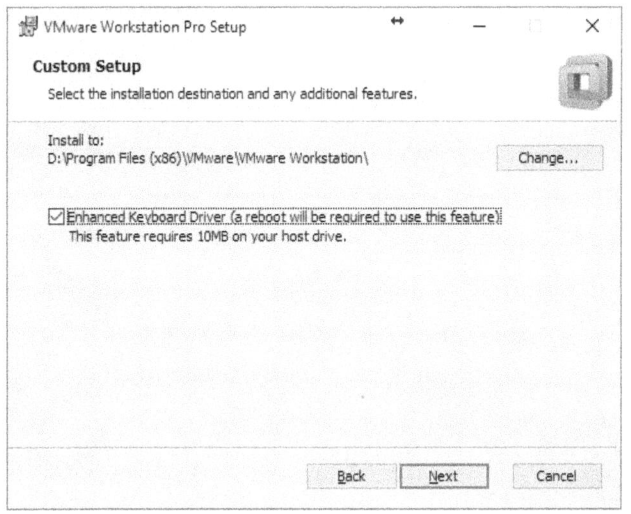

5. Now I like knowing when products have updates, yet not knowing if VMware is actually collecting what they claim to be collecting from my system, I opted out from joining their improvement program; but the choice is yours. Click *Next.*

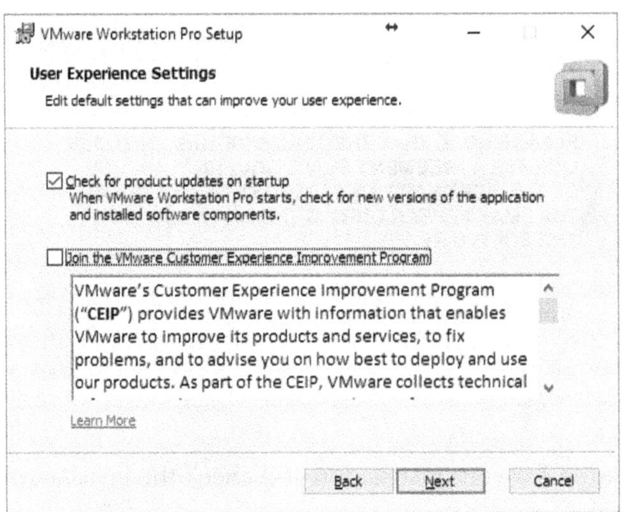

6. Again, creating shortcuts is your choice here. Click *Next.*

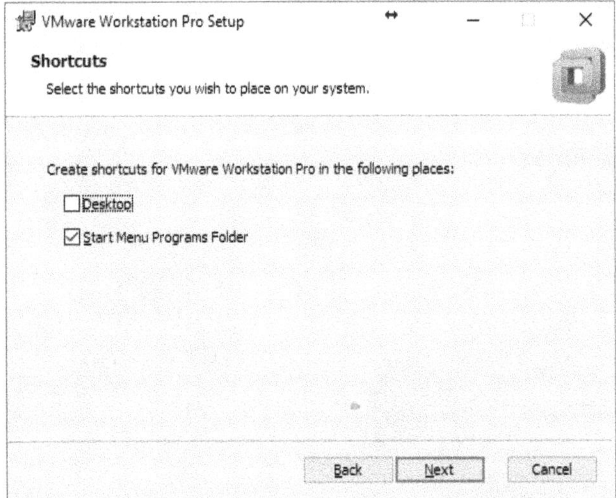

7. And finally let the installation begin. Click *Install.*

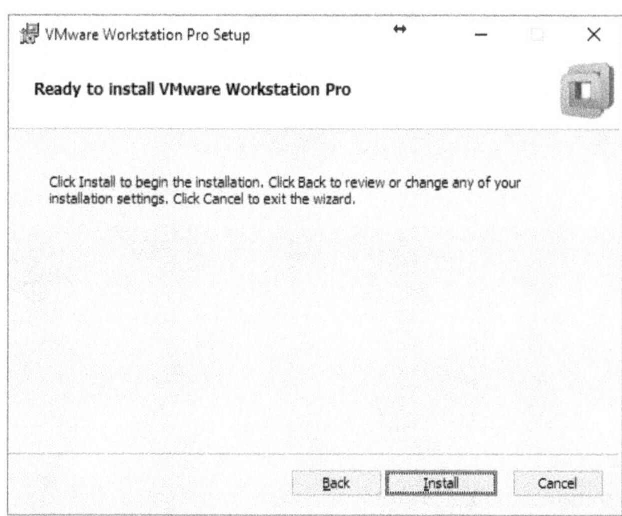

8. Choose *License*, input your license key and click *Enter.*

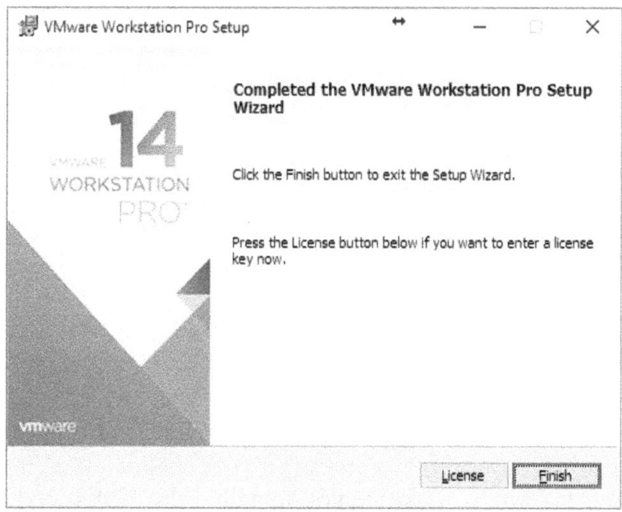

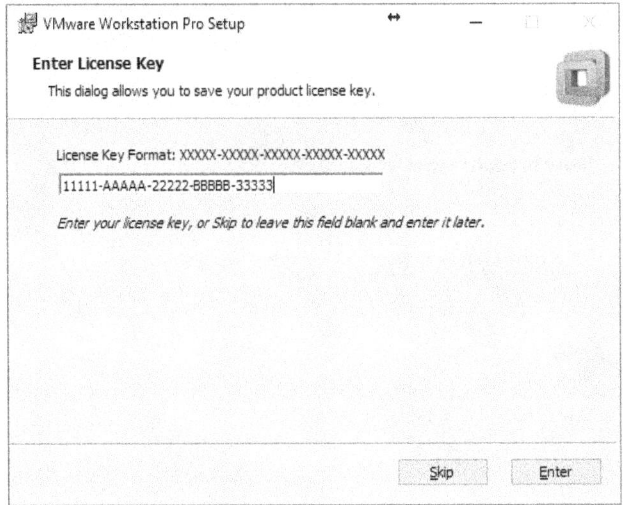

9. After the key is validated, click *Finish.*

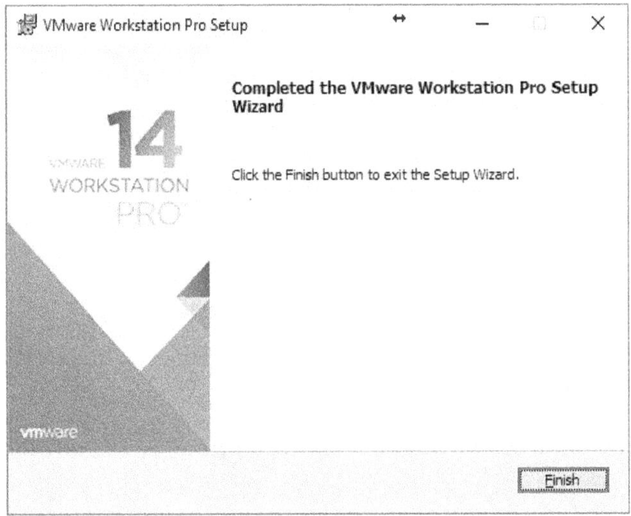

10. Please restart your system, now, since you installed the Enhanced Keyboard Driver.

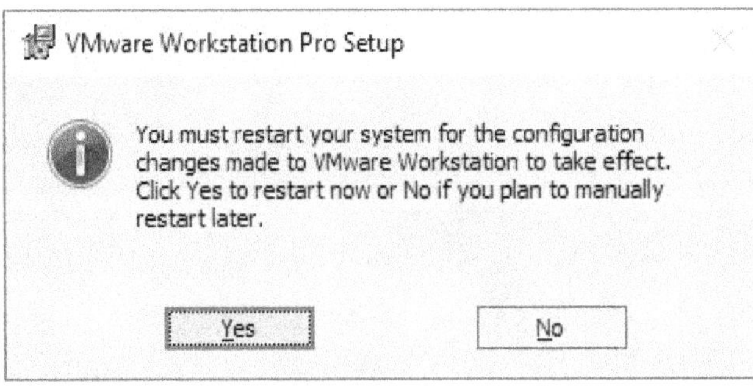

Note: Let me bring to your attention what VMware quietly performed in the background. It created 2 new VMware virtual NICs – VMnet1 and VMnet8.

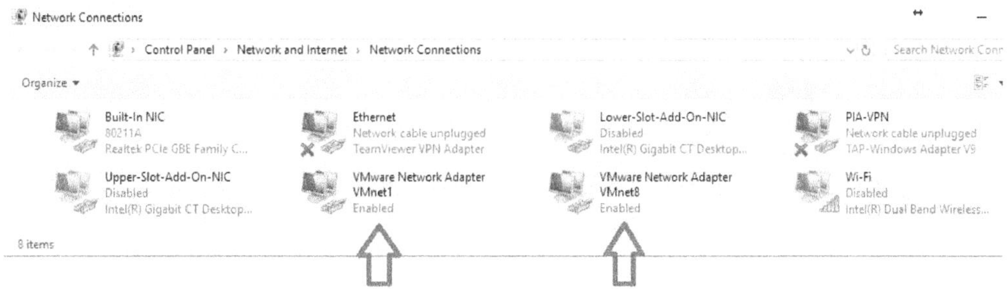

It also created VMnet 0 which is only shown in VMware and only when you click We will be modifying ⚠ Administrator privileges are required to modify the network configuration. Change Settings these in upcoming sections.

11. Once again, launch VMware Workstation. Upon my initial launch I was presented with this upgrade notice because during the installation I enabled *Check for Product Updates on Startup*. If you did not enable that checkbox, skip to the next section: *Verifying Cisco VIRL v1.5.145 Image.*

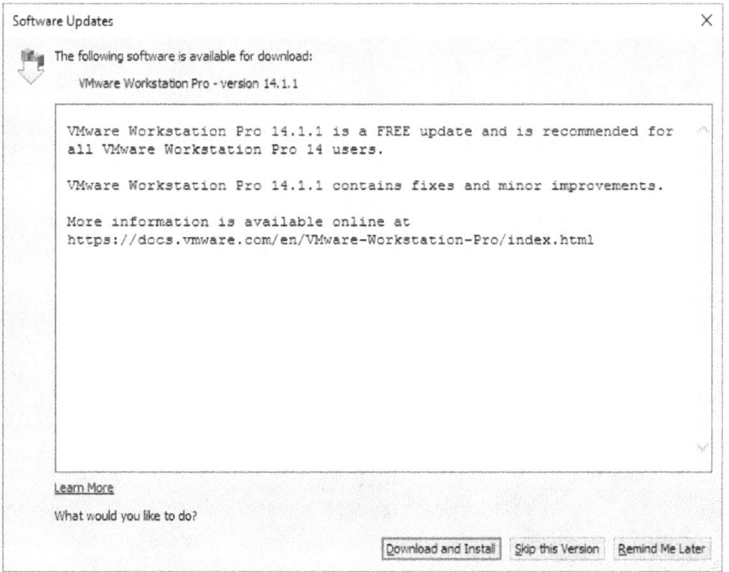

Note: If you're prompted with the next dialog box, close the program (not the upgrade process dialog box) so that the upgrade can proceed.

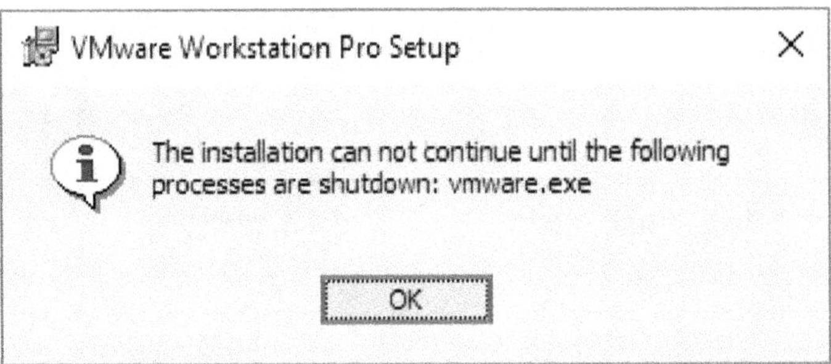

12. After choosing to download and install the updates, the setup/configuration screens are very similar to what we went through before, with the addition of uninstalling older drivers.

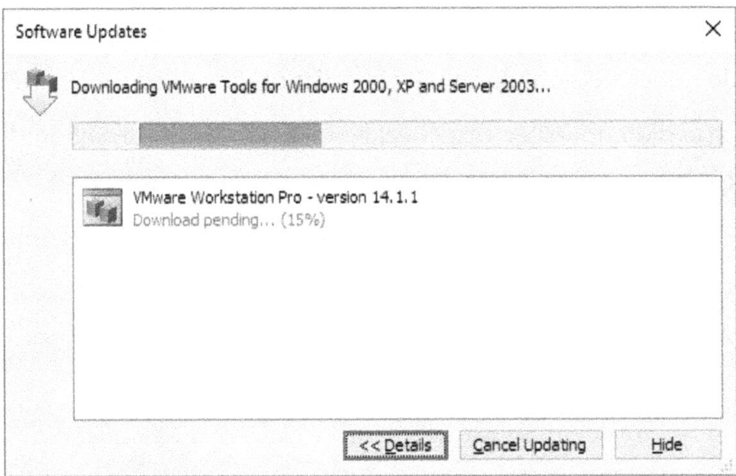

13. Please reboot your system after this upgrade.

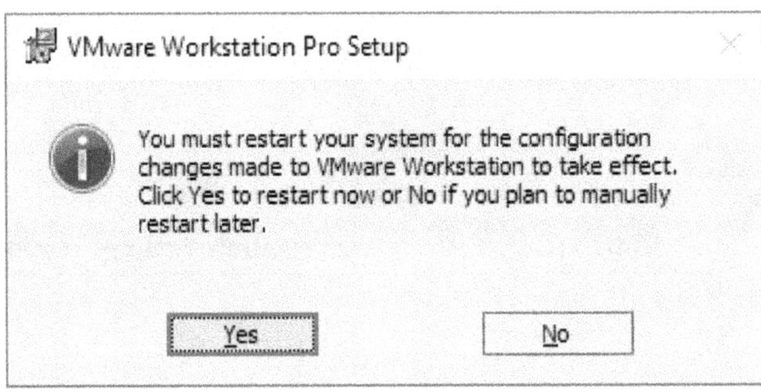

Verifying Cisco VIRL v1.5.145 Image

During your download of this rather large VIRL image, it could have possibly become corrupted. To verify it is indeed intact as Cisco intended, let's use the Windows built-in *certutil.exe* program to verify. Simply do what I've shown below – changing the path to where you downloaded the file. Notice that the MD5 hash displayed in the command prompt is exactly the same as shown on Cisco's website.

Note: Actually, any MD5 or SHA checksum program can be used to validate your download if you don't have the certutil.exe program.

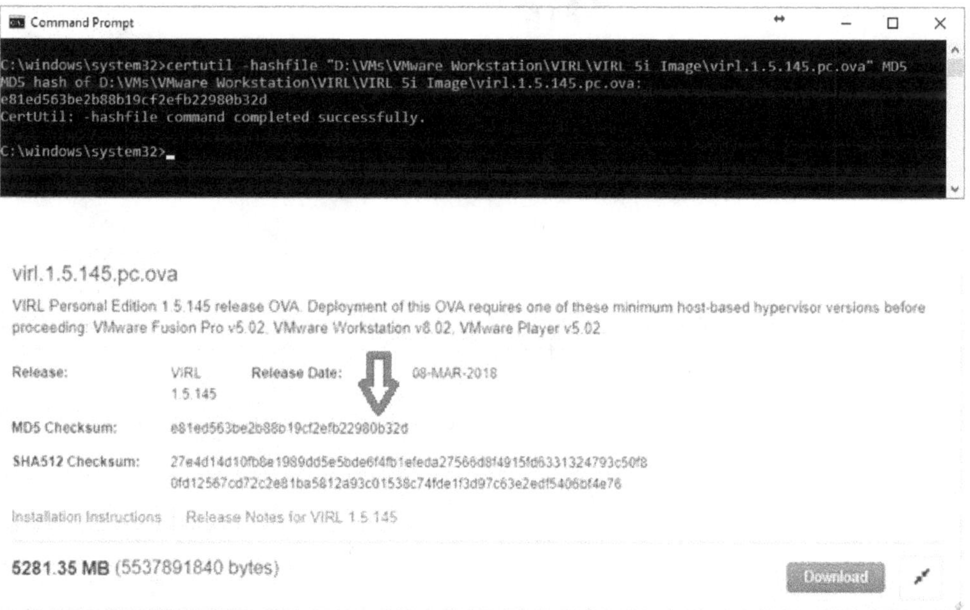

CHAPTER 6: Software Configuration

Installing and Configuring VIRL Server

1. Launch VMware Workstation, then choose *Open a Virtual Machine.*

2. Now go to the location of your downloaded .OVA image and click *Open.*

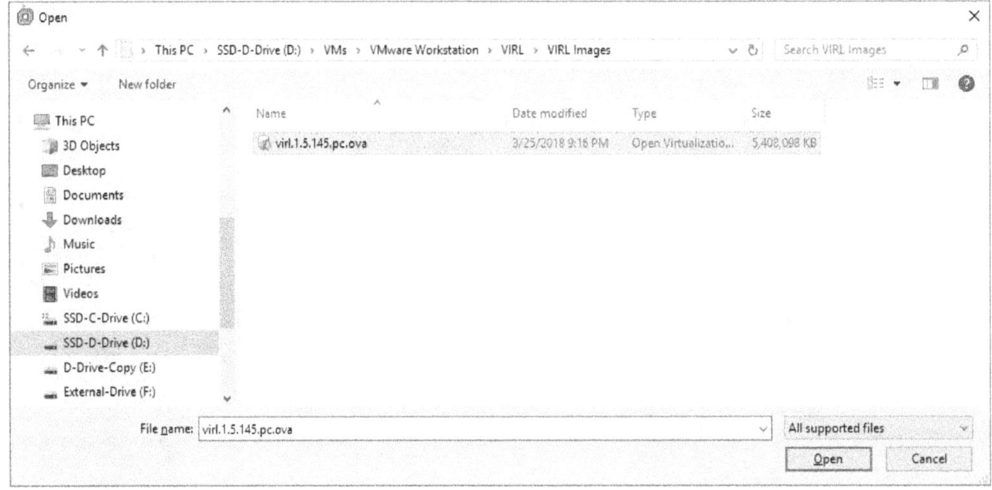

3. For the storage path of this VM I chose the same directory where the .OVA file is located (this is for good housekeeping purposes only) because the VM's operating files created during the installation are in the same directory as the original OVA file, then click *Import.*

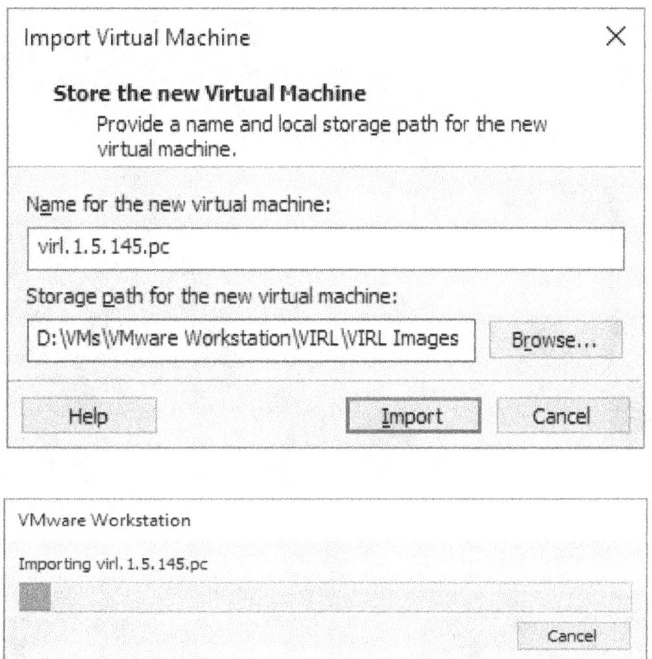

4. After the import is complete click *Power on this Virtual Machine.*

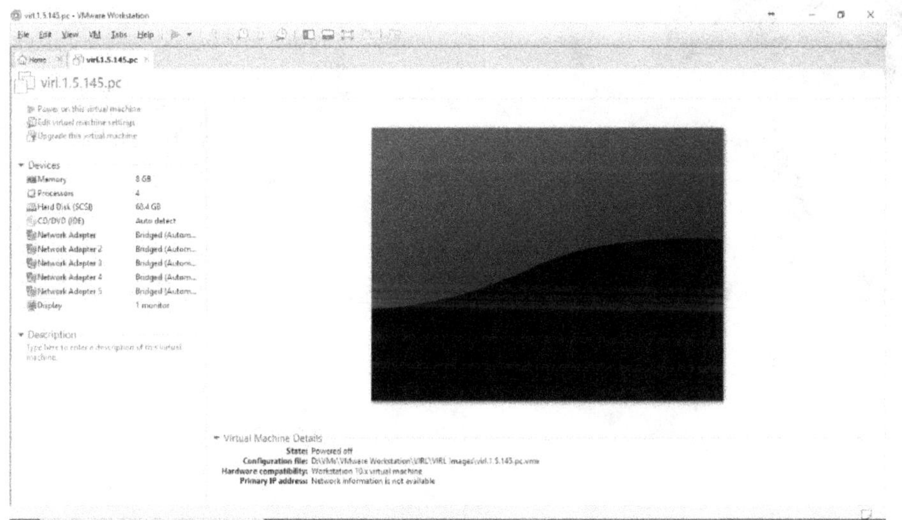

5. Since this is the first time the VM has run, you'll be presented with setup screens. Click *OK*, then *Next* to get to the screen shown. In regards to the next series of screenshots, I accepted the default options by continuing to click *Next*.

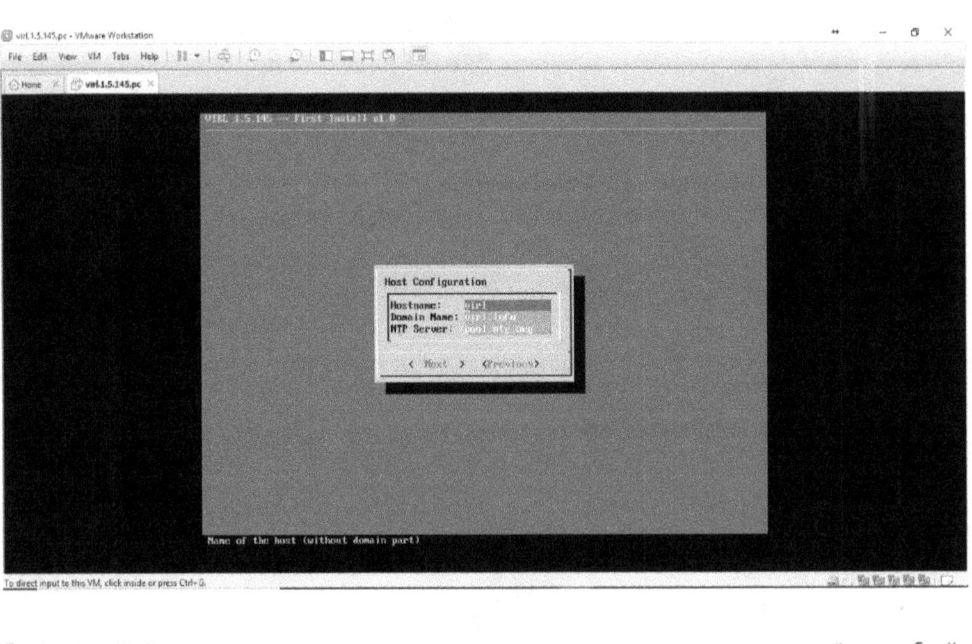

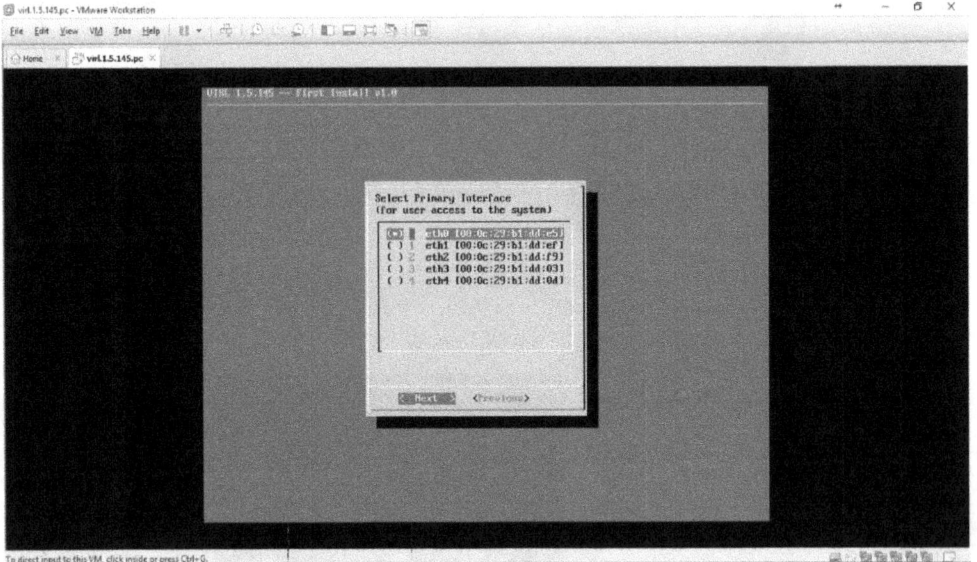

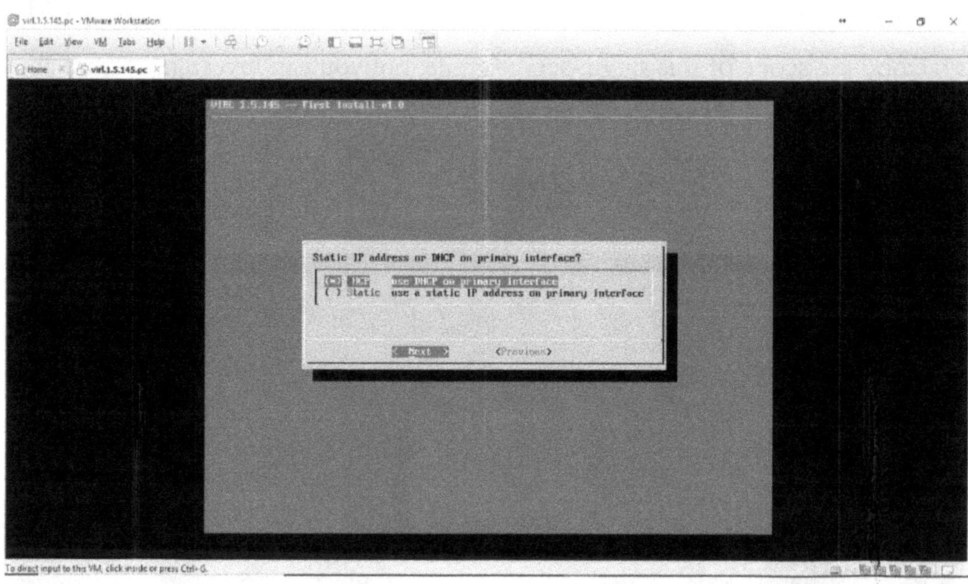
virl.1.5.145.pc - VMware Workstation
File Edit View VM Tabs Help
Home
virl.1.5.145.pc
VIRL 1.5.145 -- First Install v1.0
Static IP address or DHCP on primary interface?
(*) DHCP use DHCP on primary interface
( ) Static use a static IP address on primary interface
< Next > <Previous>
To direct input to this VM, click inside or press Ctrl+G.

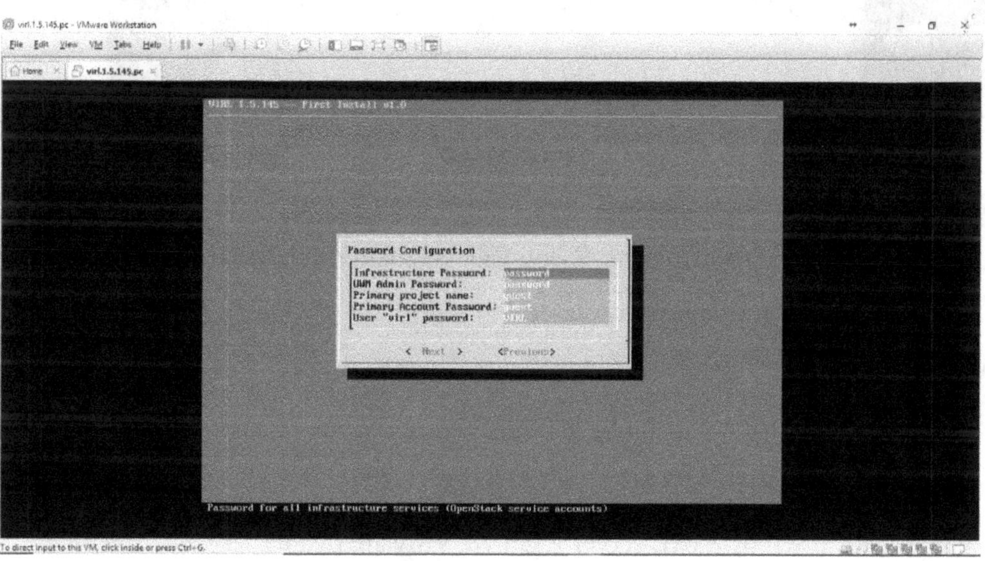
virl.1.5.145.pc - VMware Workstation
File Edit View VM Tabs Help
Home
virl.1.5.145.pc
VIRL 1.5.145 -- First Install v1.0
Password Configuration
Infrastructure Password: password
UWM Admin Password: password
Primary project name: guest
Primary Account Password: guest
User "virl" password: VIRL
< Next > <Previous>
Password for all infrastructure services (OpenStack service accounts)
To direct input to this VM, click inside or press Ctrl+G.

6. Do <u>not</u> check the *Cluster Enabled* box. We do not want to enable clustering. Clustering is beyond the scope of this single-server guide, but you can investigate more about it at: http://get.virl.info/pre.req.cluster.php

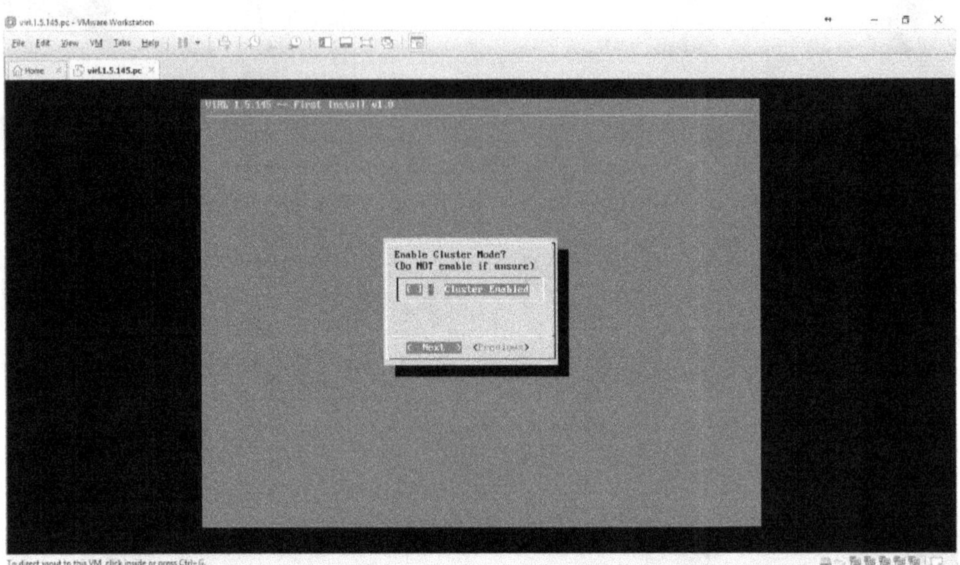

7. With all of your default options chosen, click *Confirm and Exit.* Also take note of the usernames and passwords shown because you will use them throughout the different VIRL server management programs available.

   Credentials (<username> / <password>):

   - uwmadmin / password (used by UWM)
   - guest / guest (used by UWM)
   - virl / VIRL (used by VIRL server login via VMware or PuTTY)
   - cisco / cisco (used to log into nodes)

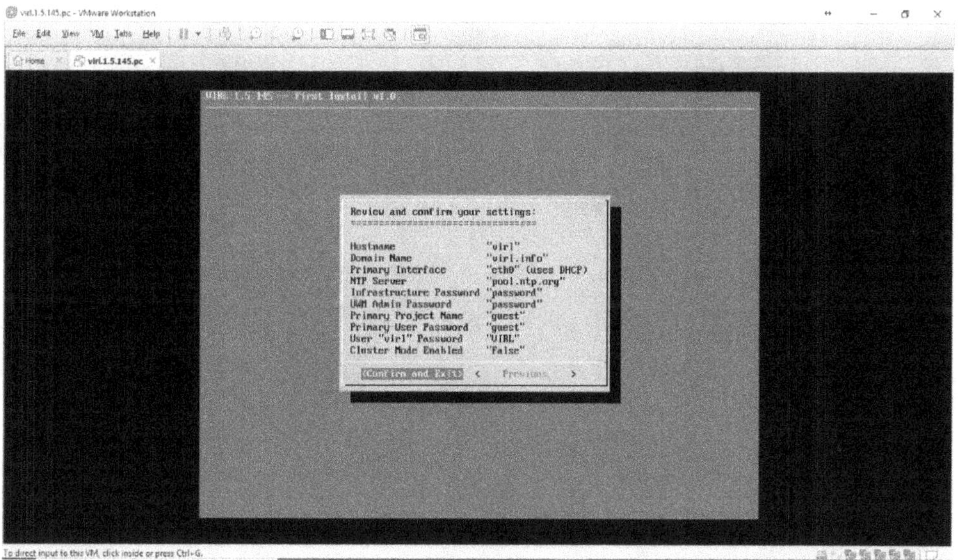

8. The VM is now being built (1st screenshot) and will restart (2nd screenshot) and ready to operate.

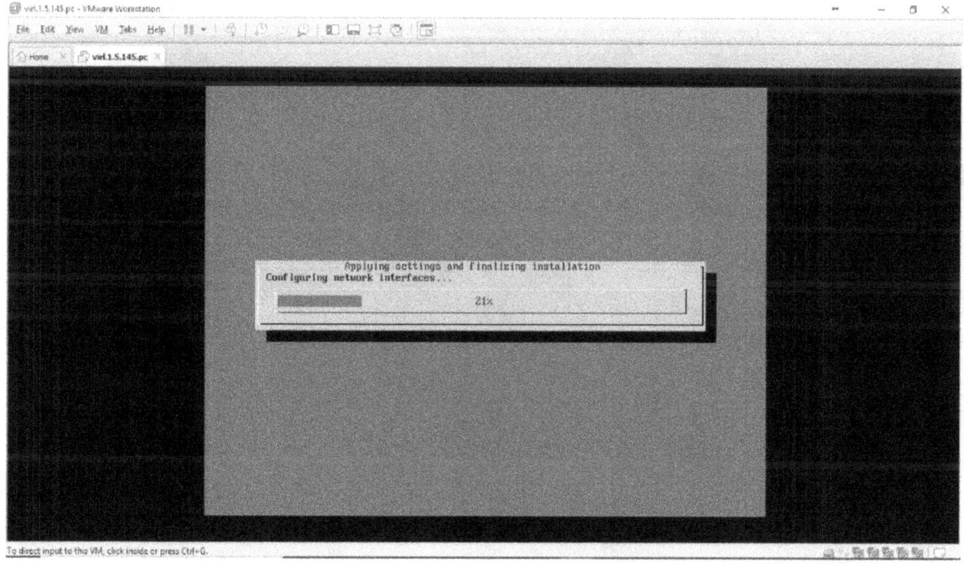

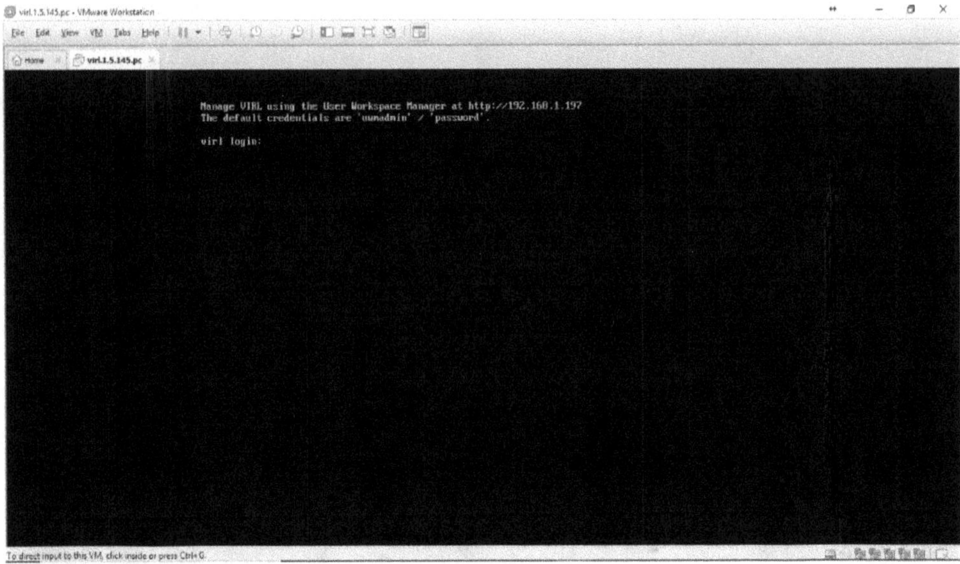

9. Let's verify that you can login to your VIRL server's backend by entering credentials: virl / VIRL.

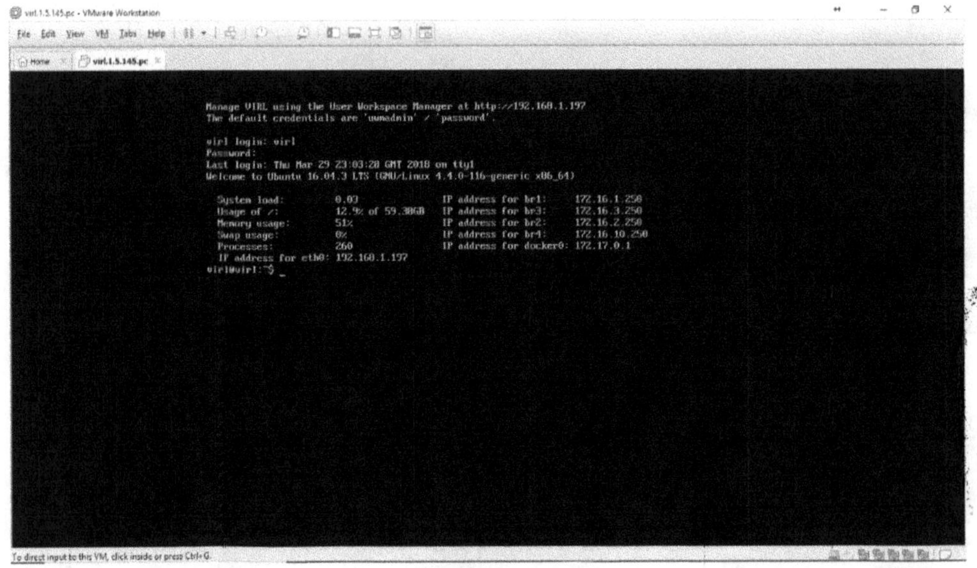

10. Let's verify connectivity to the Internet. Here I verified that I could get to Yahoo – ***ping yahoo.com***. If you cannot, verify your access rules you have running on your software- and/or hardware-based firewall.

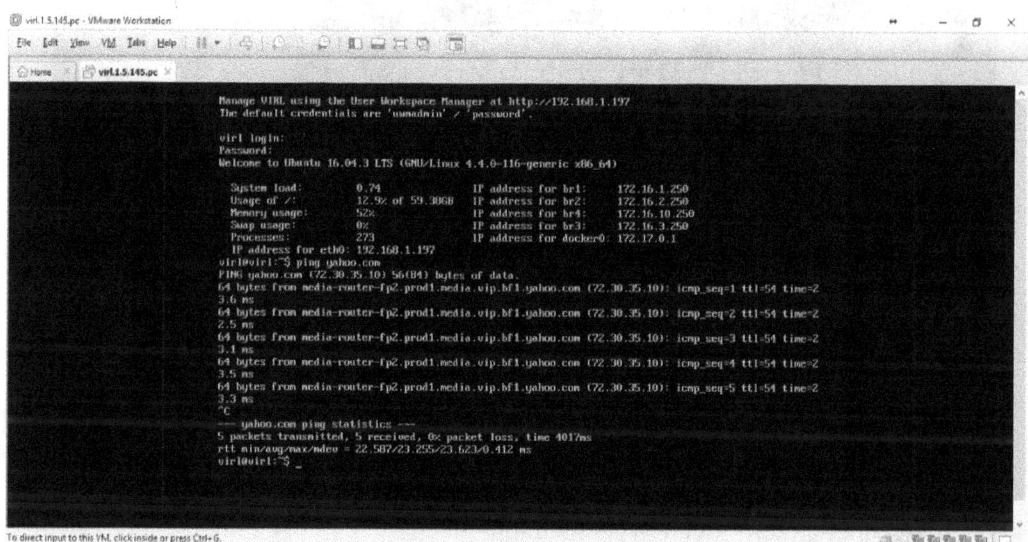

11. Depending on your geographic location, try pinging and telnetting to (at least one) Cisco SALT "license" server from the geographical list below. Choose the one(s) closest to you.

US SALT Servers

vsm-us-51.virl.info, vsm-us-52.virl.info, vsm-us-53.virl.info, vsm-us-54.virl.info

EU SALT Servers

vsm-eu-51.virl.info, vsm-eu-52.virl.info, vsm-eu-53.virl.info, vsm-eu-54.virl.info

AP SALT Servers

vsm-ap-51.virl.info, vsm-ap-52.virl.info, vsm-ap-53.virl.info, vsm-ap-54.virl.info

Type: ping <name of SALT server>

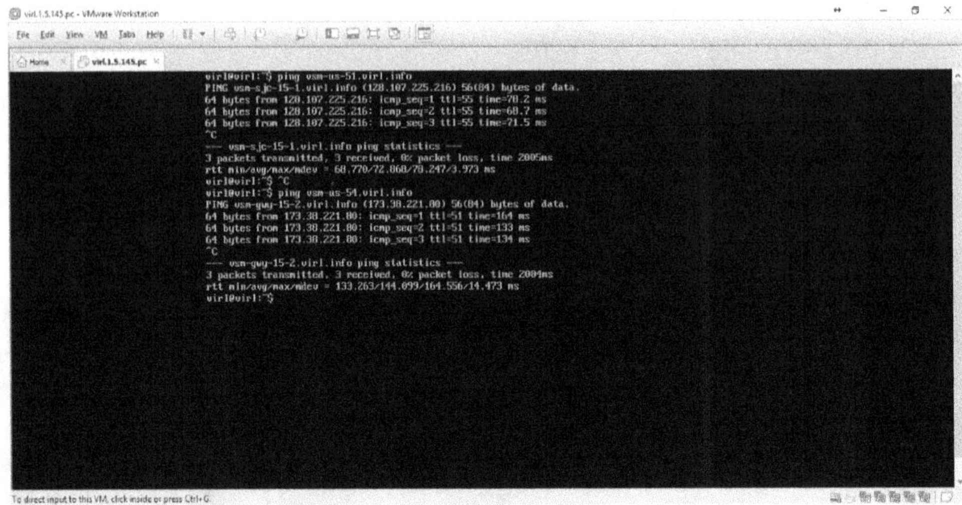

Here I'm verifying connectivity to one of the SALT server's TCP ports 4505 and 4506.

Type: telnet <name of SALT server> 4505

Type: telnet <name of SALT server> 4506

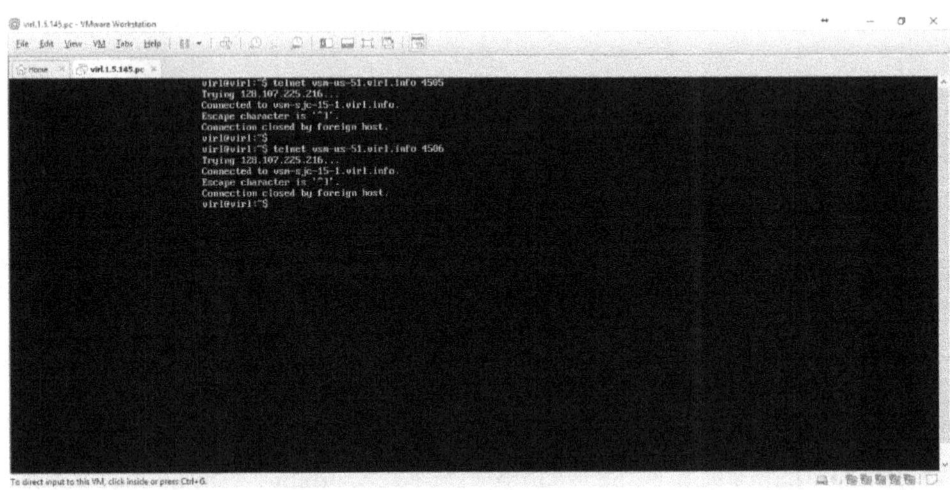

These SALT servers are the licensing servers I brought to your attention briefly in the "Hardware Requirements" section. The servers are used to verify the .PEM license file you downloaded earlier. **Your firewall must be configured to allow outbound communication from your VIRL server to these Cisco servers, via TCP ports 4505 and 4506**. If your telnet window does not display ***Connected to....***, do not proceed until you've modified your firewall accordingly and retested the connections.

12. Time to test time…or rather NTP. Your VIRL image is preconfigured to use NTP and as long as your firewall allows outbound UDP port 123 requests and its return traffic, your system's prompt should display something similar to mine after you run ***ntpq -p*** and ***timedatectl***.

    Type: *ntpq -p*

    Type: timedatectl

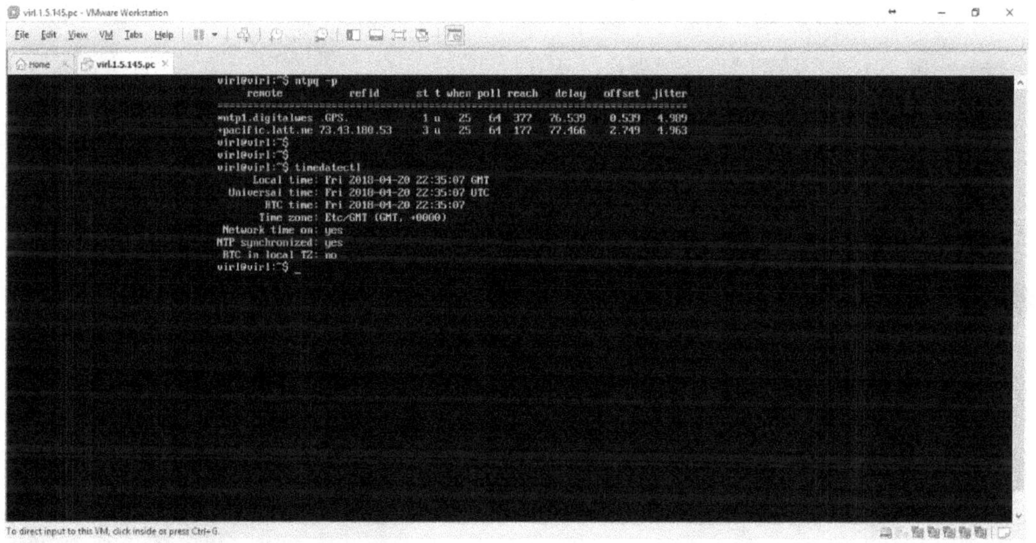

13. Lastly, let's test for KVM (Keyboard, Video and Mouse) acceleration. I see that mine failed. If your system displayed the same message, there's usually one or two things needing modification: 1) in the BIOS, verify that your system's CPU (if applicable) is enabled to support virtualization. As I mentioned earlier the latest Intel and AMD motherboards do support this feature and/or 2) we need to verify that a key VIRL configuration file has an entry needed to support "nested virtualization".

    Type: sudo kvm-ok

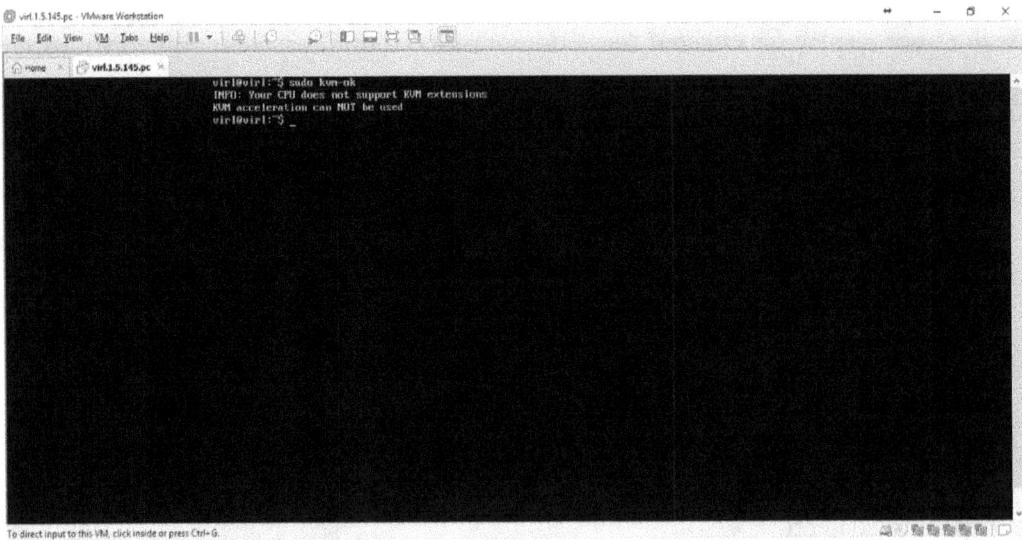

I rebooted my system and verified that the BIOS' VT-x feature was indeed enabled; thus it was on to examining one of VIRL's configuration files.

Note: <u>Before performing the next step shutdown your VIRL VM</u> by right-clicking your VM's tab in VMware and choosing *Shut Down Guest.*

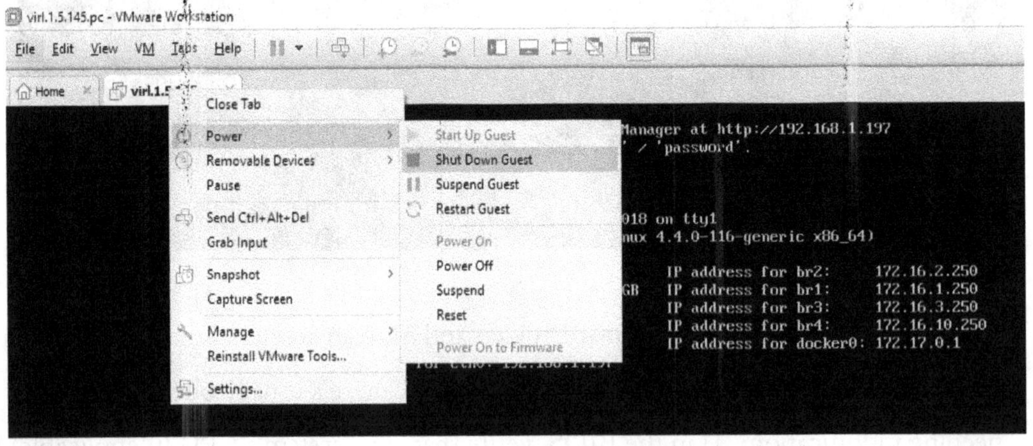

14. Using Notepad, open VIRL's configuration file: *virl.1.5.145.pc.vmx.*

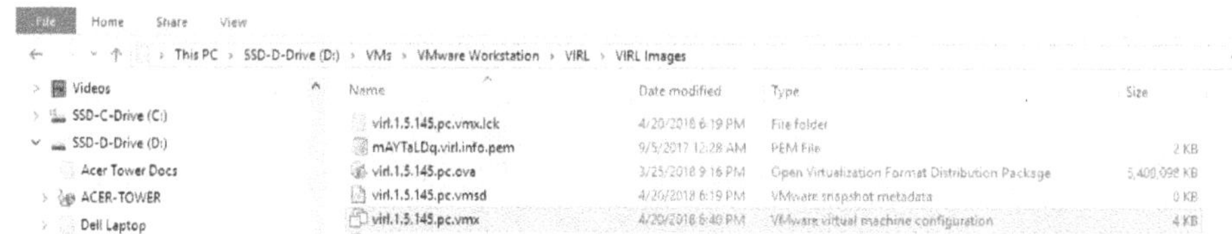

15. I then noticed the following line was missing so I added it and saved the file.

vhv.enable = "TRUE"

```
.encoding = "UTF-8"
displayname = "virl.1.5.145.pc"
guestos = "ubuntu-64"
bios.bootorder = "cdrom"
virtualhw.version = "10"
vhv.enable = "TRUE"
config.version = "8"
numvcpus = "4"
cpuid.coresPerSocket = "1"
memsize = "8192"
pciBridge0.present = "TRUE"
pciBridge4.present = "TRUE"
pciBridge4.virtualDev = "pcieRootPort"
pciBridge4.functions = "8"
pciBridge5.present = "TRUE"
```

16. Now restart the VIRL VM, login with credentials: virl / VIRL and re-run the command: *sudo kvm-ok*. KVM acceleration should be working now.

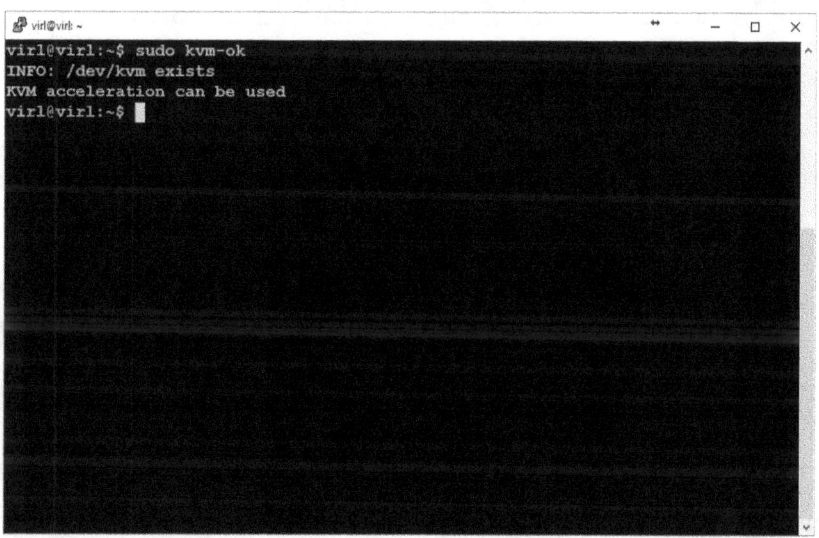

Note: KVM (Keyboard, Video and Mouse) acceleration is a feature on VT-x/AMD-V enabled systems that allows instruction set extension hardware assistance to VMs. Since we are running a "nested virtualization" environment – simulated switches and routers which are running as VMs under VIRL server (which is also a VM) running on top of a VMware hypervisor – need to pass the CPU "flags" from the host system down to VIRL (which is two levels down). This fools the switches and routers running in VIRL into thinking that they have direct access to the CPU. There are a multitude of blogs written about this on the Internet – just use: *cisco virl kvm* in your search to learn more.

17. Your .PEM license file must now be installed. Luckily your VIRL server is equipped with a browser-based management console – User Workspace Management Interface (UWM). Using FireFox or Chrome, connect to your server's IP address, which is displayed in the VMware console window:

```
Manage VIRL using the User Workspace Manager at http://192.168.1.197
The default credentials are 'uwmadmin' / 'password'.
```

18. The credentials are: uwmadmin / password.

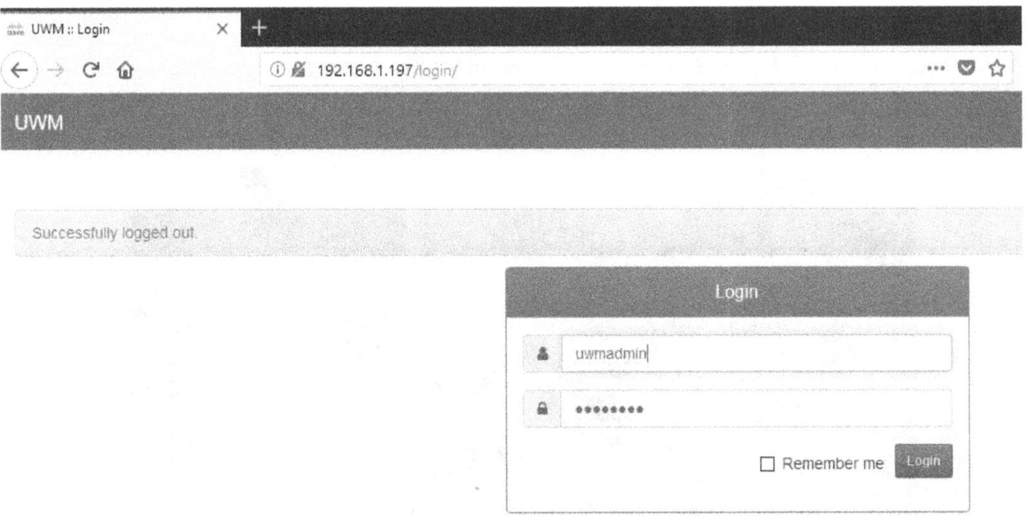

19. Notice the pink blocked text. This is what it looks like when your VIRL server is not configured properly to communicate to Cisco's SALT servers (i.e., either your firewall is

blocking communication or your license is not valid). Notice that in my case only *Connect* is in red - which is only because the license hasn't been applied and verified. Let's fix this.

In UWM's left-side pane select VIRL Server | Salt Configuration and Status.

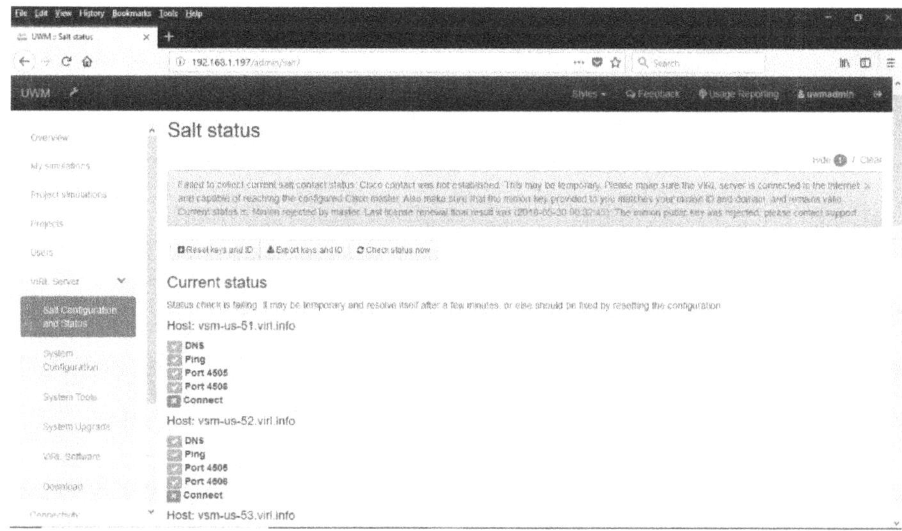

20. After clicking *Reset keys and ID*, the following screen is displayed. Here I've filled out the respective fields:

    - **Salt ID and domain**: <enter your license file name without the PEM extension included>
    - **Customer email address**: <the email address you used when you registered your account>
    - **List of Cisco salt masters**: <click on one of the regions (closest to you)>
    - Master sign public key: <do nothing>
    - **Minion private RSA key in PEM format**: Open your license file with Notepad and copy the entire contents into your system's buffer memory (Ctrl-C). Now replace all the text currently in this field with your license's text, then click *Reset.*

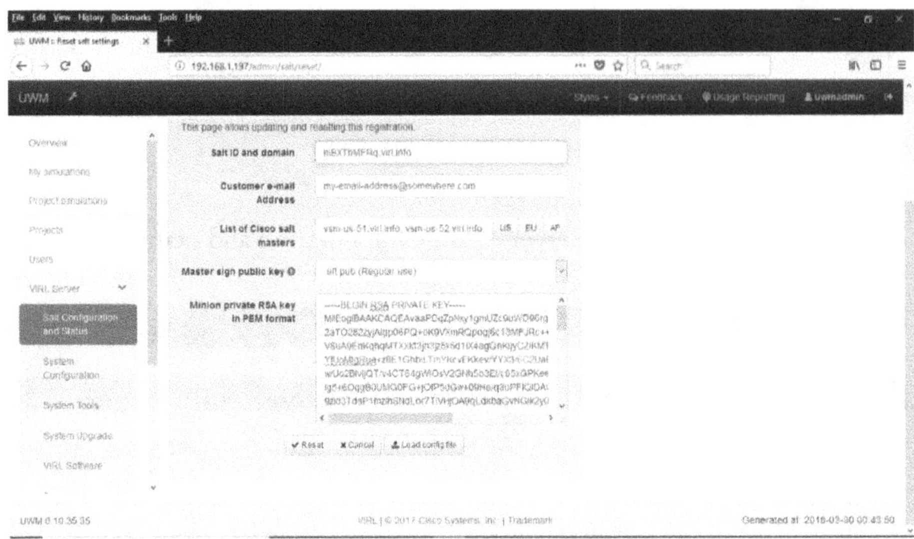

21. After a moment or so (less than a minute for me) your system should now display as mine did. If registration fails the first time, click *Check status now* and observe the green or red entry checkmarks. If it continues to fail re-verify each field in Step #20 again.

    If your screen displays all green checks, congrats, your server is now up and running!

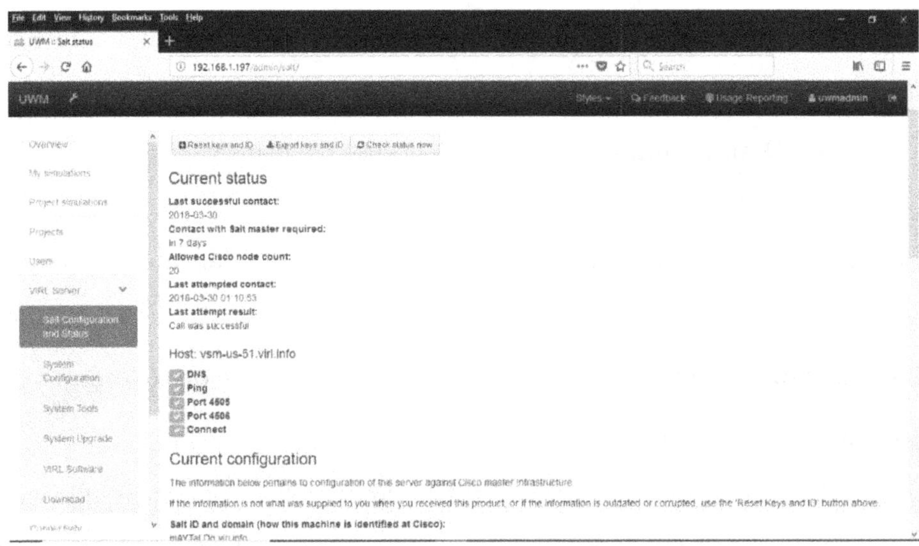

Note: Keep in mind that although you purchased this VIRL PE server license, the product is still owned by Cisco and as such they utilize your license (your PEM file's private key) to validate two very important aspects of your use of the program: 1) If the product has been shut down for nearly 7 days (or more) you will see a message similar the following in UWM:

Failed to contact Cisco for 6 days: last reason: Call has timed out; failed to connect or minion key not accepted Please make sure your minion key is valid. This is just a warning, and may be temporary. Please make sure the VIRL server is connected to the internet at regular times.

and 2) during your connection to Cisco's SALT servers they can ascertain if your PEM file is being used simultaneously from multiple systems. Now although you can install VIRL server on at least 2 different systems and use the same PEM file for licensing purposes, at least one of those systems must be off whenever the other system is on.

Also when your license expires – 1 year later – simply purchase the VIRL server again and you will be sent a new .PEM (license file). You only need to modify the contents in the **Minion private RSA key in PEM format** field, then click *Reset.*

VM Maestro Installation and Pre-Configuration

Packaged with VIRL server is the front-end component of this client/server platform, called: VM Maestro. If VMware Workstation is considered the "backbone" of your VM platform, with VIRL server being considered the "heart", then VM Maestro would be the "eyes". You will use this client-side application to configure certain aspects of the "heart" and to build and run your topologies/simulations. Now although VM Maestro could be installed on another computer (inside your network) since it does communicate with VIRL server over specific TCP ports (mentioned later), we will keep this simplified by installing it on our same Windows 10 system.

1. With your VIRL VM running, open FireFox or Chrome and connect to *http://<VIRL's IP address>/download*. Here you see the Linux, Windows and Macintosh versions of VM Maestro software, respectively. I chose to download the 64-bit Windows version.

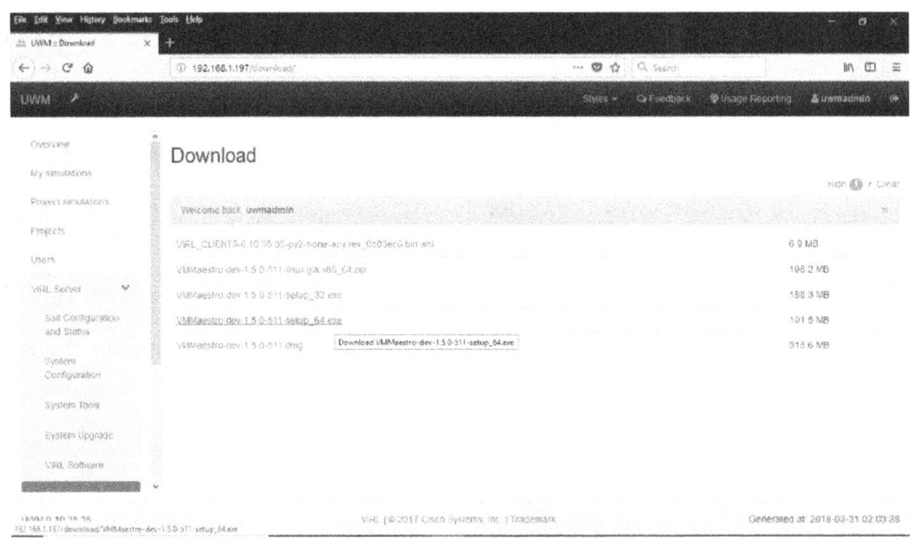

2. Based on whether you downloaded the 32- or 64-bit Windows version, run the installation as I have.

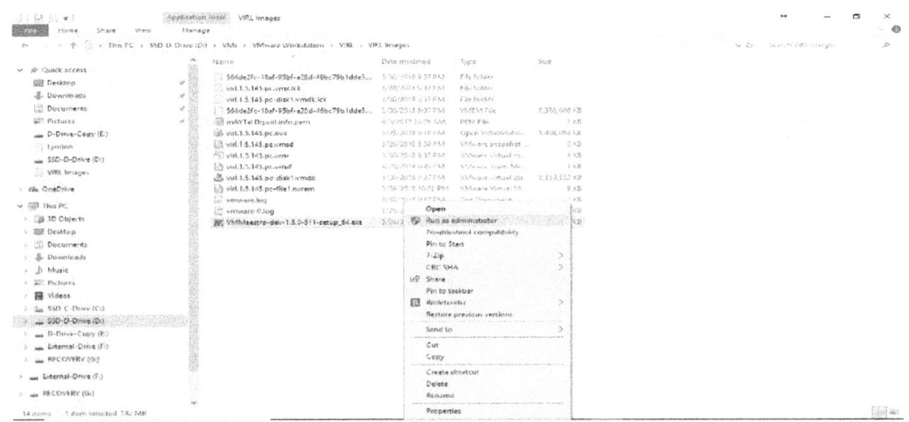

3. I chose all the default options for this software's installation, except for the installation's location (your choice here), then clicked *Install.*

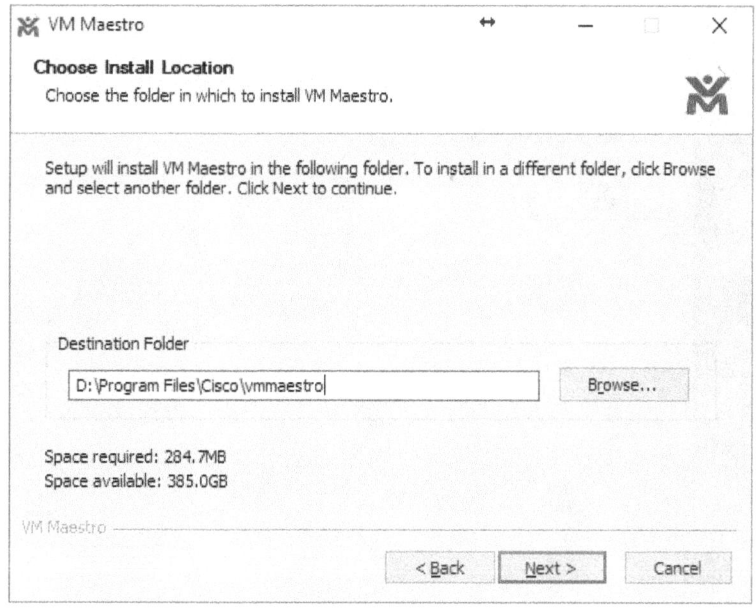

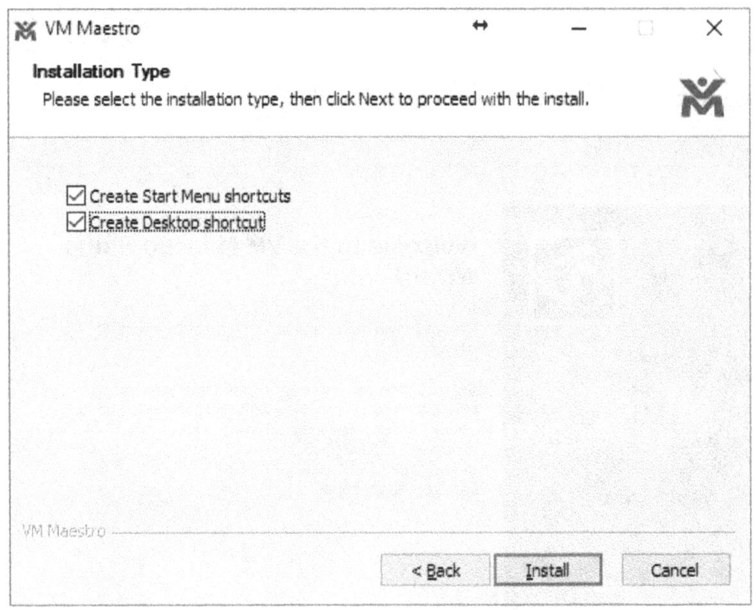

4. Now, let's run the program by clicking *Finish*.

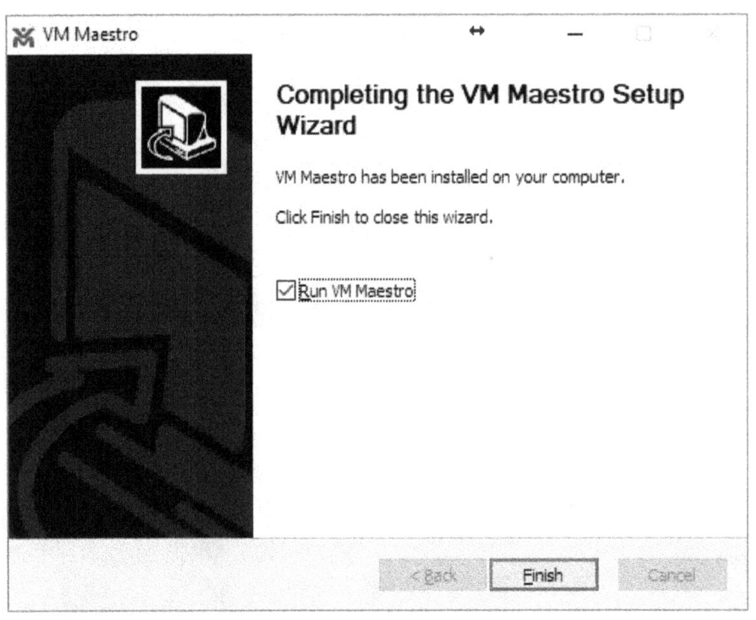

5. Check the Remember my decision box and click Agree.

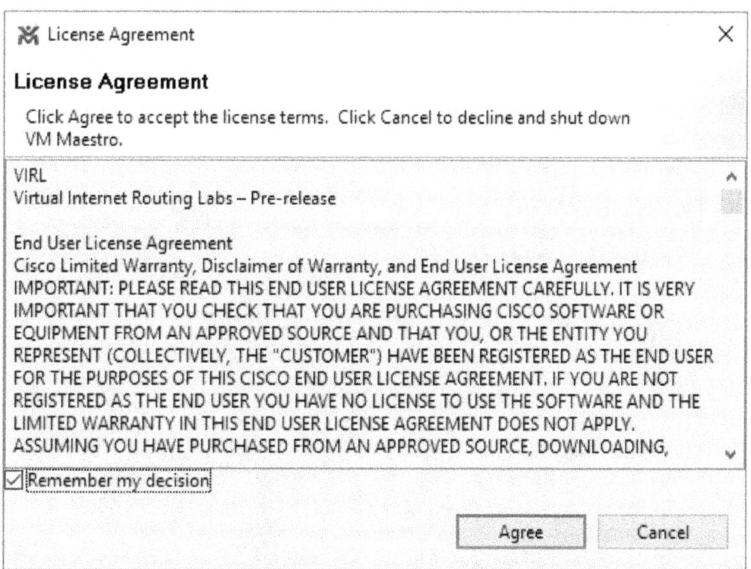

6. As mentioned earlier, I don't like sending information back to vendors about my system; yet the choice is yours. Click *OK* to continue.

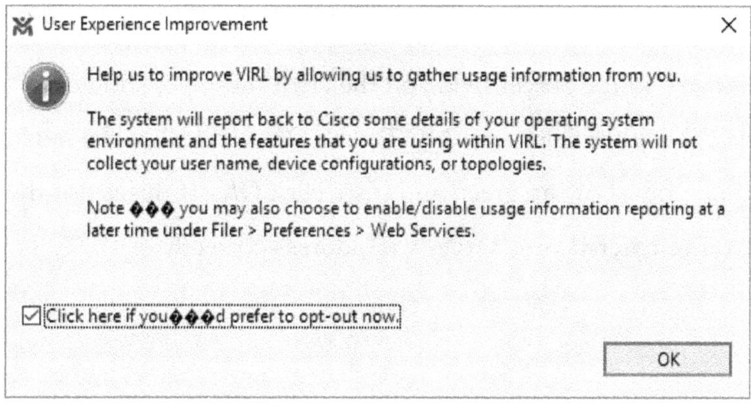

7. I was presented with the following error messages:

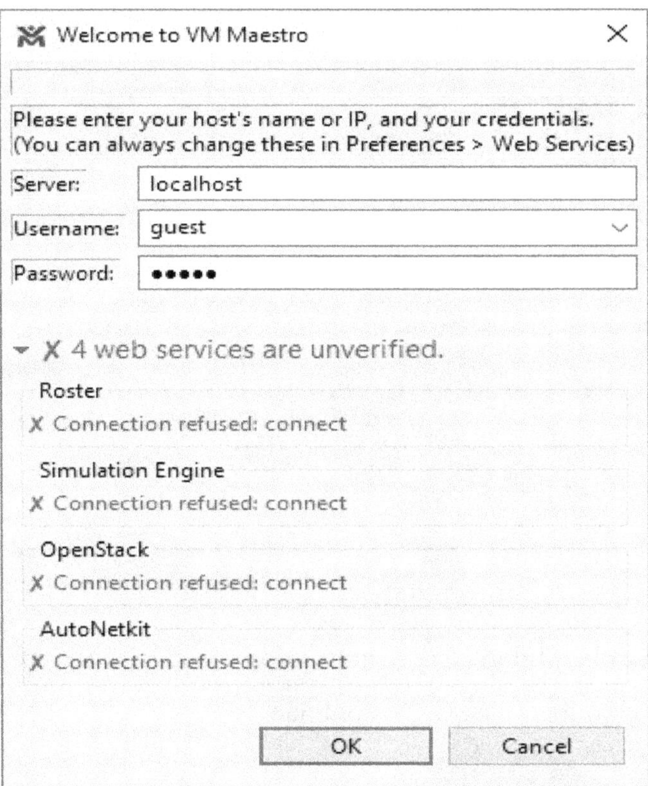

8. Enter <*VIRL Server's IP address*> in the Server field and the error messages should change. Now click in one of the other fields - do **NOT** click *OK* – and all of the red web services messages should now show up green and if so, click *OK.* If this is not the case, please re-verify that you've entered your server's IP address correctly.

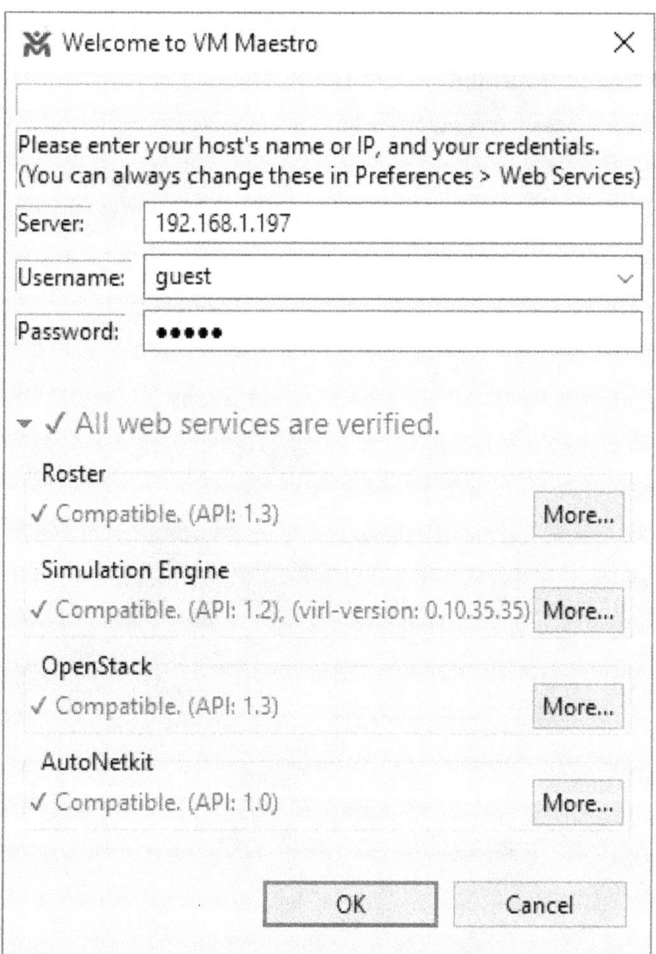

9. I was then presented with this message. Click *Yes* and enter whatever questions and answers you'd like on the next screen.

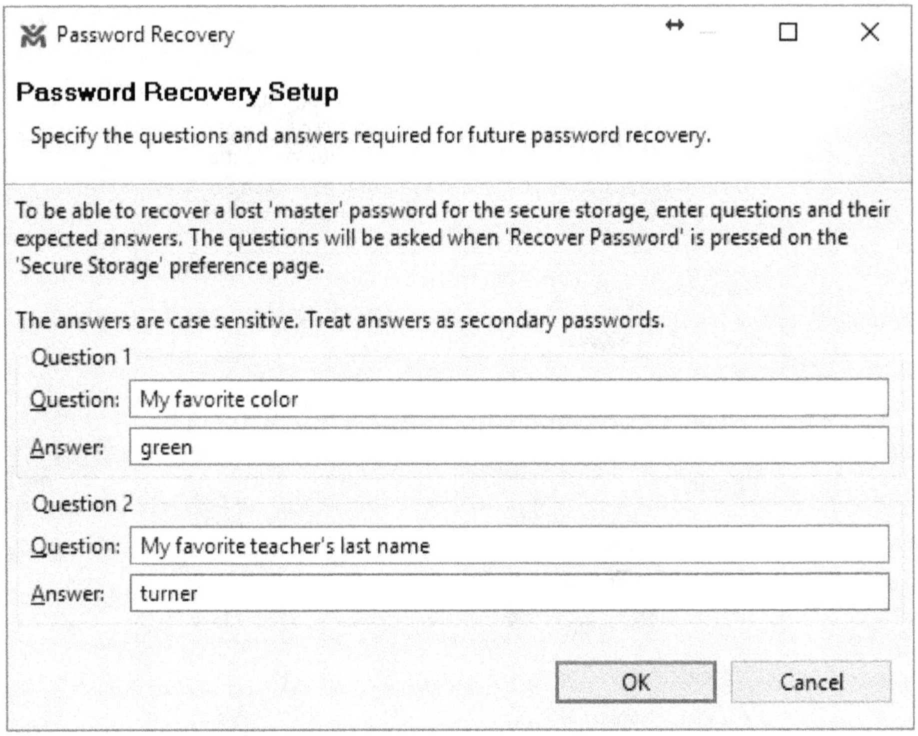

Password Recovery

Password Recovery Setup

Specify the questions and answers required for future password recovery.

To be able to recover a lost 'master' password for the secure storage, enter questions and their expected answers. The questions will be asked when 'Recover Password' is pressed on the 'Secure Storage' preference page.

The answers are case sensitive. Treat answers as secondary passwords.

Question 1

Question: My favorite color

Answer: green

Question 2

Question: My favorite teacher's last name

Answer: turner

OK Cancel

PuTTY Post-Configuration

Note: Download PuTTY from https://www.putty.org/

(Optional)

Under (VM Maestro) *File | Preferences | Terminal | Cisco Terminal*, I chose to enable *use external terminal applications* because when you open a terminal session on a node, instead of using VM Maestro's terminal window, PuTTY opens a separate SSH window for each node and allows me to move the terminal sessions to another screen while leaving my lab displayed – in VM Maestro - on my primary screen. If you prefer not to use PuTTY (or a similar external terminal client), skip this step.

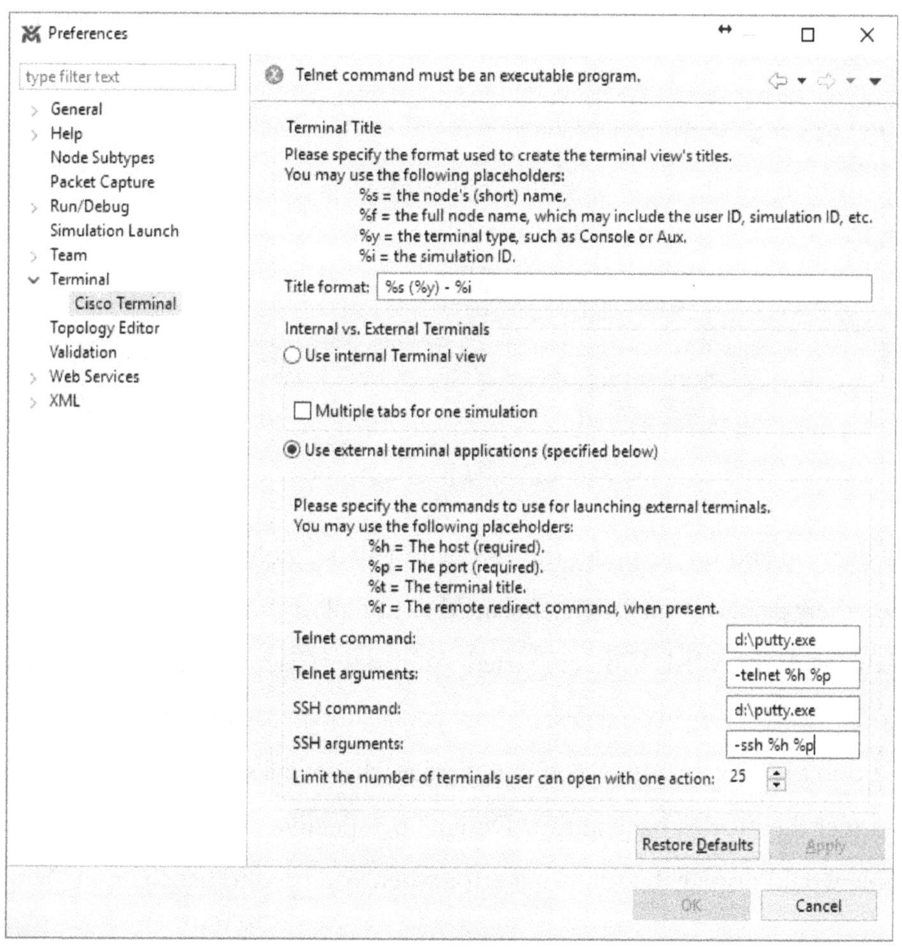

Node Subtypes Post-Configuration

Initially, VM Maestro is only aware of 13 subtypes (or nodes). To download the additional 18 subtypes, click on *File* | *Preferences* | *Node Subtypes*. Scroll down to the bottom of the screen and click *Fetch from Server*, then *OK*. VM Maestro downloads these additional subtypes from the VIRL server. Click *OK*. You should now see at least 31 different subtypes.

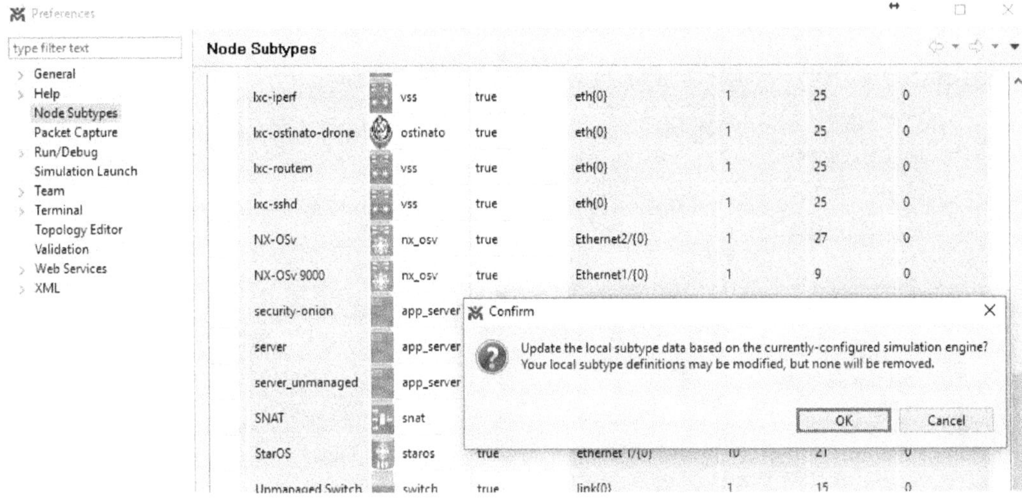

Lastly, scroll back up and notice under the "Show in Palette" column that some subtypes display "false" while others display "true". This means that not all of the subtypes shown may have images available with the VIRL VM being used. Why does Cisco put the "cart before the horse"? In other words, why would Cisco show you a subtype that's not even available yet in this image? I don't know. In any case, if you were to change all subtypes to "true" they would all show up under the **Nodes** pane in the "Design" perspective and those that don't have an image available would display the following error when you tried to use them in "Simulation" perspective:

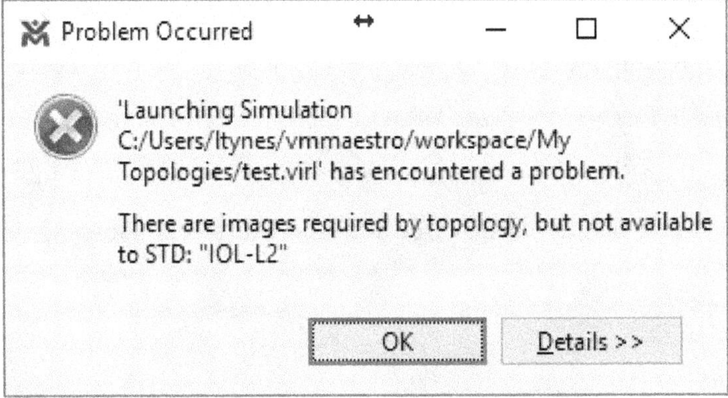

My suggestion: change <u>all</u> subtypes to "true" and those that display the previous error dialog box, when trying to use them in a simulation, simply change their subtype back to "false" – that way they won't show up in VM Maestro.

Note: Any time after a VIRL image update, or simply using a different VIRL image, you should always perform these previous steps.

CHAPTER 7: Getting to Know VM Maestro

If you recall during the installation and configuration of this application we were shown 4 web services that were not connecting. Anyway, whenever you first open VM Maestro and/or ever have issues with VM Maestro not working correctly, start by verifying that these web services are indeed connecting to the VIRL server via *File | Preferences | Web Services.* This is also where credentials: guest/guest are used.

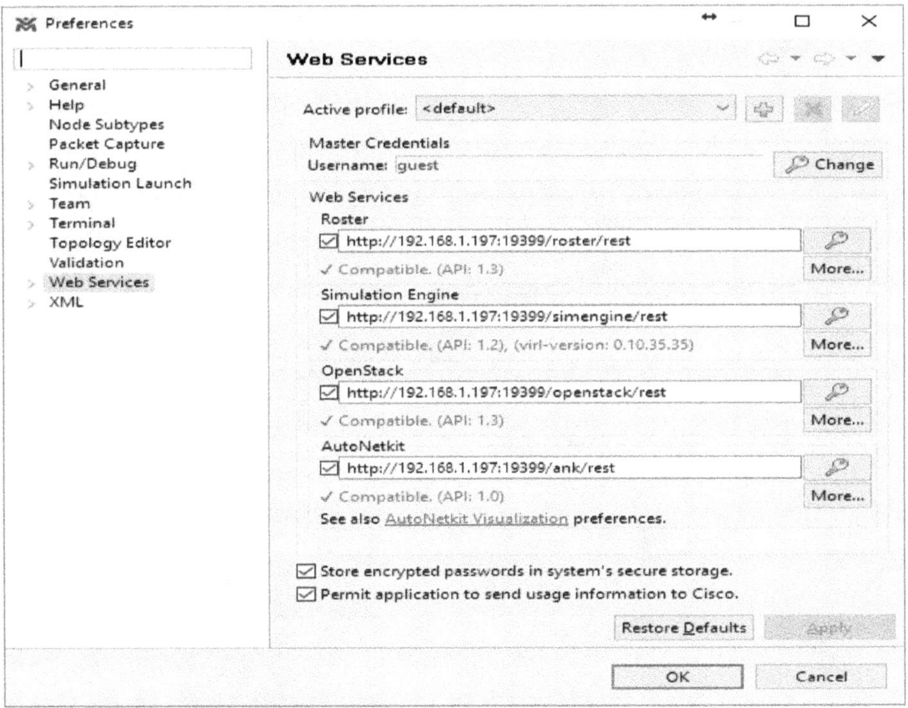

I'd be remissed if I didn't also mention two other ports (19401 and 19402) used to talk to VIRL that are editable in VM Maestro. These are used for the "AutoNetkit Webserver" and "Live Visualization Webserver" respectively. Keep in mind that once these are set (automatically during the installation), you need not worry about them – unless you change the ports in the VIRL server – which I'm certain you won't be doing.

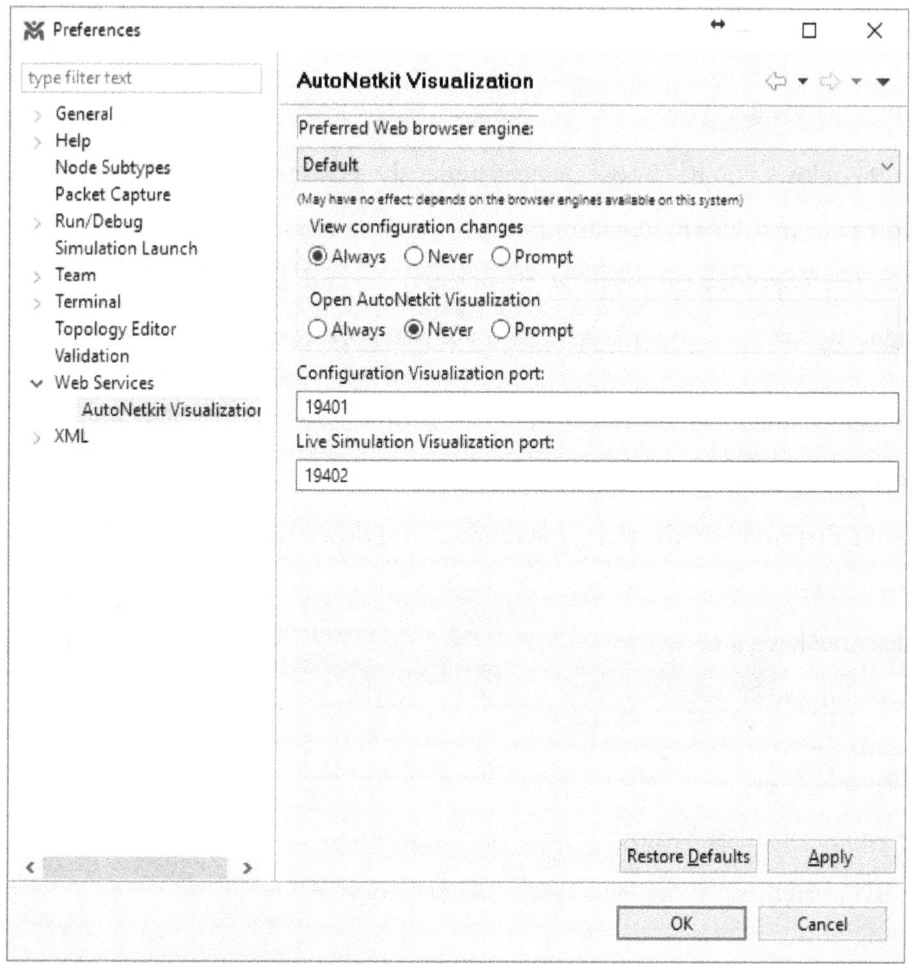

When opening VM Maestro you will always be presented with 1 of 2 perspectives: "Design" or "Simulation". By default, the design perspective is presented. Switching between perspectives is available in the upper righthand corner. Here in "design" perspective is where you create your topologies and utilize the various palette objects described next. "Simulation" perspective is where all of the nodes in your lab and their connections are started up. This is where the real hands-on work begins.

Note: If you ever inadvertently close or resize any of the following panes being described, just choose *Window* | *Reset Perspective…* and click *Yes* to resetting the perspective back to default.

Design Perspective

Topology Palette View - Tools

- **Select** – allows you to choose devices under the **Nodes** pane, add them to the Topology Editor pane and move them around. To choose a node simply click it and then click within the Topology Editor pane (there's no drag and drop here folks) to add it to your design. By the way, if you keep clicking in the workspace pane, the node you chose will keep being added. To prevent this just click on the Tools Select object again.
- **Connect** – choosing this tool allows you to make connections between nodes. Just click on your first node (in the design window), hold down the left mouse button, drag it to the second node and left mouse click. Your nodes now have a network connection between them.

Topology Palette View – Nodes

As I'm sure you're aware of by now – these are the various devices you use in designing a simulation. To learn more about each node, see Appendix A.

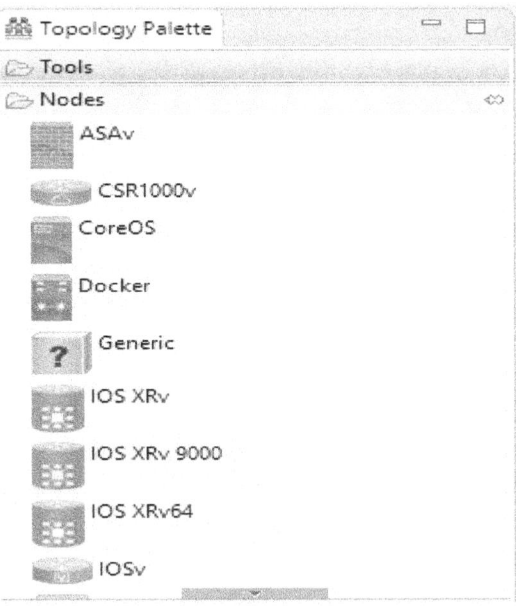

As I previously mentioned, just click/select a node and then click on the Topology Editor pane to add it to your topology.

Topology Palette View – General

Here's where you can connect your simulated lab via: a L2 external (FLAT1) switch or a L3 (SNAT) external router. Specifically, this means that:

1. L2 external (FLAT1) – allows your topology's in-band management interface IP addresses reachable externally (i.e., to a "true" physical switch).
2. L3 (SNAT) external router – allows you external connectivity via a static NAT (SNAT) L3 router. This allows you to hide (translate) your lab's topology IP addresses inbound and outbound so that your lab's addressing scheme is not propagated outside of your virtual network.

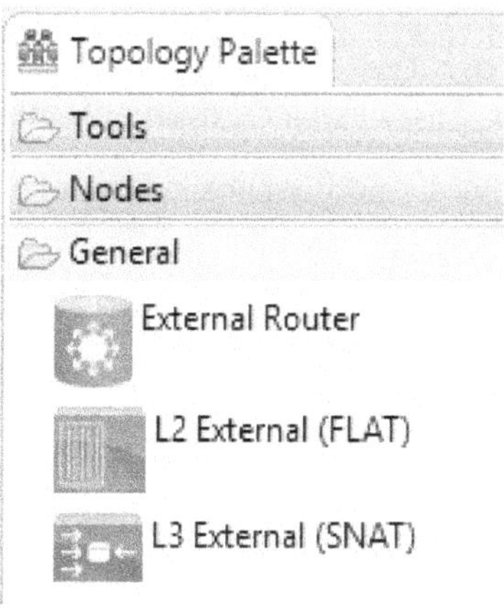

Only the L2 and L3 external connectivity types are explained in more detail in Chapter 9: Reaching Outside of Your Lab.

Topology Palette View – Annotations

Here is where notations can be made to your lab. The best use of this pane is in placing nodes into the rectangle or ellipse, then using the text tool to reference a location.

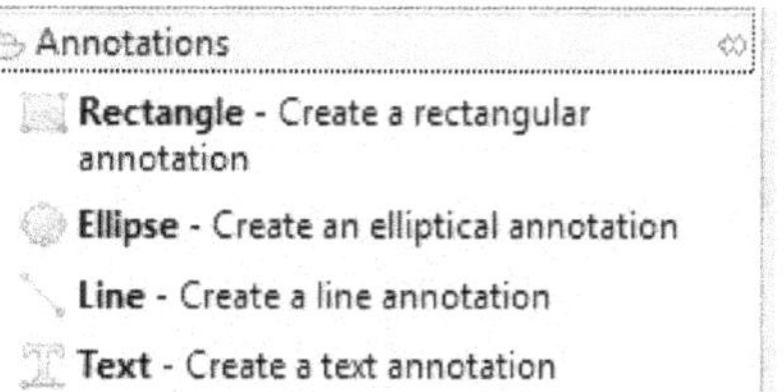

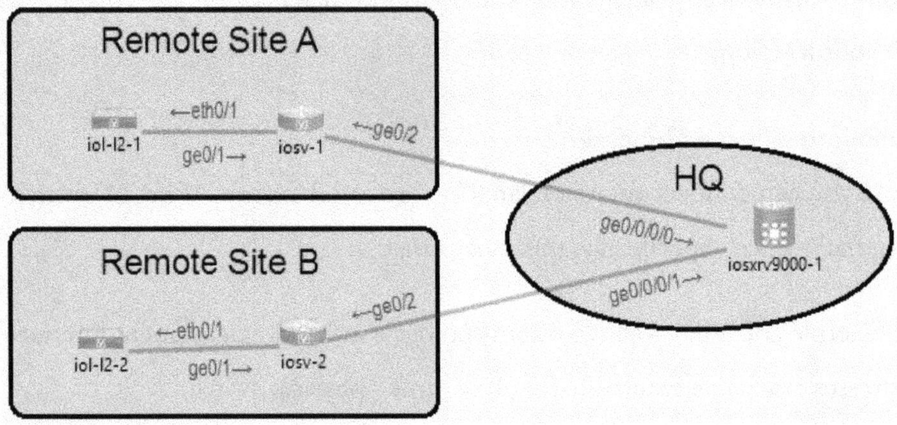

Topology Palette View – Projects

Here's where the built-in, or your manually created labs, are stored. To open one, in the "Design" perspective, just double-click it. These files all have a .virl extension and are written in .XML. Each .virl file contains node configurations, their attributes and how they're connected and laid out in the workspace pane. You can also do many other functions in this pane simply by right-clicking one of the topologies or right-clicking on a blank space. Some of the more interesting options are:

- Making a copy of an existing lab
- Importing/Exporting labs or projects
- Validating a lab
- Properties: checks the location of a lab and other aspects
- Team: applying a project patch or share projects with others.

By default labs are stored in:

My Topologies – c:\users\<username>\vmmaestro\workspace\My Topologies

Sample Topologies – c:\users\<username>\vmmaestro\workspace\Sample Topologies

Sample-topologies – c:\users\<username>\vmmaestro\workspace\git\sample-topologies\CBTNuggets

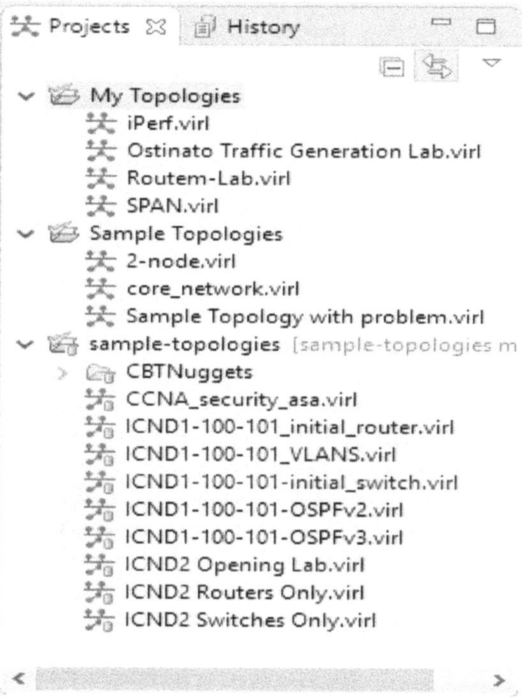

Topology Palette View – History

Historical changes made to topology files (.virl) are maintained here. This allows you to replace a current file with a previous one or even restore a file that's been deleted. Each file's history is uniquely displayed with a date and timestamp noting when the file was saved.

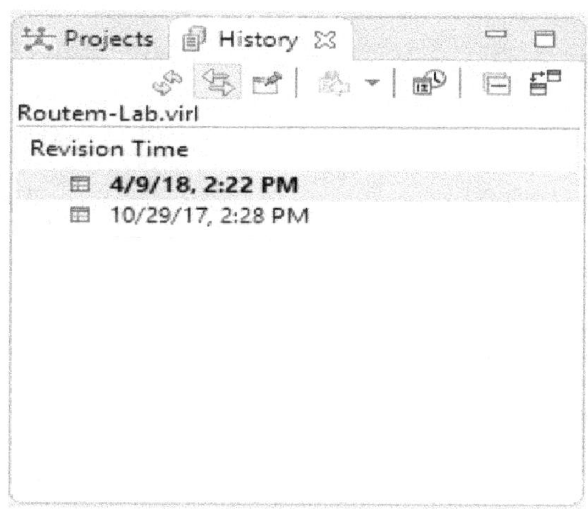

Note: You must have saved your .virl file first, before you'll see the multiple revisions (timestamps) of that file. Also note that projects and folders do not retain history retention - only .virl topology files retain history retention.

Overwrite Current Revision?
Do you wish to overwrite the current revision with the selected revision?
Yes
Cancel

One of the things I like best about this pane is right-clicking one of the timestamped revisions and choosing *Get Contents*. This will prompt you - as shown - whether or not you want to replace what's currently in your workspace's topology.

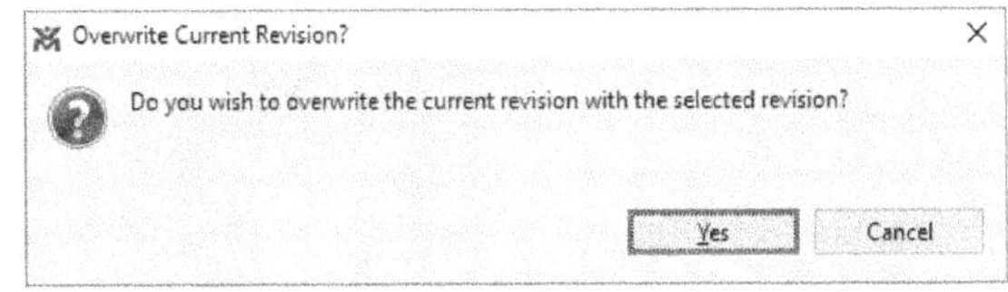

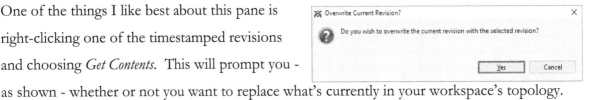

Properties View

When a topology is placed in the Topology Editor pane, properties pertaining to that lab – the number of nodes, your IP addressing schema, routing protocols used, etc - are displayed.

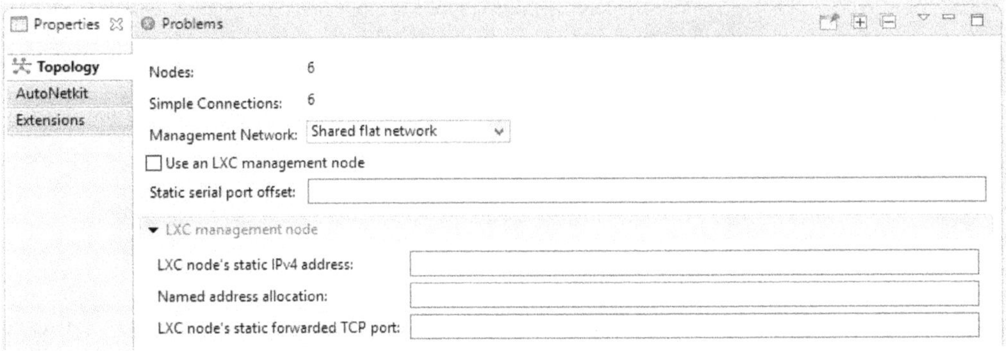

Properties
Problems
Topology
AutoNetkit
Extensions
Nodes: 6
Simple Connections: 6
Management Network: Shared flat network
Use an LXC management node
Static serial port offset:
LXC management node
LXC node's static IPv4 address:
Named address allocation:
LXC node's static forwarded TCP port:

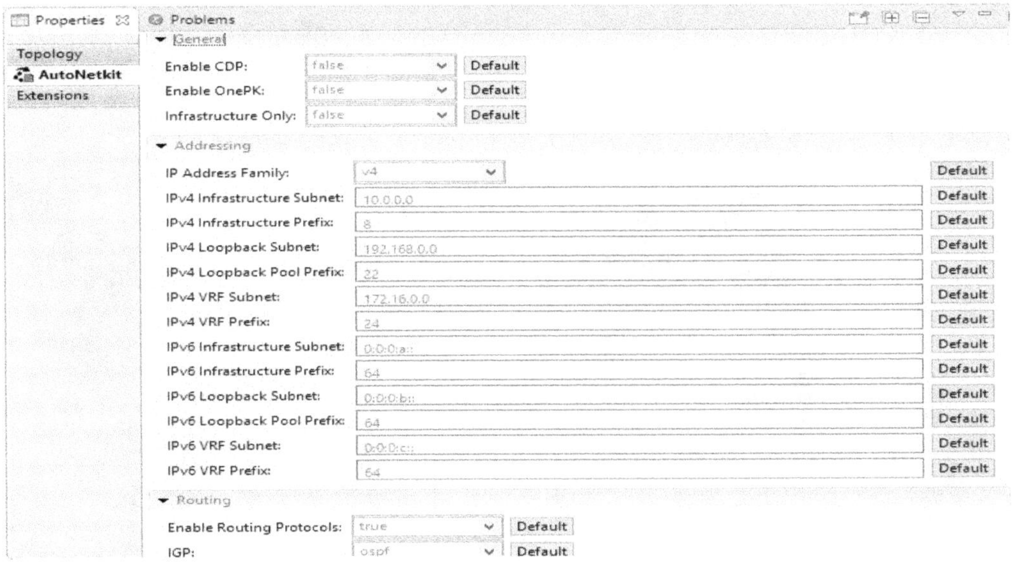

Properties
Problems
Topology
AutoNetkit
Extensions
General
Enable CDP: false Default
Enable OnePK: false Default
Infrastructure Only: false Default
Addressing
IP Address Family: v4 Default
IPv4 Infrastructure Subnet: 10.0.0.0 Default
IPv4 Infrastructure Prefix: 8 Default
IPv4 Loopback Subnet: 192.168.0.0 Default
IPv4 Loopback Pool Prefix: 22 Default
IPv4 VRF Subnet: 172.16.0.0 Default
IPv4 VRF Prefix: 24 Default
IPv6 Infrastructure Subnet: 0:0:0:a:: Default
IPv6 Infrastructure Prefix: 64 Default
IPv6 Loopback Subnet: 0:0:0:b:: Default
IPv6 Loopback Pool Prefix: 64 Default
IPv6 VRF Subnet: 0:0:0:c:: Default
IPv6 VRF Prefix: 64 Default
Routing
Enable Routing Protocols: true Default
IGP: ospf Default

Now, if a particular node - within a topology - is selected, its properties are displayed (based on the Property tab selected):

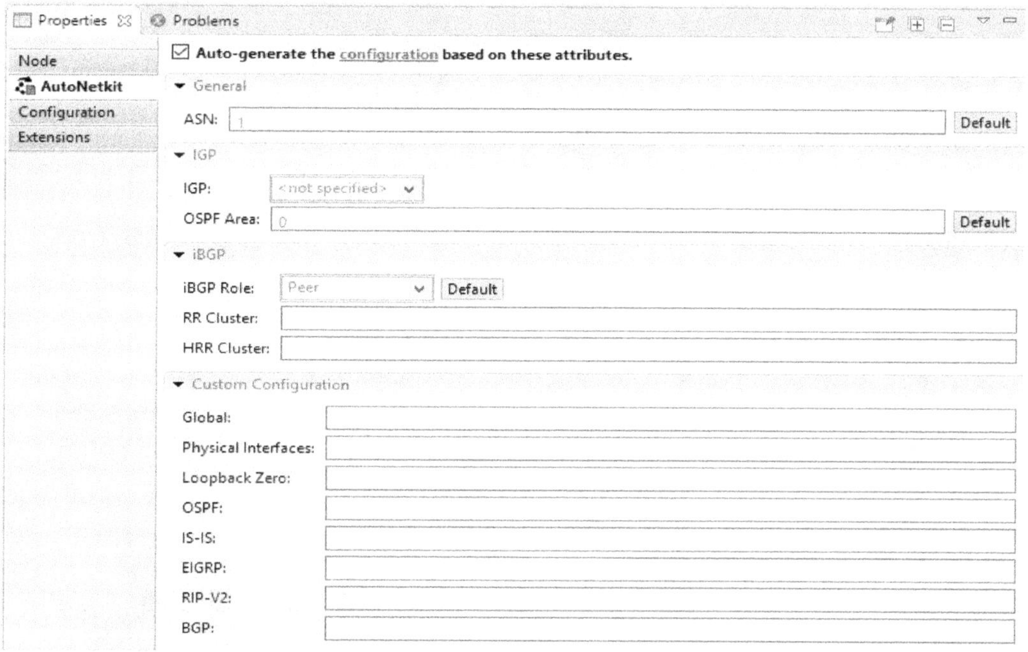

Properties | Problems

Node
AutoNetkit
Configuration
Extensions

☑ Auto-generate the configuration based on these attributes.

▾ General

ASN: 1 [Default]

▾ IGP

IGP: <not specified>

OSPF Area: 0 [Default]

▾ iBGP

iBGP Role: Peer [Default]

RR Cluster:

HRR Cluster:

▾ Custom Configuration

Global:

Physical Interfaces:

Loopback Zero:

OSPF:

IS-IS:

EIGRP:

RIP-V2:

BGP:

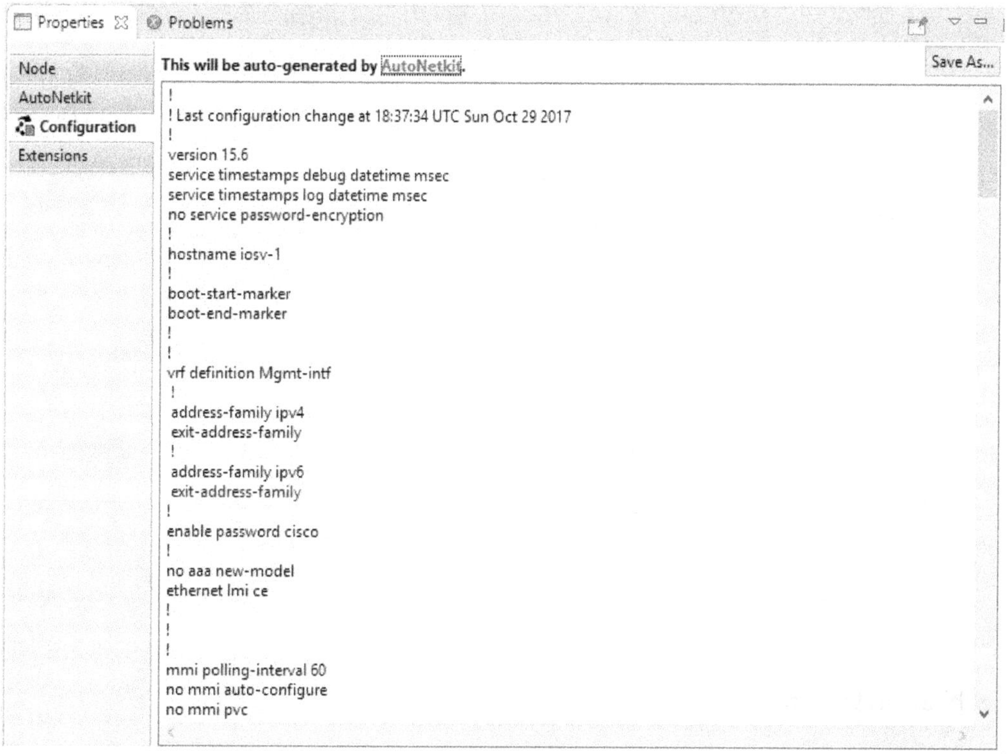

Properties | Problems

Node
AutoNetkit
Configuration
Extensions

This will be auto-generated by AutoNetkit. [Save As...]

```
!
! Last configuration change at 18:37:34 UTC Sun Oct 29 2017
!
version 15.6
service timestamps debug datetime msec
service timestamps log datetime msec
no service password-encryption
!
hostname iosv-1
!
boot-start-marker
boot-end-marker
!
!
vrf definition Mgmt-intf
 !
 address-family ipv4
 exit-address-family
 !
 address-family ipv6
 exit-address-family
!
enable password cisco
!
no aaa new-model
ethernet lmi ce
!
!
!
mmi polling-interval 60
no mmi auto-configure
no mmi pvc
```

I'd like to bring your attention the **AutoNetkit** tabs shown in the previous screenshots. AutoNetkit is an automated feature of VIRL that provisions basic IP addressing, routing protocols and more. This allows you more time working with labs and learning the various technologies as opposed to wasting time configuring basic settings.

In regards to a topology, AutoNetkit allows you to globally configure all devices within your specific lab to take into account settings such as: CDP, auto IP addressing (IPv4, IPv6, both, or none), routing protocols and MPLS. To disable this feature, choose *None* or *False* from each area.

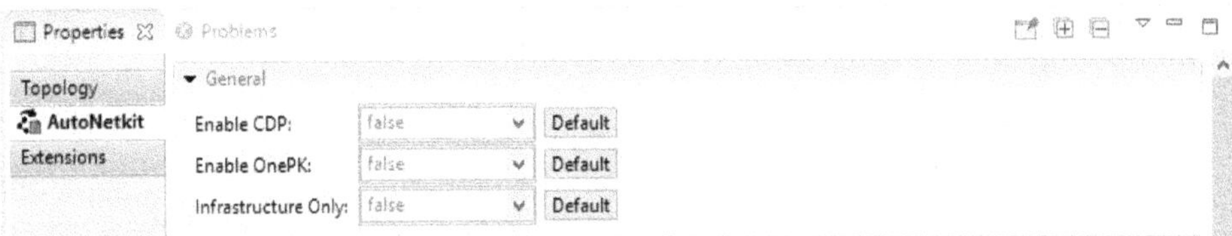

In regards to individual nodes, AutoNetkit can be enabled or disabled. Enabling it auto-generates settings from the topology's AutoNetkit settings plus additional settings such as: ASNs, the type of routing protocol (if any) and its specific settings, VRFs, GRE tunnels and more. To disable this feature, uncheck *Auto-generate the configuration based on these attributes.*

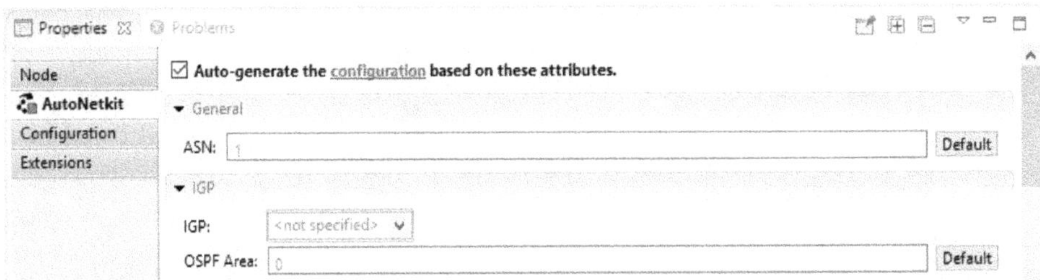

So if you chose not to use AutoNetkit, per topology or per node, you can manually configure these settings; thus getting even more hands-on with the various configuration options.

What a cool tool huh?! Starting with an automatically converged network will save you hours of setup time and although it's not necessarily needed, it is advisable to leave it enabled at least initially while you learn more about the product.

Simulation Perspective

The "Simulation" perspective is activated when a lab/topology is launched by clicking

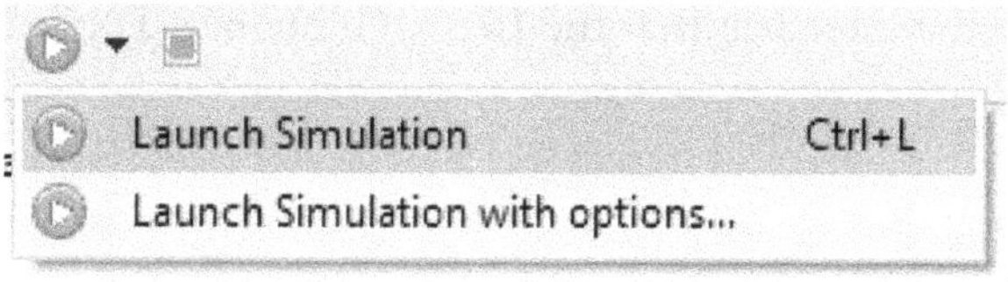

.

The **Projects, Topology Editor**, **Simulations,** and **Console** views are all part of this perspective.

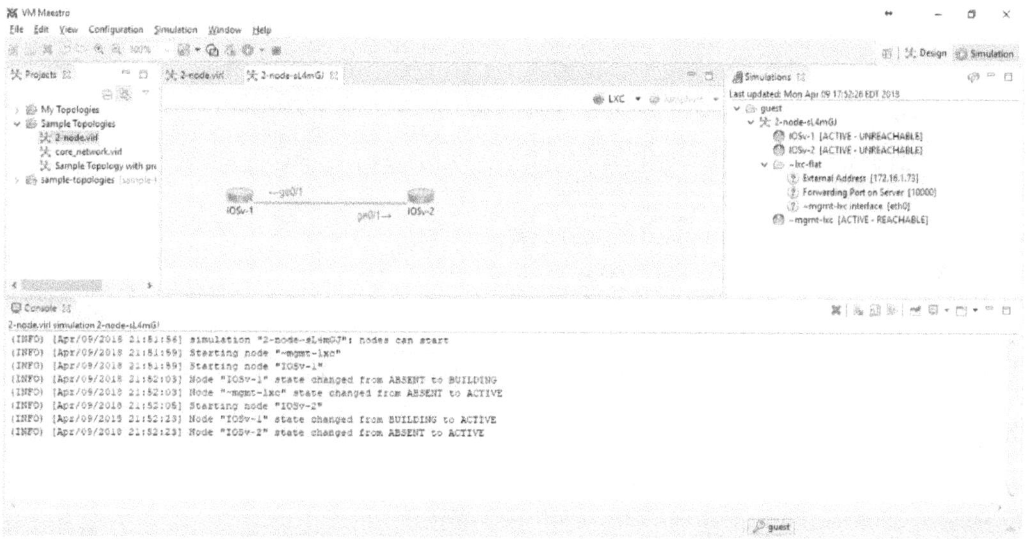

Using the built-in ***2-node.virl*** sample topology as my example, pay special attention to the **Simulations** and **Console** panes during the launch of your topology. Here's where each node's status is reported and this is the first place to look at if problems are encountered. The **Simulations** pane displays a green icon – per node – if that particular node launched successfully. This icon will display as blue (if the node is building) or clear (if the node is stopped) with the **Console** pane explaining why the node's icon is the color that it is.

You may have noticed that nodes **IOSv1** and **IOSv2**; although displayed with a green icon, are also showing [ACTIVE – UNREACHABLE]. The reason "unreachable" is displayed is because it's Gi0/0 interface is "administratively down" – by default. Simply "unshutting" the interface fixes this.

Gi0/0 also happens to be the interface that the Linux Container (LXC) or "jump server" uses to manage/communicate with this node.

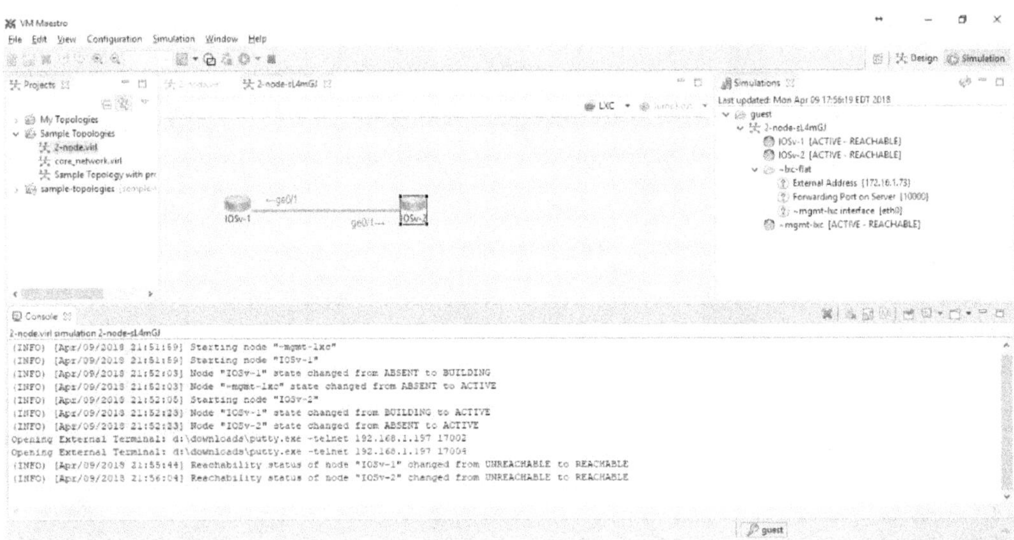

Special Note: Enabling the checkbox to include a Linux Container (LXC) in a topology is something you should always enable. It's a "jump" box you can use to ping or SSH/telnet to other topology nodes; among many other things (i.e., testing for open ports on other topology nodes using telnet).

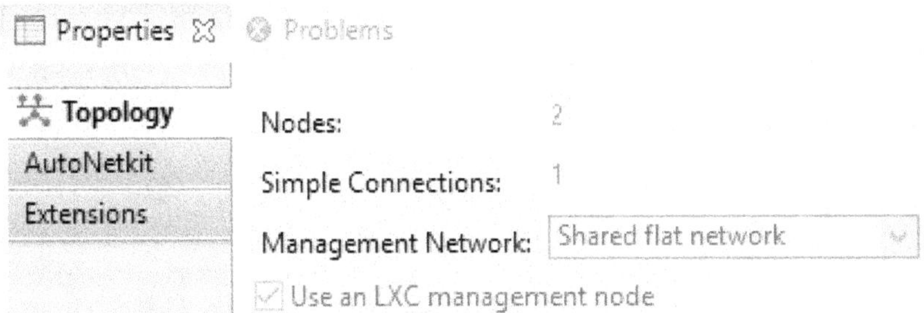

To access a node's console, right-click it and choose *Telnet… | to its Console port.* You may have to hit <enter> a couple times to get a response.

Note: Attempting to connect to a node via its management port (172.16.1.x) will always fail. Remember the default management network only exists inside the VIRL VM; thus why it's so important to create an LXC management node with each topology. As demonstrated earlier you can configure PuTTY to SSH from your Win10 workstation to VIRL's server via 192.168.1.197 and then use its 172.16.1.250 address to connect to any node's management IP address.

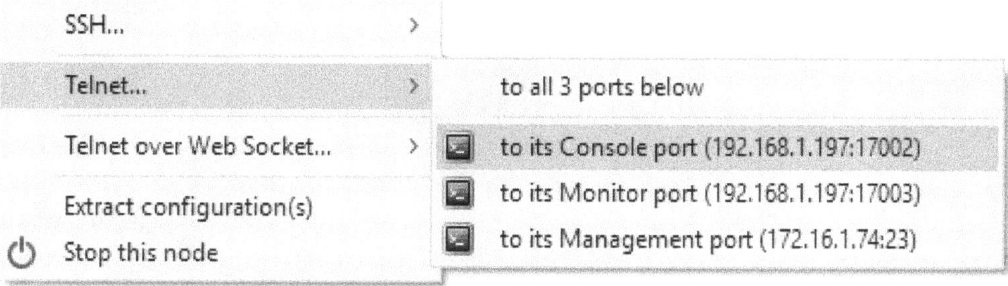

To access your LXC via its management port, click LXC ▾ , *SSH… | to its Management (via server) port.* The credentials to login are: guest / guest.

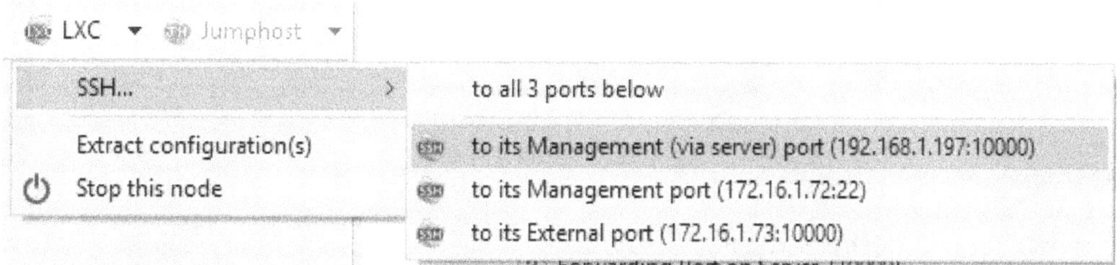

Notice how the command prompt's suffix (i.e., sL4mGJ) is the same name displayed in the VM Maestro Topology Editor tab. This proves helpful if you have multiple LXC's running from multiple active topologies.

192.168.1.197 - PuTTY

```
login as: guest
guest@192.168.1.197's password:
guest@mgmt-sL4mGJ$
```

Whew! We've accomplished a lot just to get our environment up and running just how we want it. This seems like an appropriate time to mention backing up your VIRL server. In VMware Workstation we have the option of creating a snapshot – whether the VM is running or not – so let's do that.

Right-click on your VIRL Server's tab, choose Snapshot | Take Snapshot.

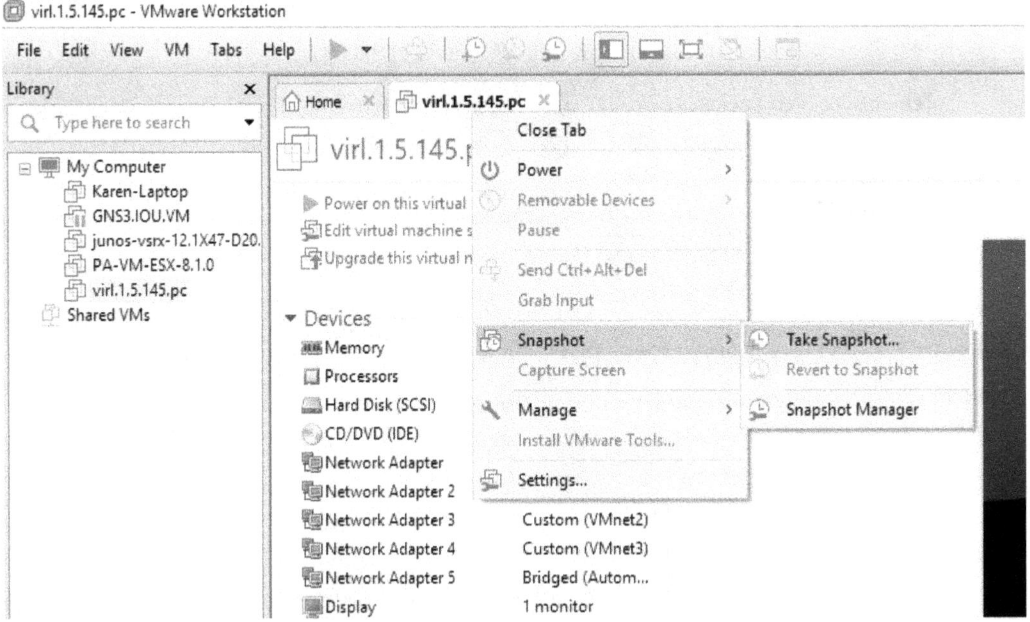

Name it whatever you desire and click *Take Snapshot.*

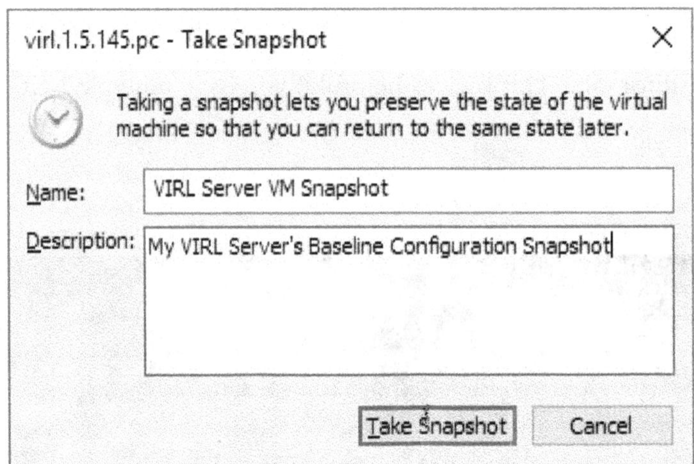

Note: Remember that this snapshot only pertains to the virtual machine's memory, settings, and state of its virtual disk(s) from the VMware Workstation perspective.

The internal VIRL server's configuration settings are stored in various files – in my case under D:\VMs\VMware Workstation\VIRL\VIRL Server VM. **I highly advise you to backup these files to another directory** – in my case to D:\VMs\VMware Workstation\VIRL\VIRL Server Backup. You could then use these files to restore your running VIRL server's files if they ever become corrupted or you've misconfigured VIRL server in such a way that it will not run properly.

CHAPTER 8: Getting to Know User Workspace Management

In Chapter 6 you were first introduced to some of the uses of the User Workspace Management (UWM) Interface by configuring your VIRL server with its license key. As you saw at that time, UWM was used for backend configuration; but it's also used for frontend configuration, user account management, projects, monitoring, and other miscellaneous purposes. As I mentioned before: "…VIRL server being considered the "heart" and VM Maestro being considered the "eyes…" – let's think of UWM as the embodiment of both of these.

During your VIRL server configuration the following two accounts were automatically created: **uwmadmin** and **guest**, using (default) passwords: **password** and **guest**, respectively. Each of these accounts has different permissions inside of UWM. The following table depicts these differences:

User Account	UWM Feature	Permission?	Note
Uwmadmin	My Simulations	No	Not able to run simulations
Guest	My Simulations	Yes	Given by default during installation as the primary account/owner for all simulations.
Uwmadmin	Project Simulations	No	Not able to run simulations
Guest	Project Simulations	Yes	Given by default during installation as the primary account/owner for all simulations.

Uwmadmin	Projects	Yes	Can modify all of guest's project settings, but can only modify uwmadmin's project quotas
Guest	Projects	Yes	Can modify all of uwmadmin's project settings, but can only modify guest's project quotas
Uwmadmin	VIRL Server | System Config, System Upgrade and VIRL software	Yes	Default system admin permissions
Guest	VIRL Server | System Config, System Upgrade and VIRL software	No	Granted no system admin permissions
Uwmadmin	Repositories	No	Is not presented
Guest	Repositories	Yes	Git hub repositories can be added

Now that you know what each account can/cannot perform while in UWM, let's dive a little deeper into what many of the features do.

Note: A comprehensive search index and documentation library is included with your VIRL server and located at the following URL: http://192.168.1.197/doc.

UWM Feature	Purpose
Overview Resource usage by host Resource usage of simulations Simulations	Displays the versions of software used by the different VIRL components Displays your VIRL server's (number of CPUs, RAM, and disk size) VMware configuration. You can modify this at any time. When running a simulation, displays how many instances, virtual RAM and virtual CPUs are being used per simulation. This is controllable under "Projects" Displays the simulation's name, the user whose context it's running under, its status, time it started, expiration date (if set) and you can also stop the simulation.
My Simulations (as "guest") Launch new simulation Resource usage of user guest	Displays the simulation's name, its status, time it started, expiration date (if set), a "live visualization" that allows you to collect specific information (i.e., ARP, route path, etc) as mentioned in chapter 11, and allows you to stop the simulation. Method used to launch a simulation via a local or remote .virl file. Displays the (instances, virtual CPUs and virtual RAM) resources running under a user's context. This is controllable under "Projects"
Project Simulations (as "guest") Resource usage of	Displays the simulation's name, the user context the simulation is running under, its status, time it started, and expiration date (if set). Displays the (instances, virtual CPUs and virtual RAM) resources running under a user's project. This is controllable under "Projects"

project guest	
Projects Export	Displays user accounts that have projects running under its context. Exports a selected project and all its users to a JSON or TSV file.
Users	Project user account creation
VIRL Server Salt Configuration and Status System Configuration (as "uwmadmin")	 Verifies the status of your VIRL server, resets the configuration (i.e., license file, etc), export your VIRL license, and check/recheck the connection to Cisco's SALT (license) servers. Remote Connections: used to configure an NTP server, proxy and DNS servers. Hardware: mainly used for RAM and CPU overcommit to allow more nodes to run in a simulation when your physical host's resources are rather limited. Shared Networks: used to configure OOB management and L2 external connectivity. L3 SNAT: used to configured L3 external connectivity. Service Ports: TCP ports used by various features. Users: used to modify default user accounts and set other user permissions. Simulation Details: VM serial port timeout inactivity. OpenVPN: used to configure OpenVPN. Cisco Call-Home: sends anonymous information to Cisco and checks for software updates automatically. Display Statistics: displays memory usage, the number of nodes,

System Tools System Upgrade VIRL Software Download	projects and users run in simulations over a day, week and month. Check System Health: displays details of the various hardware components (i.e., disk partitioning and utilization, RAM usage, etc), configuration and services running in the VIRL VM. System Operation Check: runs thorough tests to verify proper operation of your VIRL system. Download System Logs: exports your entire system's logs to a zipped file. System Console: provides a terminal session to the server – similar to what you have in VMware or via and SSH session – using "virl" account credentials. Provides the mechanism to upgrade VIRL either partially or in its entirety. Provides a list of the last upgraded components that were installed. VMMaestro client software
Connectivity	Displays L2, L3 and management IP allocations and connections. Here you can also add static IP / MAC address allocations.
VM Control Nodes	Use with caution as this feature is used for troubleshooting purposes only. (If simulation is running) Displays active nodes. Nodes can also be deleted. (If simulation is running) Displays the network type (i.e., flat, flat1, ext-

Networks	net) and number of interfaces on active nodes. Nodes can also be deleted.
Ports and Floating IPs	(If simulation is running) Displays each node's IP address based on the type (i.e., flat, flat1, ext-net) of network its interface is on. Nodes can also be deleted.
Hosts	Displays services and agent running on the VIRL host.
Allocated Ports	(If simulation is running) Displays the active service ports being used. This is based on ports configured under *VIRL Server | System Configuration | Service Ports.*
Node Resources	
Flavors	Displays each subtype's run-time image which includes its RAM, vCPU and disk space each requires to run.
Images	Displays each subtype's image version. This is also where you import 3rd party images and can modify the characteristics of any image.
Containers	Displays container images and templates. This is where you can import docker images.
Subtypes	Displays the characteristics of each subtype (i.e., the amount of RAM it needs to run, the number of interfaces it can have, etc).
Documentation	
STD API	API providing various server information

UWM API	API for developing and management
Routem	Simply mentions "Routem" (see Chapter 11 for more comprehensive explanation and usage).
Installation & Tutorial	Various resources for obtaining and deploying VIRL; as well as tutorials and external resources for further support.
Simulation Concepts	Link to your VIRL server's comprehensive search and documentation library
Community	
Community Forum	As the name implies – a community for VIRL support, How-To's and Troubleshooting.
Online Videos	Cisco's VIRL YouTube channel

CHAPTER 9: Reaching Outside of Your Lab

As briefly mentioned in Chapter 7, there are several external connectivity methods your VIRL server's simulated lab can connect to. I will only focus on the ones that you would want to use.

1. Out-of-Band (OOB) FLAT Management Access
2. FLAT1 (L2 connectivity)
3. SNAT (L3 connectivity).

Out of Band (OOB) FLAT Management Access

Some in the VIRL community may argue that this isn't considered one of the external connectivity methods, while I would claim that since it allows your Win10 workstation direct connectivity to your simulated topology nodes – rather than having to connect/communicate directly to the nodes via the LXC "jumpbox" – it is indeed used for external connectivity outside of your lab.

This procedure is only required if you desire the ability for your Win10 workstation to directly access topology nodes; as well as the VIRL server's default management NIC (172.16.1.250). The use of PuTTY or other external applications can prove reachability to these nodes and can be used for other purposes. **I highly recommend that you configure this**.

Note: Make certain that although your VIRL server is running; no simulations are running.

Login to the UWM interface – http://192.168.1.197/login/ with credentials: uwmadmin | password.

In the left-side pane, click VIRL Server | System Configuration.

Click *Shared Networks* and make certain the category: *flat* is highlighted and choose *eth1* under the host interface, then click *Apply Changes*.

We must make this change – or any major changes to the VIRL VM – while in “maintenance mode” so click Apply Changes, then Enable maintenance mode, next Enable and lastly Apply Changes.

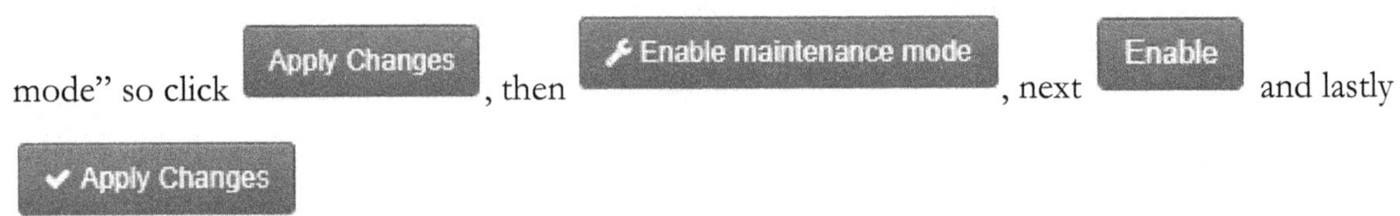

You will see a screen similar to this – Jobs in Progress…

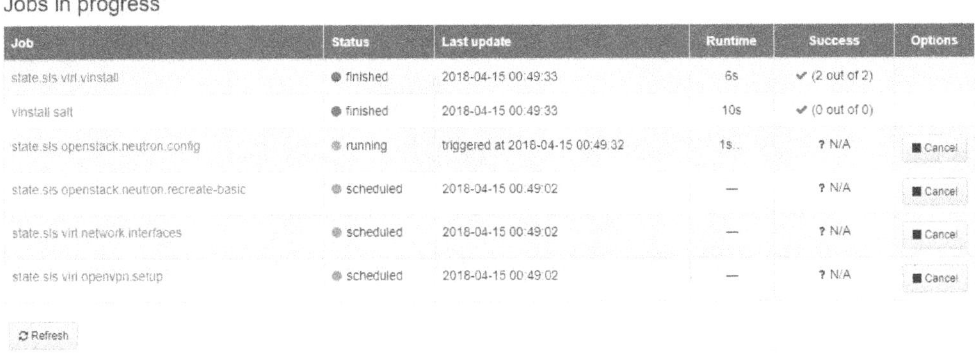

Jobs in progress

Job	Status	Last update	Runtime	Success	Options
state.sls virl.vinstall	finished	2018-04-15 00:49:33	6s	✔ (2 out of 2)	
vinstall salt	finished	2018-04-15 00:49:33	10s	✔ (0 out of 0)	
state.sls openstack.neutron.config	running	triggered at 2018-04-15 00:49:32	1s..	? N/A	Cancel
state.sls openstack.neutron.recreate-basic	scheduled	2018-04-15 00:49:02	—	? N/A	Cancel
state.sls virl.network.interfaces	scheduled	2018-04-15 00:49:02	—	? N/A	Cancel
state.sls virl.openvpn.setup	scheduled	2018-04-15 00:49:02	—	? N/A	Cancel

Refresh

Please wait until the above jobs are finished ...

Although your browser window may automatically refresh the status, you can also click

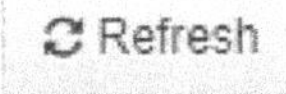

until the status column for all jobs shows **finished**.

Jobs in progress

Job	Status
state.sls virl.vinstall	finished
vinstall salt	finished
state.sls openstack.neutron.config	finished
state.sls openstack.neutron.recreate-basic	finished
state.sls virl.network.interfaces	finished
state.sls virl.openvpn.setup	finished

Now click **Disable maintenance mode**, then click **Disable**. Lastly, click **OK**. All configuration controls are now grayed out showing you are out of maintenance mode.

System Configuration Controls

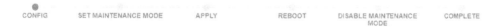

As briefly mentioned in the **VMware Workstation 14** installation section, when you installed VMware it created 3 VMnet NICs (VMnet0, VMnet1 and VMnet8). Let's make the modifications we need that will allow your Win10 workstation to communicate to the VIRL server, and any topology nodes, via their management interface.

1. Under the VMware Workstation's pull-down **Edit** menu, choose *Virtual Network Editor.*
2. Click **Change Settings**.
3. Highlight VMnet1 and modify it as I've shown below. This NIC will be used for directly accessing the VIRL server's management interface (172.16.1.250) as well as topology nodes' management interfaces.

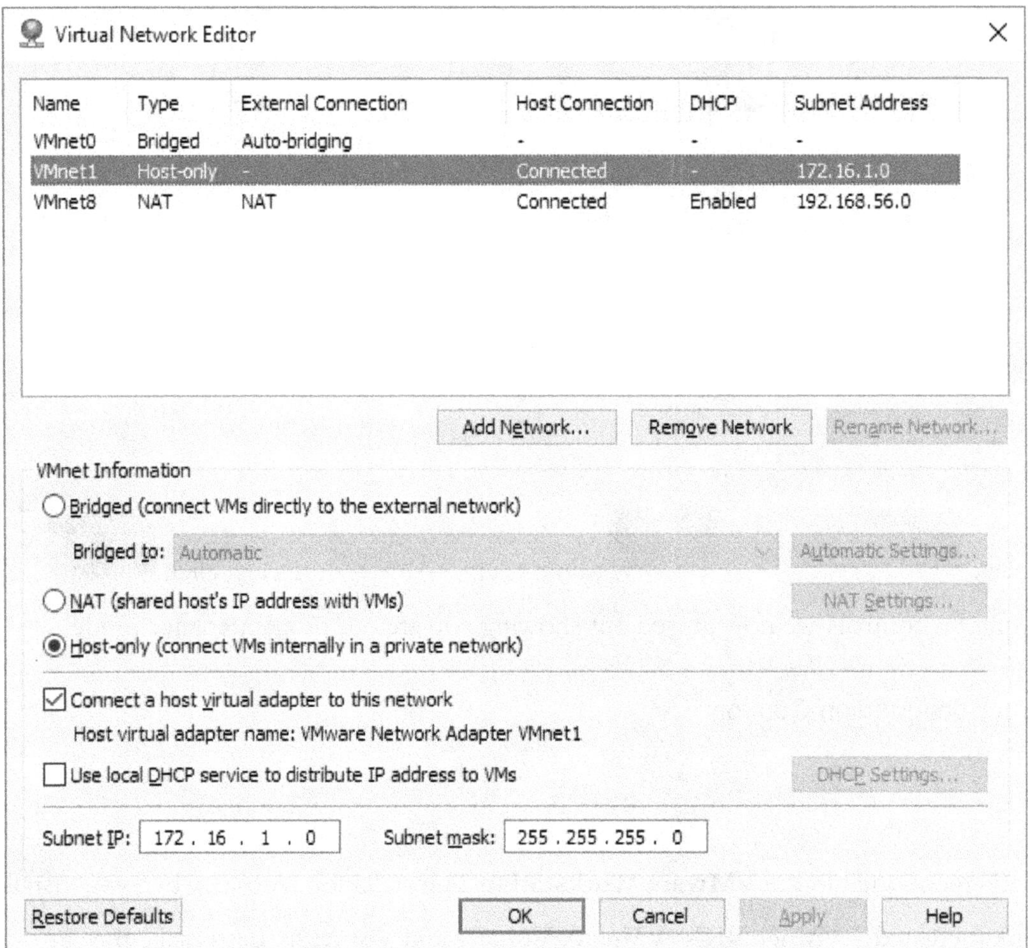

4. Now go under Control Panel | Network and Sharing Center | Change Adapter Settings and right-click **VMnet1** to bring up its Properties. Uncheck Internet Protocol Version 6 (TCP/IPv6) – unless you intend on using IPv6 - then double-click Internet Protocol Version 4 (TCP/IPv4) and (if not already set) statically assign IP address 172.16.1.1 and 255.255.255.0 as the subnet mask. Click OK twice to complete this.
5. Under VMware, right-click the VIRL server's tab and choose *Settings…*

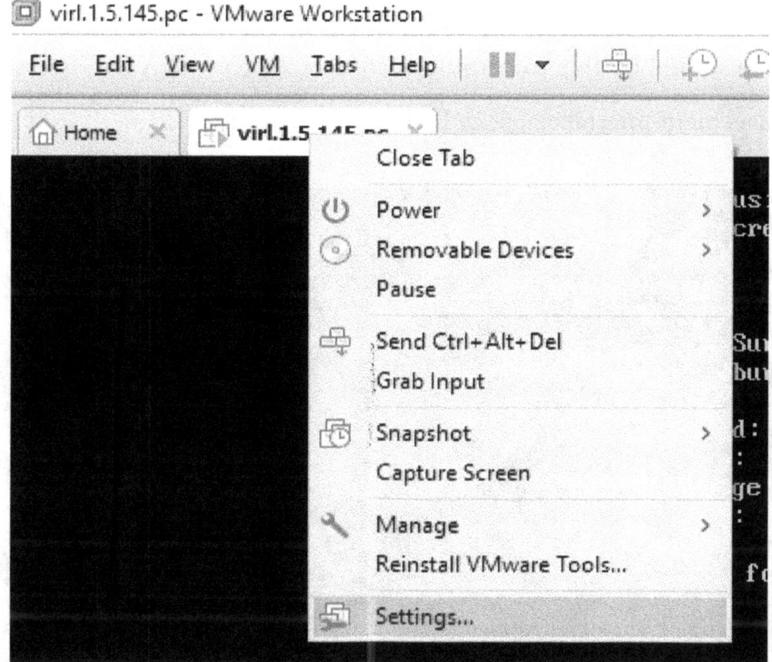

6. Now change **Network Adapter** 2 to use **VMnet1 (Host-only)** interface, as shown below, then click *OK.*

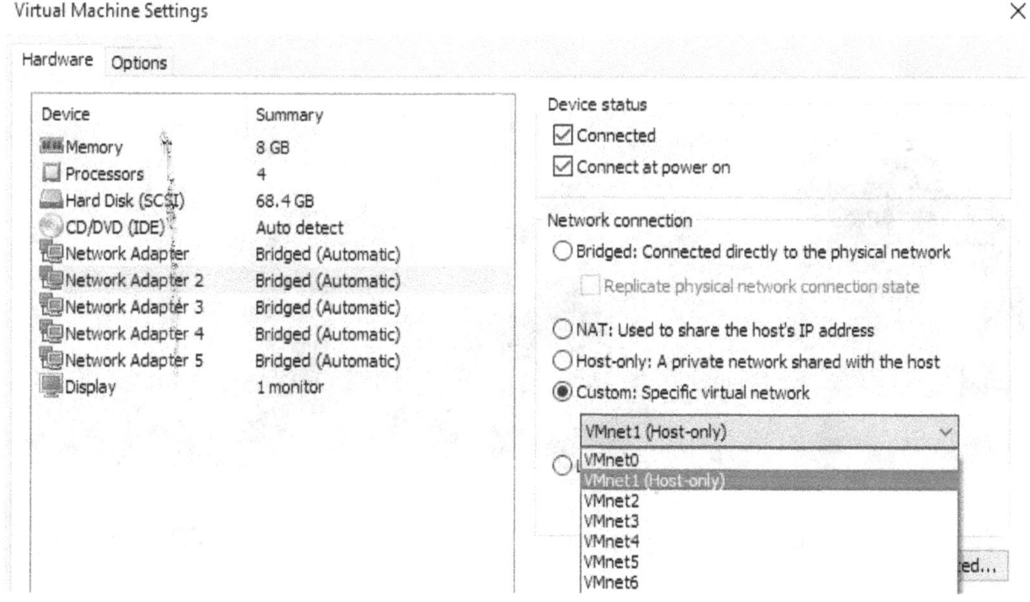

7. Run a continuous ping (give it a moment) – *ping -t 172.16.1.*250 – and now your Win10 workstation should be able to communicate directly to your VIRL's server's 172.16.1.250 (br1) management interface; just as I have.

```
C:\windows\system32>ping -t 172.16.1.250

Pinging 172.16.1.250 with 32 bytes of data:
Reply from 172.16.1.1: Destination host unreachable.
Request timed out.
Request timed out.
Request timed out.
Request timed out.
Request timed out.
Request timed out.
Request timed out.
Request timed out.
Request timed out.
Request timed out.
Request timed out.
Request timed out.
Reply from 172.16.1.250: bytes=32 time<1ms TTL=64
Reply from 172.16.1.250: bytes=32 time<1ms TTL=64
Reply from 172.16.1.250: bytes=32 time<1ms TTL=64
Reply from 172.16.1.250: bytes=32 time<1ms TTL=64
Reply from 172.16.1.250: bytes=32 time<1ms TTL=64
Reply from 172.16.1.250: bytes=32 time<1ms TTL=64
Reply from 172.16.1.250: bytes=32 time<1ms TTL=64
```

8. Using PuTTY, you should also be able to SSH to your VIRL server (172.16.1.250); using the credentials: virl | VIRL. This now proves external FLAT connectivity to your VIRL server.

```
virl@virl: ~
login as: virl
virl@172.16.1.250's password:
Welcome to Ubuntu 16.04.3 LTS (GNU/Linux 4.4.0-116-generic x86_64)

  System load:          0.09                IP address for br1:     172.16.1.250
  Usage of /:           14.8% of 59.38GB    IP address for br2:     172.16.2.250
  Memory usage:         54%                 IP address for br4:     172.16.10.250
  Swap usage:           0%                  IP address for br3:     172.16.3.250
  Processes:            267                 IP address for docker0: 172.17.0.1
  IP address for eth0: 192.168.1.197
Last login: Sun Apr 22 03:33:10 2018 from 172.16.1.1
virl@virl:~$
```

Note: The next procedure will prove external FLAT connectivity to any VIRL topology node.

To allow any topology node the ability to connect to your FLAT management external Win10 host network:

1. In the “Design” perspective of VM Maestro, create or open an existing topology.
2. Click within the **Topology Editor** canvas
3. Choose the *Properties* (pane), then the *Topology* tab.
4. Under **Management Network**, choose *Shared flat network* from the drop-down list.

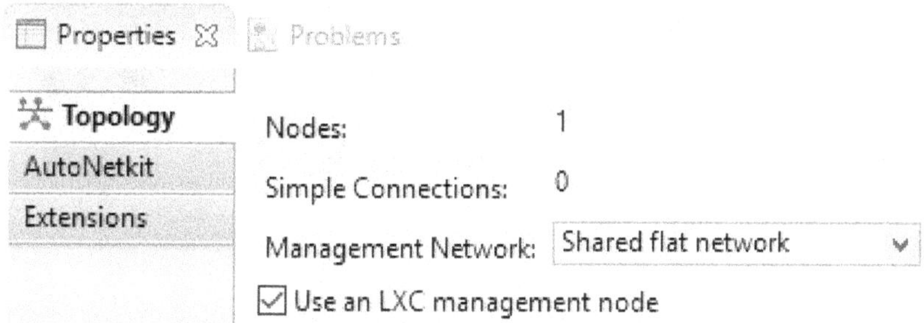

5. Click the (Build Initial Configurations) button in order to save your topology – if needed.

Now launch the simulation

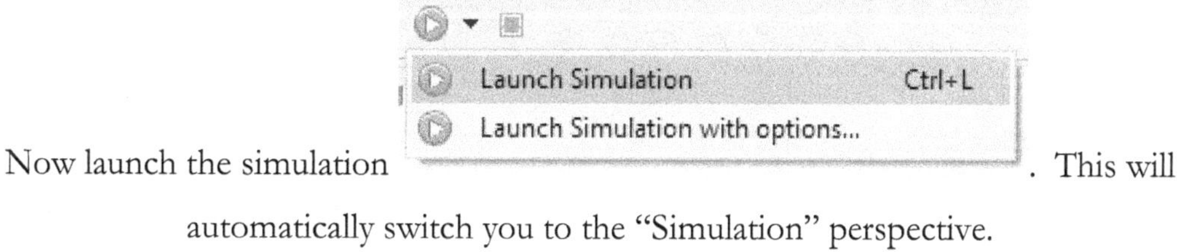

. This will automatically switch you to the “Simulation” perspective.

6. Right-click the node to view its Management port’s IP Address as shown.

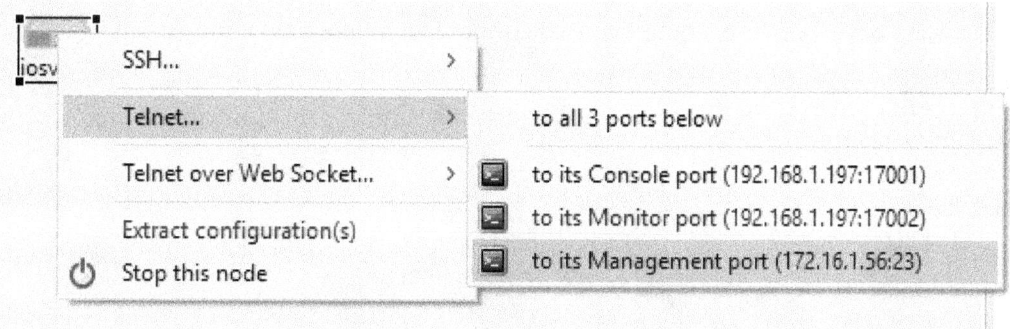

7. Ping the node from your Win10 workstation – in our case: 172.16.1.56. It should be successful. Congratulations - you now know how to directly access a topology node

using your external Win10 host. Remember you can also use PuTTY to connect to this node as well.

```
C:\windows\system32>ping 172.16.1.56

Pinging 172.16.1.56 with 32 bytes of data:
Reply from 172.16.1.56: bytes=32 time=2ms TTL=255
Reply from 172.16.1.56: bytes=32 time=1ms TTL=255
Reply from 172.16.1.56: bytes=32 time=1ms TTL=255
Reply from 172.16.1.56: bytes=32 time<1ms TTL=255
```

FLAT1 (L2) External Access

Note: You will need an additional "physical" NIC in your Win10 system for this to work.

So you want to connect your VIRL "simulated" topology to an external "physical" topology via a L2 connection. Reasons for doing this may be to:

- Propagate/block VLANs from one side of the network to the other
- Use/advertise LLDP (non-Cisco gear) vs CDP (Cisco gear) traffic between environments
- You want to convert Spanning-Tree from one type (i.e., RSTP) to another (i.e., MST) and observe/capture convergence changes
- Use SPAN or RSPAN between both environments and capture the traffic.

Whatever your L2 reason for needing external connectivity, here's how it's done.

Note: Make certain that although your VIRL server is running; no simulations are running in VM Maestro.

Login to the UWM interface – http://192.168.1.197/login/ with credentials: uwmadmin | password.

In the left-side pane, click VIRL Server | System Configuration.

Click *Shared Networks* and make certain the category: *flat1* is highlighted and choose *eth2* under the host interface, then click *Apply Changes.*

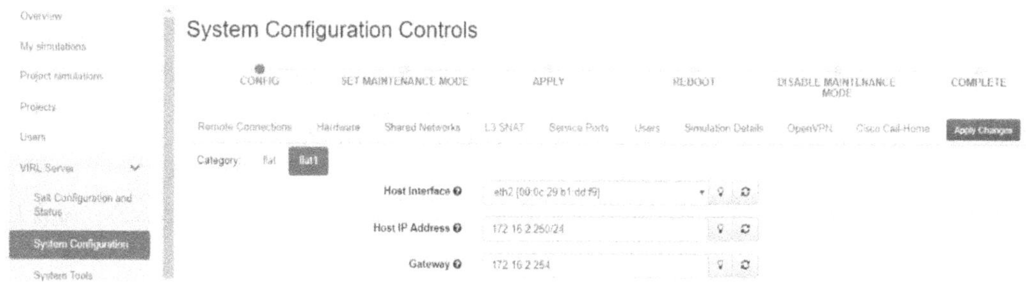

We must make this change – or any major changes to the VIRL VM – while in "maintenance mode" so click , then , next and lastly .

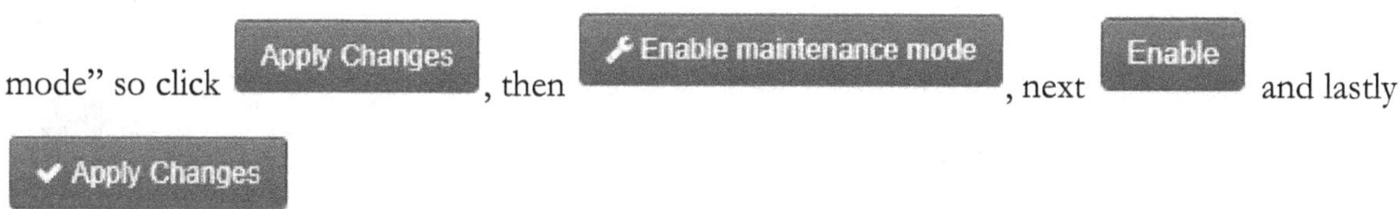

You will see a screen similar to this – Jobs in Progress…

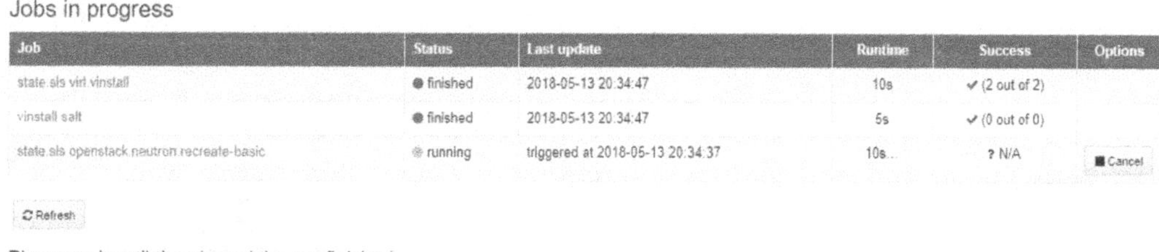

Jobs in progress

Job	Status	Last update	Runtime	Success	Options
state.sls virl.vinstall	● finished	2018-05-13 20:34:47	10s	✔ (2 out of 2)	
vinstall salt	● finished	2018-05-13 20:34:47	5s	✔ (0 out of 0)	
state.sls openstack.neutron.recreate-basic	running	triggered at 2018-05-13 20:34:37	10s...	? N/A	■ Cancel

Refresh

Please wait until the above jobs are finished ...

Although your browser window may automatically refresh the status, you can also click

until the status column for all jobs shows **finished**.

Jobs in progress

Job	Status	Last update	Runtime	Success	Options
state.sls virl.vinstall	● finished	2018-05-13 20:35:49	10s	✔ (2 out of 2)	
vinstall salt	● finished	2018-05-13 20:35:49	5s	✔ (0 out of 0)	
state.sls openstack.neutron.recreate-basic	● finished	2018-05-13 20:35:49	50s	✔ (29 out of 29)	

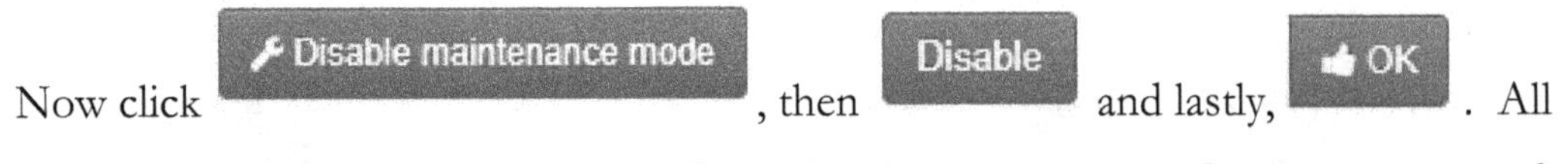

Now click Disable maintenance mode, then Disable and lastly, OK. All configuration controls are now grayed out showing you are out of maintenance mode.

We'll now create a new NIC (switch), VMnet2, that with the additional physical NIC will bridge your VIRL server's "simulated" topology to the "physical" topology.

1. Under the VMware Workstation's pull-down **Edit** menu, choose *Virtual Network Editor.*
2. Click Change Settings.
3. Click *Add Network…*. choose VMnet2 and click *OK.*

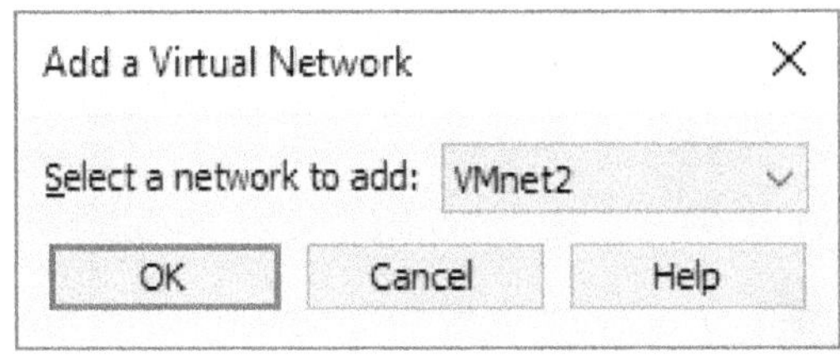

4. Highlight VMnet2, modify it as I've shown below and click *OK.*

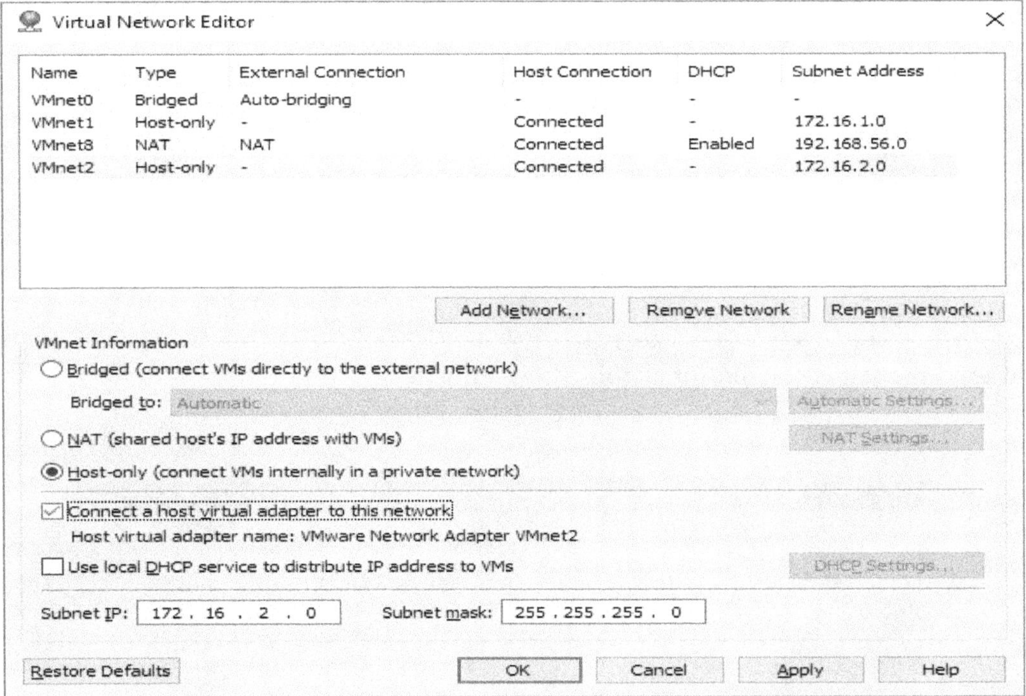

5. While in VMware, right-click the VIRL server's tab and choose *Settings…*

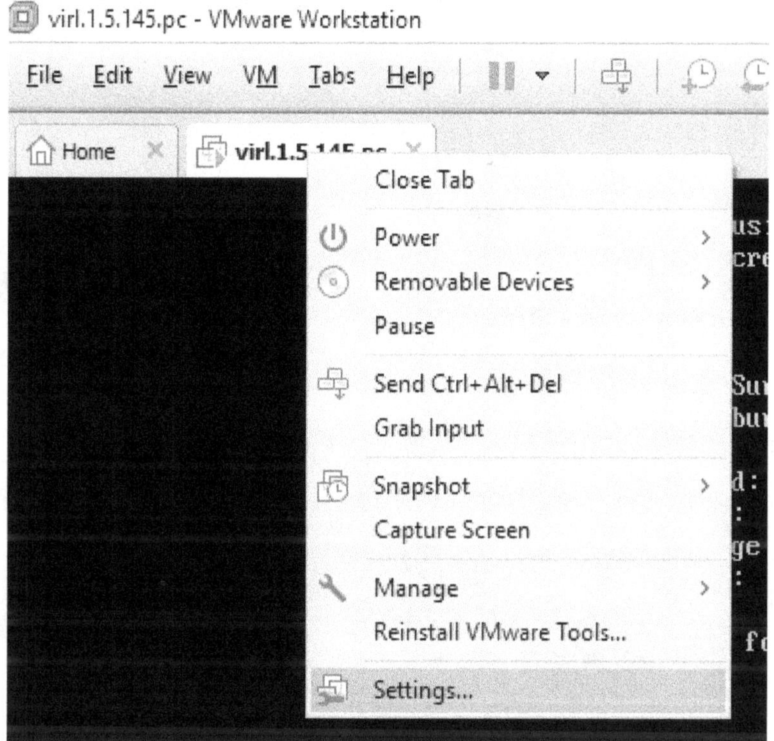

6. Now change **Network Adapter 3** to use **VMnet2 (Host-only)** interface, as shown below, then click *OK.*

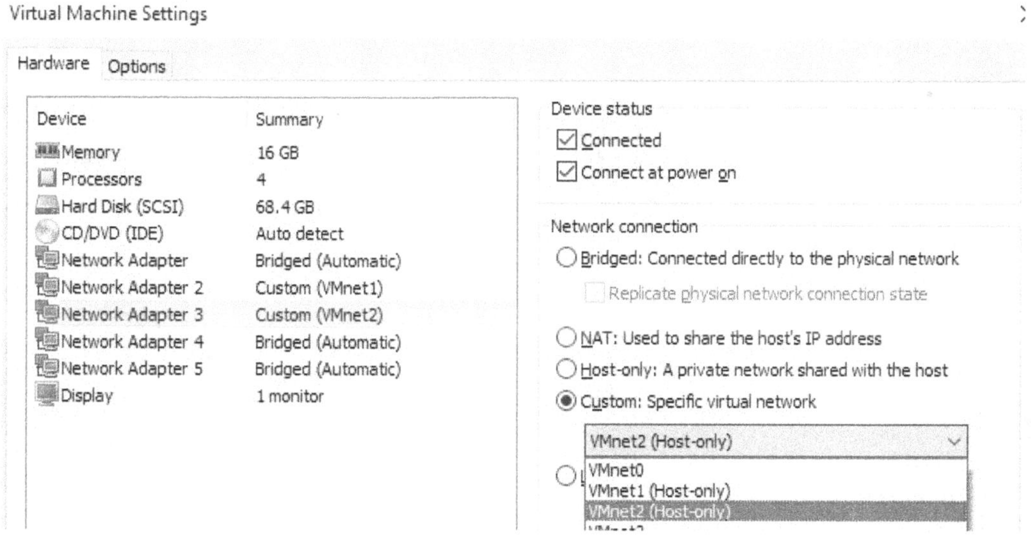

7. Now go under Control Panel | Network and Sharing Center | Change Adapter Settings and right-click **VMnet2** to bring up its Properties. If required, remove any IP address assigned under Internet Protocol Version 4 (TCP/IPv4).

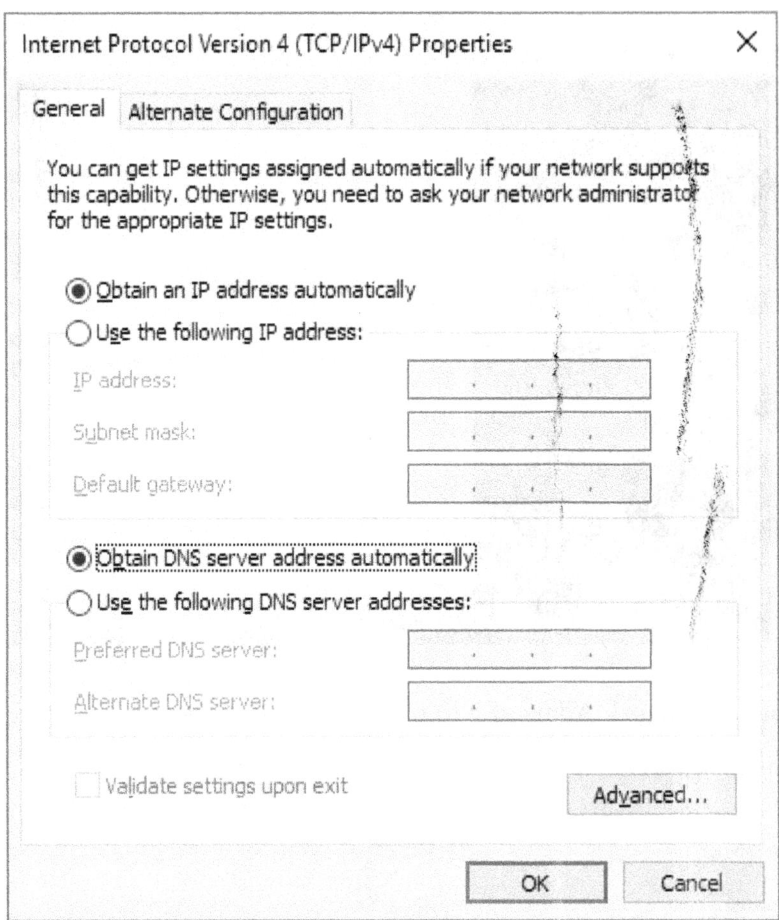

8. Now let's configure that additional "physical" NIC I mentioned that you needed, earlier. Just as we did with VMnet2, make certain that this NIC is not assigned an IP address.
9. Before I continue further, let me show you how this network is laid out.

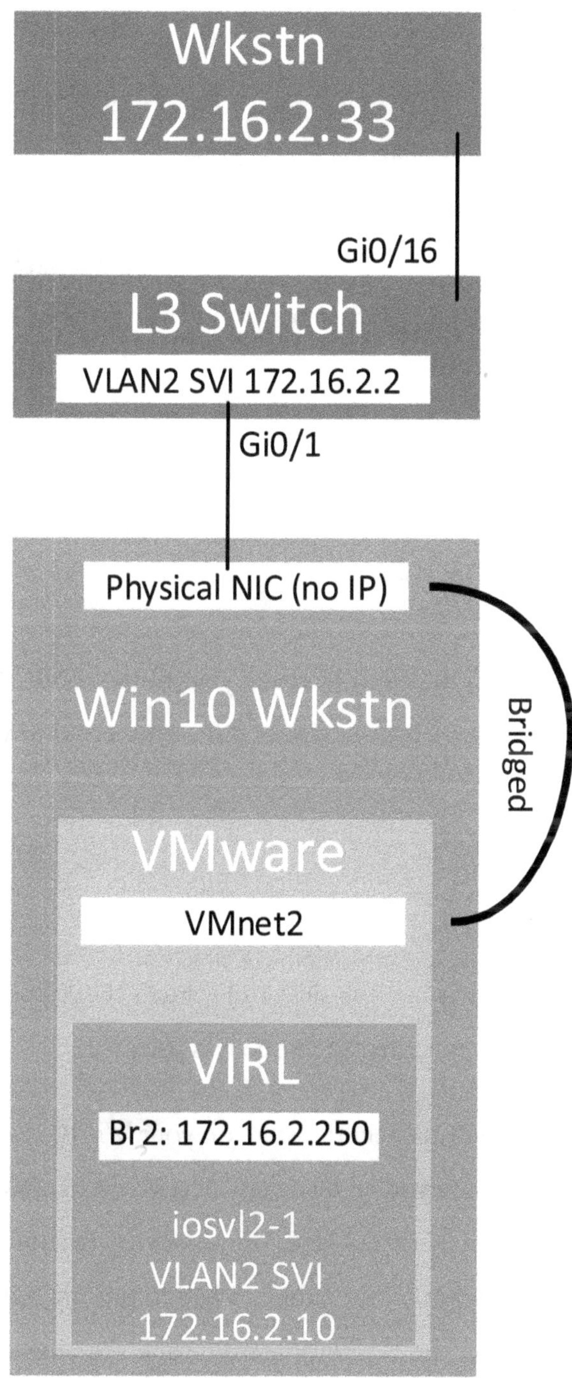

10. Now let's bridge the 2 NICs. Under *Control Panel | Network and Sharing Center | Change Adapter Settings*, click on your "physical" NIC, hold down the *Ctrl* key, click VMnet2, right-click and choose *Bridge Connections*.

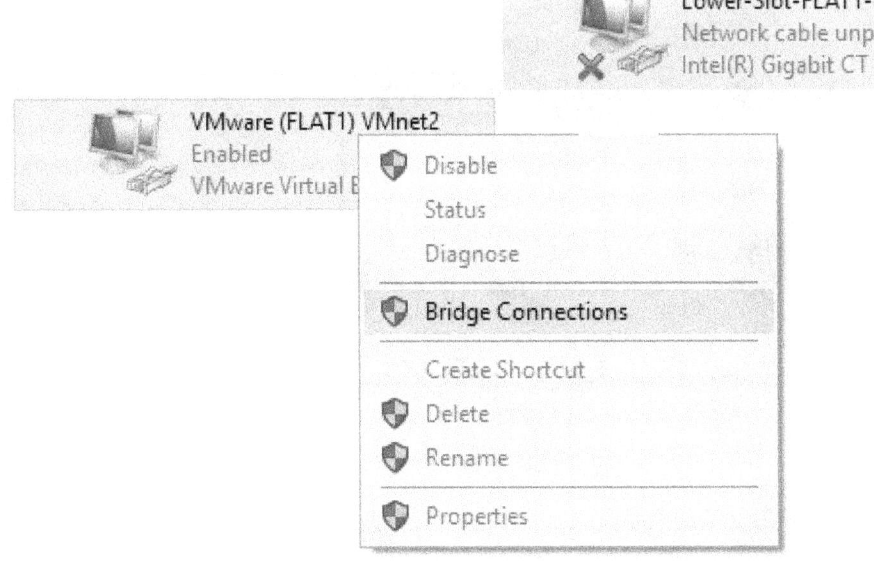

11. You've now bridged the connection between your physical NIC (connected to your external topology) and your VMware virtual NIC (connected to your VIRL server).

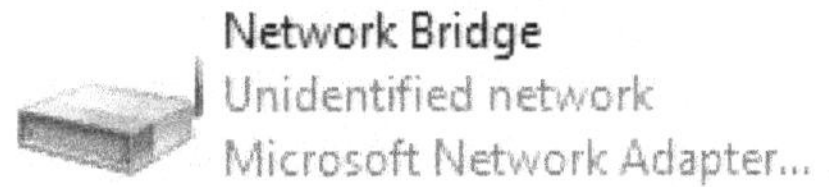

Notes: You might have noticed that the (physical and virtual) NICs I used were renamed in order for me to simply make sense of what each one was used for.

Also if you happen to have an Internet Security suite on your Win10 system – I happen to use BitDefender – (if needed) make sure you've made any necessary changes to allow communication to this and any other virtual NIC. For instance, firewall software has a tendency to categorize NICs as either home/office or public. I had to put my NICs in my *Home/Office* network, as well as having to make the NIC visible inside and allowing access to it via all applications.

12. In building this L2 simulation topology, I:
    - Utilized AutoNetkit
    - Connected the topology to the **Shared flat network**
    - Used an LXC management node
    - Configured **iosvl2-1** with VLAN2 SVI 172.16.2.10/24.
    - On the **flat-1** connector (node) I connected it to the **flat1** network on **VLAN 2.** I could have left this on VLAN1 (which works) but I wanted to validate that FLAT1 also works on other VLANs as well.

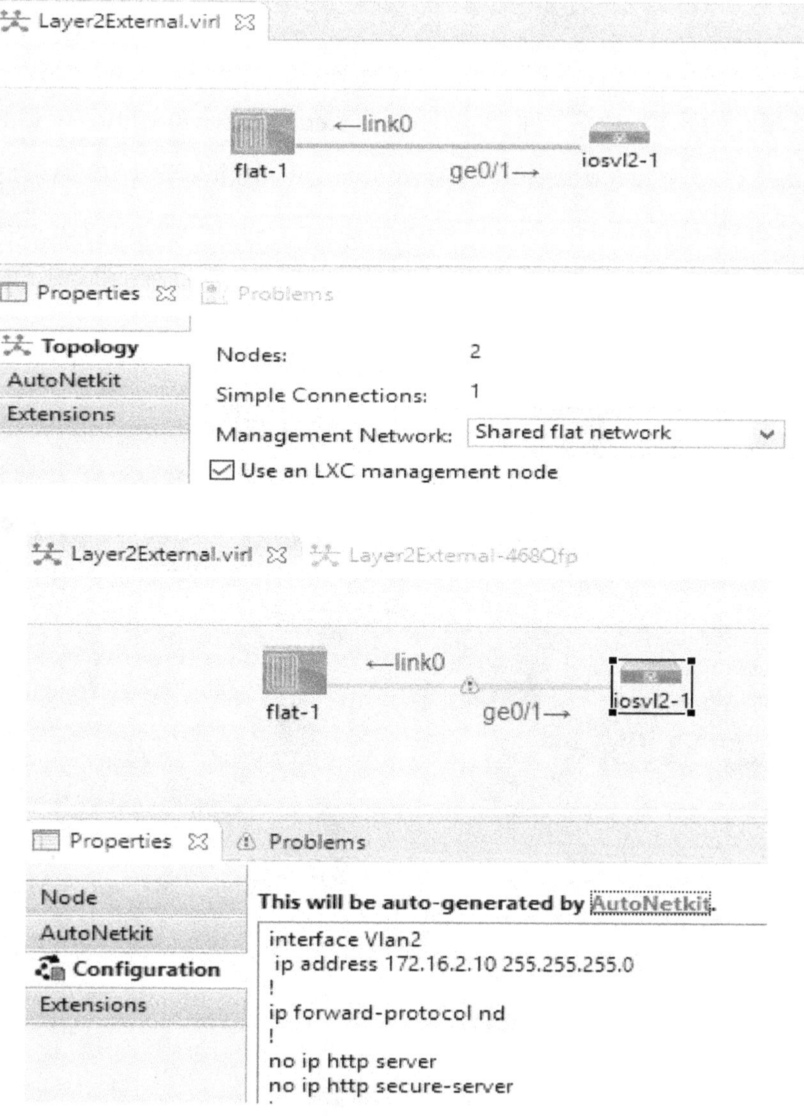

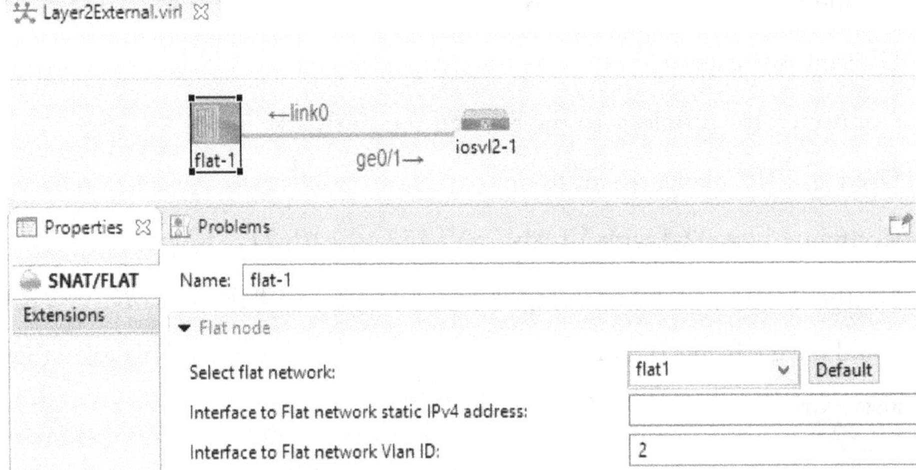

13. While the simulation was starting up, I consoled into the external L3 switch and configured it's L3 VLAN2 SVI (as shown in Step #9 above) with IP address 172.16.2.2/24. I immediately ran a continuous ping to **iosvl2-1** (172.16.2.10) from both the external switch and the workstation and once **iosvl2-1** was up, connectivity was verified. I then performed a traceroute so that you can see how the NICs are viewed – as transparent - (a bump in the wire) to the switch.

```
External-Switch#ping 172.16.2.10 repeat 100

Type escape sequence to abort.
Sending 100, 100-byte ICMP Echos to 172.16.2.10, timeout is 2 seconds:
.........!!!!!!!!!!!!!!!!!!!!!!!!!!!!!!!!!!!!!!!!!!!!!!!!!!!!!!!!!!!!!!
!!!!!!!!!!!!!!!!!!!!!!!!!!!!!!
Success rate is 91 percent (91/100), round-trip min/avg/max = 1/3/9 ms
External-Switch#
External-Switch#traceroute 172.16.2.10

Type escape sequence to abort.
Tracing the route to 172.16.2.10

  1 172.16.2.10 0 msec 0 msec *
```

Note: Although I used, by default, subnet 172.16.2.0/24 under VIRL and VMware to connect to my external 172.16.2.0/24 subnet, you don't have to accept using this subnet if in fact the external network you're trying to connect to is numbered differently (i.e., 192.168.168.0/24). To make your L2 connection simply change 172.16.2.x accordingly in VIRL's UWM and VMware to 192.168.168.x.

SNAT (L3) External Access

Note: You will need an additional NIC in your Win10 system for this to work.

In the previous section we connected our "simulated" topology to an external "physical" topology via a L2 connection. The connectivity externally via a L3 Static Network Address Translation (SNAT) is nearly identical; yet with distinguishable differences.

Reasons for needing a L3 SNAT connection may be to:

- Simulate a customer-to-ISP scenario whereas your "simulated" nodes - behind the L3 SNAT device – are using a single public IP address to access the external "physical" ISP topology. All of your "simulated" nodes are protected behind this single IP address.
- You're constructing a lab and need your "simulated" nodes to be able to access the Internet via your production network's ISP connection.

Whatever your L3 reason for needing this, here's how it's done.

Note: Make certain that although your VIRL server is running; no simulations are running in VM Maestro.

Login to the UWM interface – http://192.168.1.197/login/ with credentials: uwmadmin | password.

In the left-side pane, click VIRL Server | System Configuration.

Click *L3 SNAT* and configure it to use VIRL's Eth3 interface, as shown, then click *Apply Changes.*

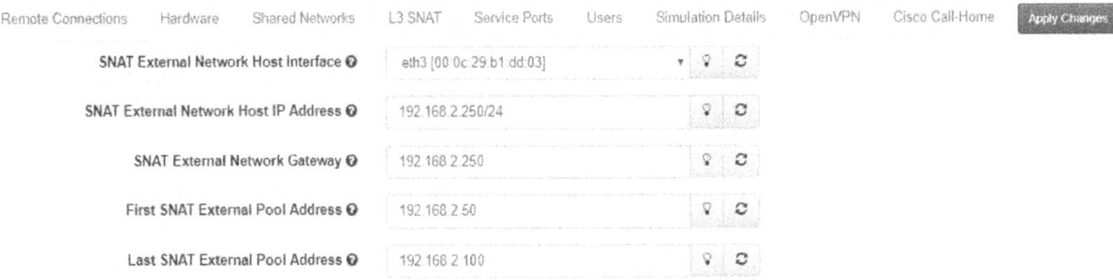

Note: The subnet shown above has been modified from UWM's default – reason being is that I want to show you how you can make it whatever you need in order to talk to the external "physical" topology subnet needed .

We must make this change – or any major changes to the VIRL VM – while in "maintenance

mode" so click , then , next and lastly .

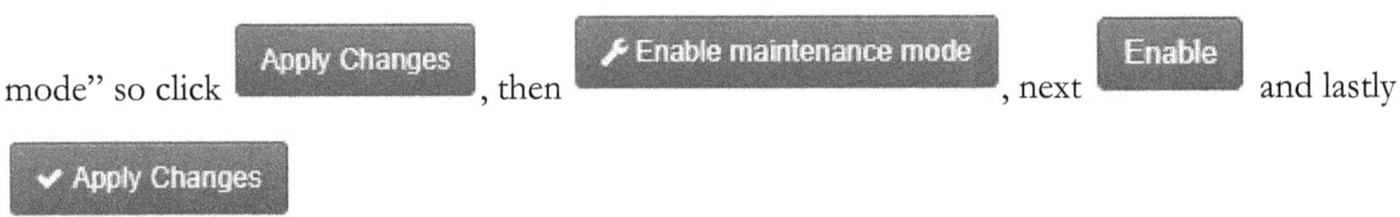

You will see a screen similar to this – Jobs in Progress…

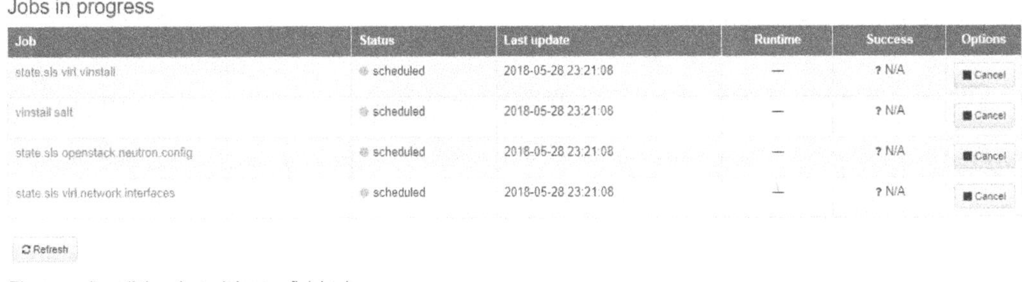
Jobs in progress

Job	Status	Last update	Runtime	Success	Options
state.sls virl.vinstall	scheduled	2018-05-28 23:21:08	—	? N/A	Cancel
vinstall salt	scheduled	2018-05-28 23:21:08	—	? N/A	Cancel
state.sls openstack.neutron.config	scheduled	2018-05-28 23:21:08	—	? N/A	Cancel
state.sls virl.network.interfaces	scheduled	2018-05-28 23:21:08	—	? N/A	Cancel

Refresh

Please wait until the above jobs are finished ...

Although your browser window may automatically refresh the status, you can also click

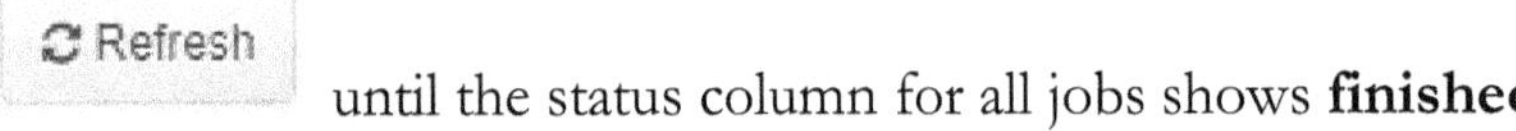

until the status column for all jobs shows **finished**.

Jobs in progress

Job	Status	Last update	Runtime	Success	Options
state sls virl vinstall	finished	2018-05-28 23:22:09	10s	✓ (2 out of 2)	
vinstall salt	finished	2018-05-28 23:22:09	10s	✓ (0 out of 0)	
state sls openstack neutron config	finished	2018-05-28 23:22:09	30s	✓ (49 out of 49)	
state sls virl network interfaces	finished	2018-05-28 23:22:09	8s	✓ (22 out of 22)	

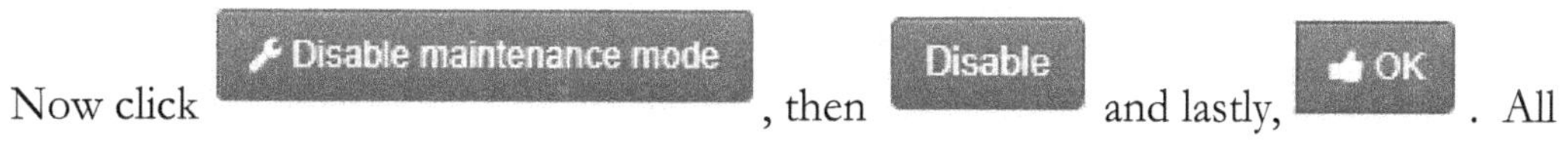

Now click [Disable maintenance mode], then [Disable] and lastly, [OK]. All configuration controls are now grayed out showing you are out of maintenance mode.

We'll now create a new NIC (switch), VMnet3, that with the additional physical NIC will bridge your VIRL server's "simulated" topology to the "physical" topology.

1. Under the VMware Workstation's pull-down **Edit** menu, choose *Virtual Network Editor.*
2. Click Change Settings.
3. Click *Add Network….* choose VMnet3 and click *OK.*

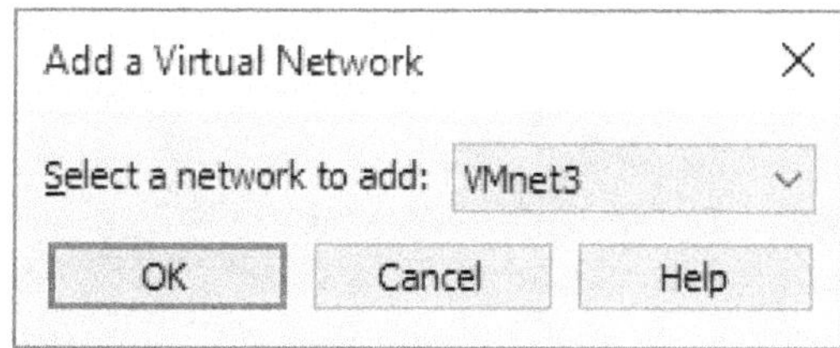

4. Highlight VMnet3, modify it as I've shown below (choosing your specific "physical" NIC under *External Connection*) and click *OK.*

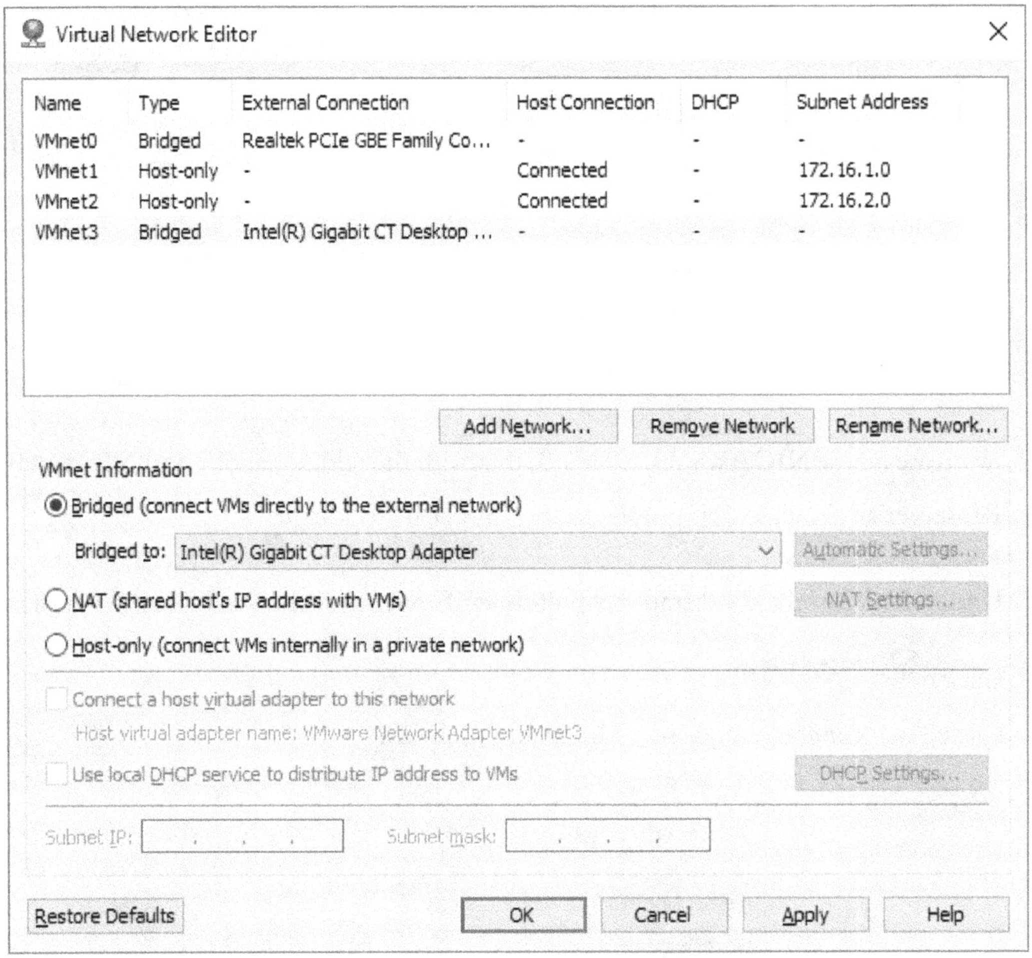

Virtual Network Editor
Name Type External Connection Host Connection DHCP Subnet Address
VMnet0 Bridged Realtek PCIe GBE Family Co... - - -
VMnet1 Host-only - Connected - 172.16.1.0
VMnet2 Host-only - Connected - 172.16.2.0
VMnet3 Bridged Intel(R) Gigabit CT Desktop ... - - -
Add Network...
Remove Network
Rename Network...
VMnet Information
Bridged (connect VMs directly to the external network)
Bridged to: Intel(R) Gigabit CT Desktop Adapter
Automatic Settings...
NAT (shared host's IP address with VMs)
NAT Settings...
Host-only (connect VMs internally in a private network)
Connect a host virtual adapter to this network
Host virtual adapter name: VMware Network Adapter VMnet3
Use local DHCP service to distribute IP address to VMs
DHCP Settings...
Subnet IP:
Subnet mask:
Restore Defaults
OK
Cancel
Apply
Help

5. While still in VMware, right-click the VIRL server's tab and choose *Settings…*

virl.1.5.145.pc - VMware Workstation
File Edit View VM Tabs Help
Home
virl.1.5
Close Tab
Power
Removable Devices
Pause
Send Ctrl+Alt+Del
Grab Input
Snapshot
Capture Screen
Manage
Reinstall VMware Tools...
Settings...

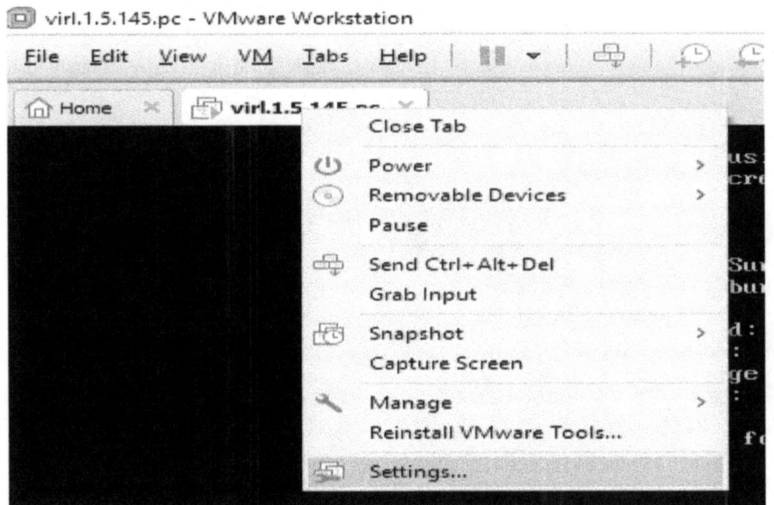

6. Now change VIRL's **Network Adapter 4** to use the **VMnet3** interface, as shown below, then click *OK*.

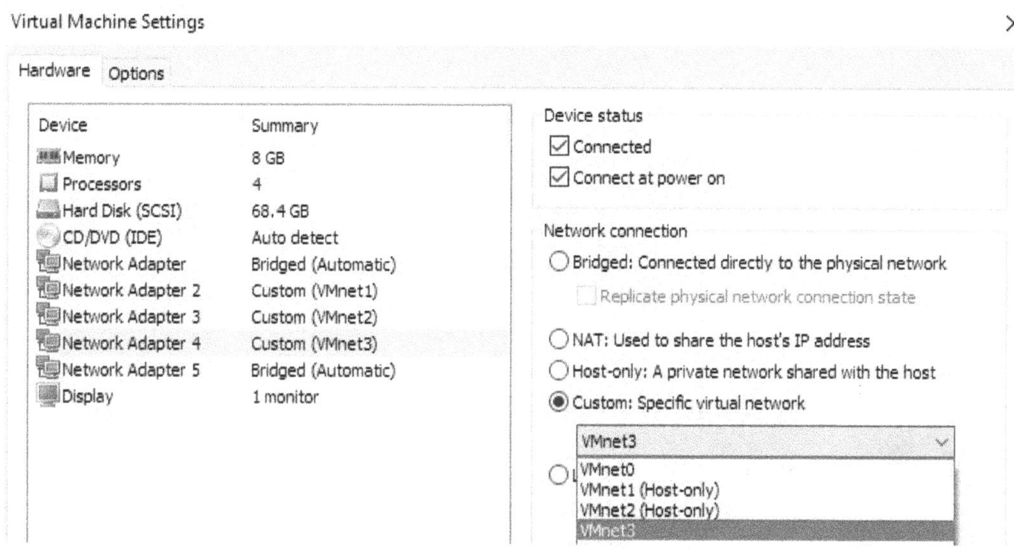

7. Under *Control Panel | Network and Sharing Center | Change Adapter Settings* you will not see **VMnet3** since what we've done is to bridge it to our SNAT "physical" interface in Step #4 (in my case to my Intel® Gigabit CT Desktop Adapter)
8. Now let's configure that additional "physical" NIC I mentioned that you needed, earlier.

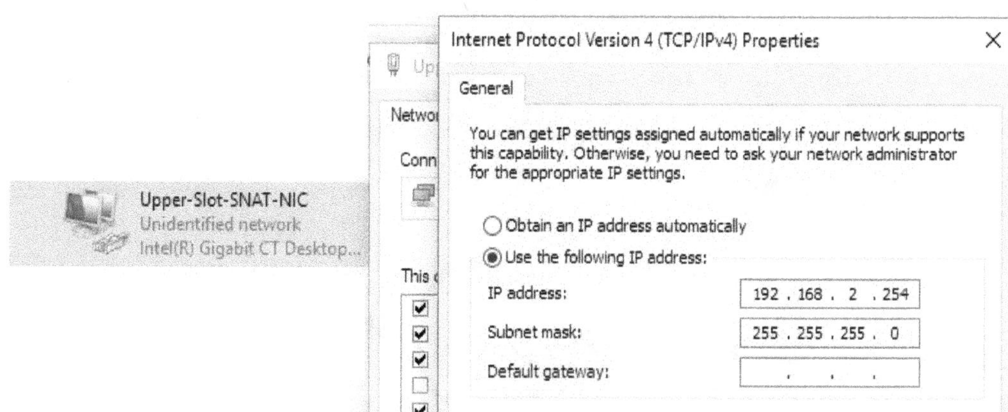

9. Before I continue further, let me show you how this network is laid out.

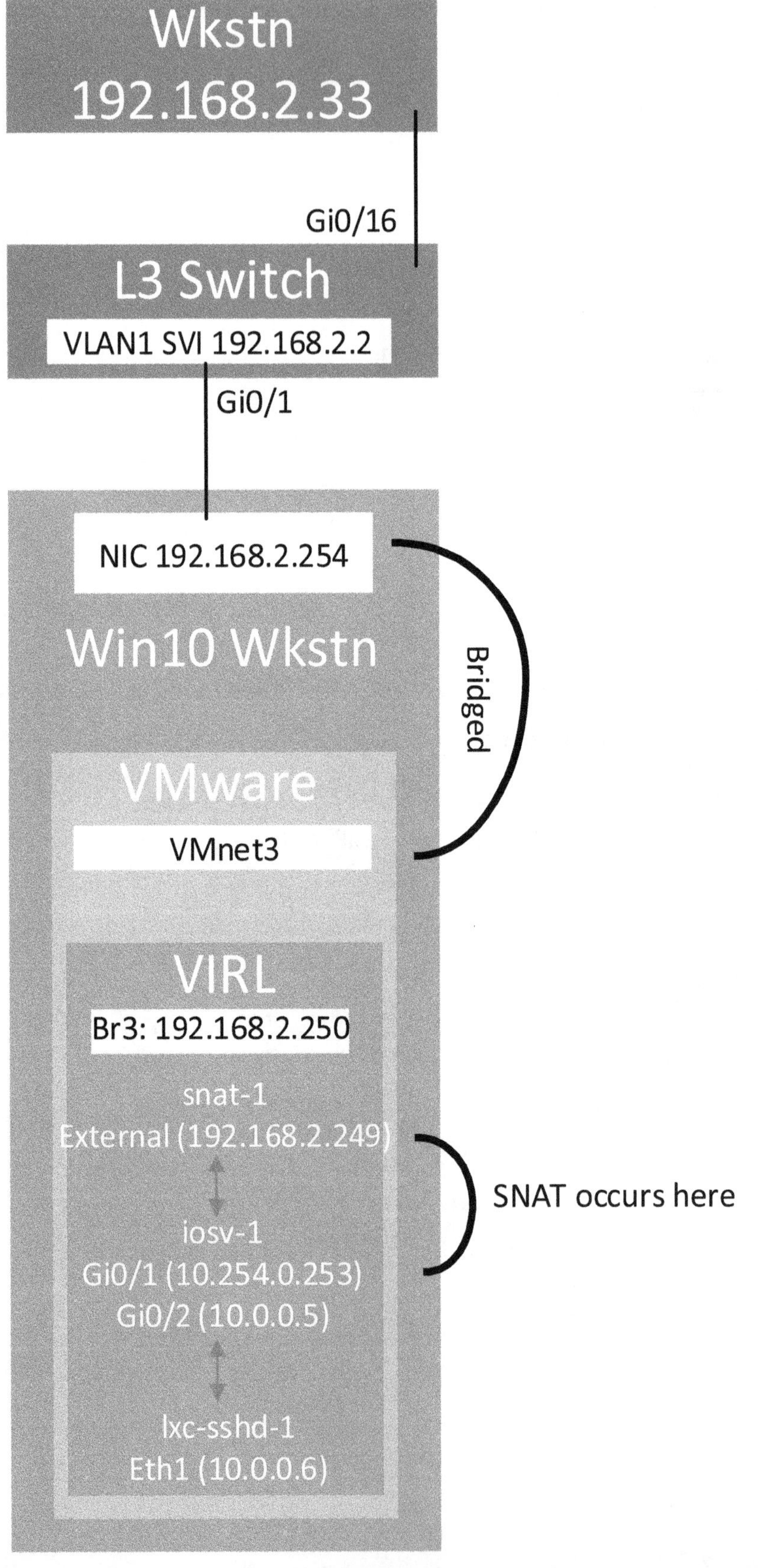
Wkstn
192.168.2.33
Gi0/16
L3 Switch
VLAN1 SVI 192.168.2.2
Gi0/1
NIC 192.168.2.254
Win10 Wkstn
Bridged
VMware
VMnet3
VIRL
Br3: 192.168.2.250
snat-1
External (192.168.2.249)
SNAT occurs here
iosv-1
Gi0/1 (10.254.0.253)
Gi0/2 (10.0.0.5)
lxc-sshd-1
Eth1 (10.0.0.6)

The above diagram depicts the hierarchical construction of the logical (from VMware downward) and physical (from Win10 Wkstn's physical NIC upward) layout. In it the **snat-1** node acts as the NATing node so that the "simulation" topology can reach the "physical" topology. What it does is it uses **iosv-1's** Gi0/1 external IP address (10.254.0.253) and translates any traffic from the 10.0.0.x subnet nodes – in our case just **lxc-sshd-1** – into the NATed external IP address (192.168.2.249); but another important configuration must take place. The **iosv-1** router must be manually configured for NATting (as shown later). This traffic traverses the VIRL server's L3 SNAT medium (192.168.2.250) and allows any 10.0.0.x node access to any 192.168.2.x/24 node, and vice-verse – pending routing statements that will be needed next.

Notes: The physical NIC I used was renamed in order for me to simply make sense of what its purpose is.

At this point you should be able to successfully ping the VIRL server's BR3 interface (192.168.2.250) from the workstation (192.168.2.33) – showing that you can at least move partially from the "physical" to "simulated" infrastructure.

Also if you happen to have an Internet Security suite on your Win10 system – I happen to use BitDefender – (if needed) make sure you've made any necessary changes to allow communication to this and any other virtual NIC. For instance, firewall software has a tendency to categorize NICs as either home/office or public. I had to put my NICs into my *Home/Office* network, as well as having to make the NICs visible inside and allowing access to it via all applications.

10. In building this "simulated" L3 topology, I:
    - Used **AutoNetkit**, but disabled the use of a routing protocol
    - Connected the topology to the **Shared flat management network**
    - Used an LXC management node

- Configured the **snat-1** connector (node) to use 10.254.0.253 on its inside interface (actually what **snat-1** does is to use **iosv-1's** Ge0/1's IP address) and 192.168.2.249 on its outside interface.

Properties | Problems

Topology
AutoNetkit
Extensions

IPv4 VRF Prefix: 24
IPv6 Infrastructure Subnet: 0:0:0:a::
IPv6 Infrastructure Prefix: 64
IPv6 Loopback Subnet: 0:0:0:b::
IPv6 Loopback Pool Prefix: 64
IPv6 VRF Subnet: 0:0:0:c::
IPv6 VRF Prefix: 64

Routing
Enable Routing Protocols: false Default
IGP: ospf Default

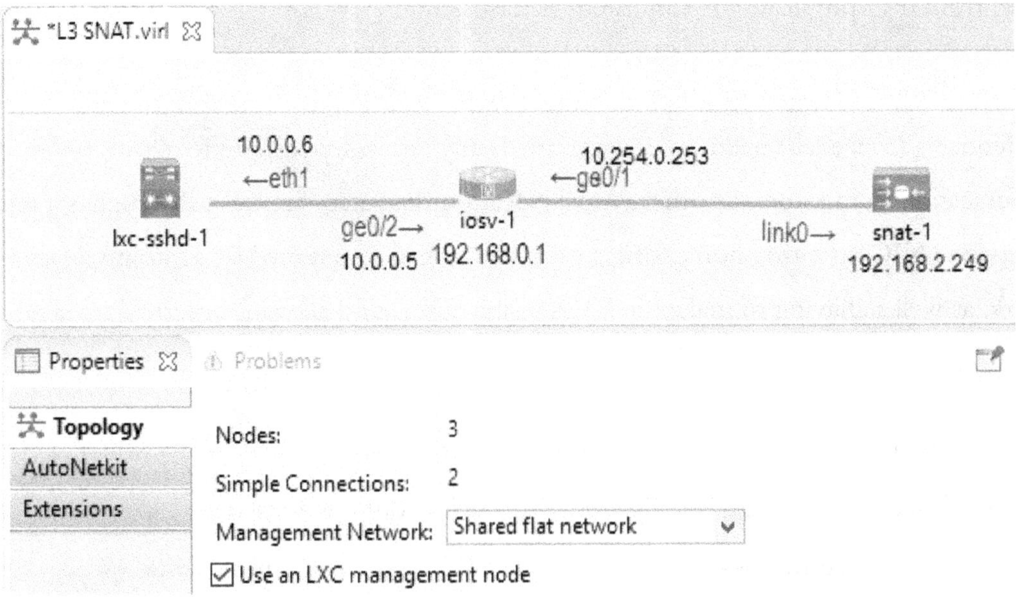

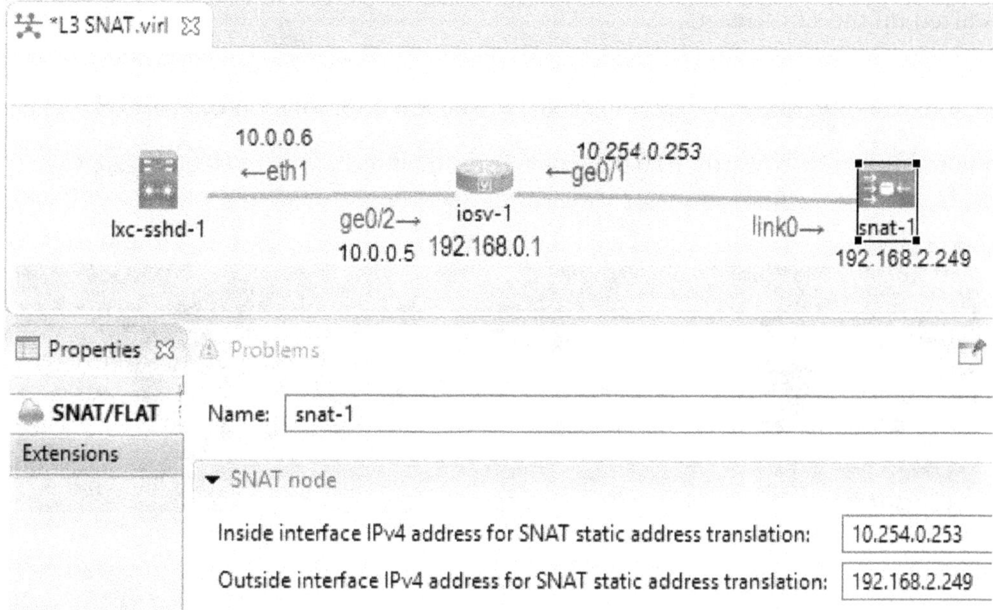

11. I then configured the following device's route statements:

On lxc-sshd-1:
route del -net 0.0.0.0 netmask 0.0.0.0 dev eth0
route add -net 0.0.0.0 netmask 0.0.0.0 gw 10.0.0.5

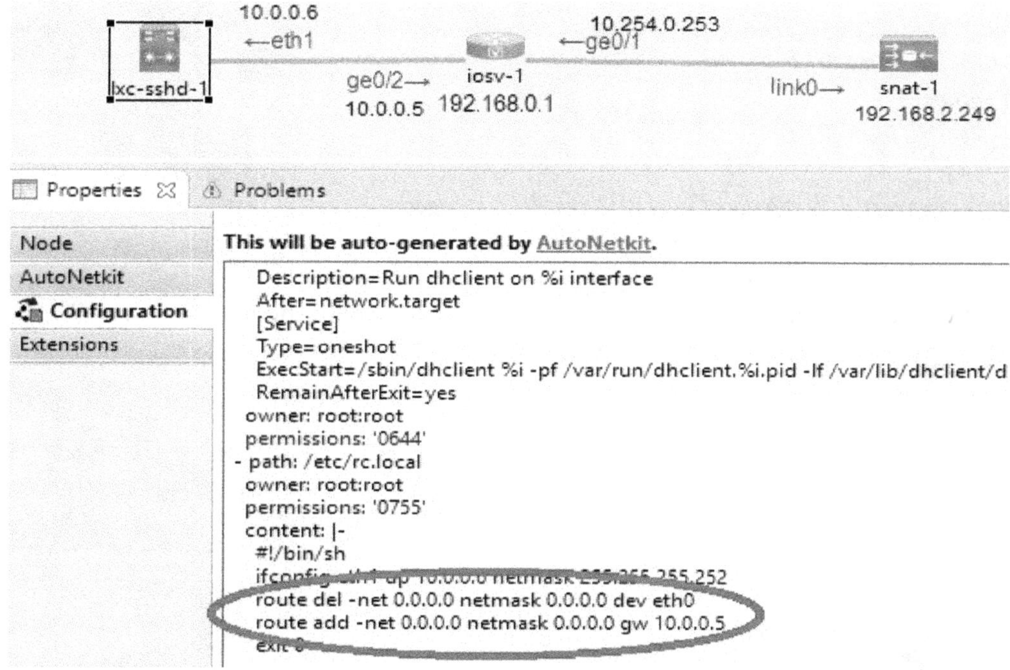

Here I started up the simulation…

The next screenshot verifies the previous route statement additions on **lxc-sshd-1.** This shows how I pointed the node towards 10.0.0.5 (**iosv-1**) inside interface – it's default gateway.

172.16.1.58 - PuTTY

```
Using username "cisco".
cisco@172.16.1.58's password:
cisco@lxc-sshd-1$ route
Kernel IP routing table
Destination     Gateway         Genmask         Flags Metric Ref    Use Iface
default         10.0.0.5        0.0.0.0         UG    0      0        0 eth1
10.0.0.4        *               255.255.255.252 U     0      0        0 eth1
172.16.1.0      *               255.255.255.0   U     0      0        0 eth0
cisco@lxc-sshd-1$
```

On iosv-1: create a default route towards the **snat-1** connector.

```
iosv-1(config)#ip route 0.0.0.0 0.0.0.0 GigabitEthernet0/1 192.168.2.249
```

Note: Now at this point you should be able to successfully ping 192.168.2.249 from your workstation (192.168.2.33).

On iosv-1: configured PATing using access-list 100.

interface GigabitEthernet0/1
Ip nat outside
interface GigabitEthernet0/2
Ip nat inside
ip nat inside source list 100 interface GigabitEthernet0/1 overload
access-list 100 permit ip 10.0.0.0 0.255.255.255 any

Note: Now at this point you should be able to successfully ping the workstation (192.168.2.33) from **lxc-sshd-1** (10.0.0.6).

```
172.16.1.58 - PuTTY
cisco@lxc-sshd-1$ ping 192.168.2.33
PING 192.168.2.33 (192.168.2.33) 56(84) bytes of data.
64 bytes from 192.168.2.33: icmp_seq=1 ttl=126 time=2.12 ms
64 bytes from 192.168.2.33: icmp_seq=2 ttl=126 time=1.35 ms
64 bytes from 192.168.2.33: icmp_seq=3 ttl=126 time=1.48 ms
^C
--- 192.168.2.33 ping statistics ---
3 packets transmitted, 3 received, 0% packet loss, time 2003ms
rtt min/avg/max/mdev = 1.354/1.655/2.128/0.338 ms
cisco@lxc-sshd-1$
```

Next I ran wireshark to confirm what IP address, **lxc-sshd-1** (10.0.0.6), showed up as when its icmp echo packet (ping) reached 192.168.2.33. As you can see it was NATed by **snat-1's** 192.168.2.249.

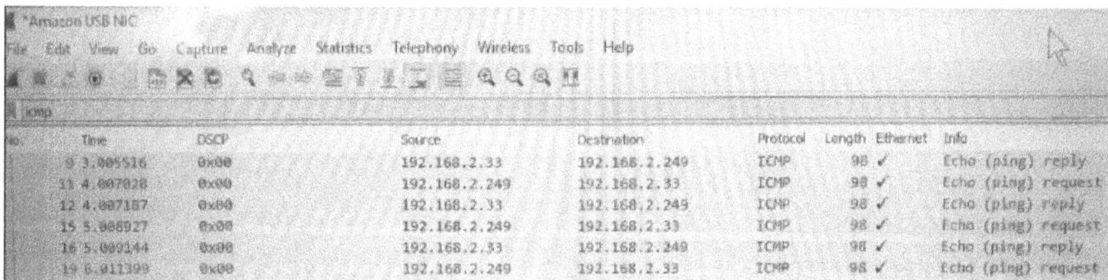

No.	Time	DSCP	Source	Destination	Protocol	Length	Ethernet	Info
9	3.005516	0x00	192.168.2.33	192.168.2.249	ICMP	98	✓	Echo (ping) reply
11	4.007028	0x00	192.168.2.249	192.168.2.33	ICMP	98	✓	Echo (ping) request
12	4.007187	0x00	192.168.2.33	192.168.2.249	ICMP	98	✓	Echo (ping) reply
15	5.008927	0x00	192.168.2.249	192.168.2.33	ICMP	98	✓	Echo (ping) request
16	5.009144	0x00	192.168.2.33	192.168.2.249	ICMP	98	✓	Echo (ping) reply
19	6.011399	0x00	192.168.2.249	192.168.2.33	ICMP	98	✓	Echo (ping) request

To further test connectivity to my workstation (192.168.2.33) from **lxc-sshd-1**, I started a portable app webserver on 192.168.2.33 and then used the ***wget*** command to confirm connectivity.

```
172.16.1.58 - PuTTY
cisco@lxc-sshd-1$ wget -p http://192.168.2.33
--2018-08-01 01:47:01--  http://192.168.2.33/
Connecting to 192.168.2.33:80... connected.
HTTP request sent, awaiting response... 200 OK
Length: unspecified [text/html]
Saving to: '192.168.2.33/index.html'

192.168.2.33/index.html        [ <=>                                       ]   1.40K  --.-KB/s    in 0s

2018-08-01 01:47:01 (222 MB/s) - '192.168.2.33/index.html' saved [1436]

Loading robots.txt; please ignore errors.
--2018-08-01 01:47:01--  http://192.168.2.33/robots.txt
Reusing existing connection to 192.168.2.33:80.
HTTP request sent, awaiting response... 404 Not Found
2018-08-01 01:47:01 ERROR 404: Not Found.

--2018-08-01 01:47:01--  http://192.168.2.33/format.css
Reusing existing connection to 192.168.2.33:80.
HTTP request sent, awaiting response... 200 OK
Length: 4522 (4.4K) [text/css]
Saving to: '192.168.2.33/format.css'
```

Immediately after the wget command was executed I verified that **iosv-1** was indeed NATing my traffic. As you can see a NAT entry was created for 10.0.0.6 (lxc-sshd-1); showing that it was connecting to 192.168.2.33 via TCP port 80.

```
iosv-1#sh ip nat trans
Pro Inside global         Inside local         Outside local        Outside global
tcp 10.254.0.253:33700    10.0.0.6:33700       192.168.2.33:80      192.168.2.33:80
```

Congratulations! At this point, traffic originating from behind **iosv-1** is able to reach out to your "physical" topology.

CHAPTER 10: Using OpenVPN to Reach Inside of Your Lab

In Chapter 9 I discussed the ability in accessing your VIRL simulation nodes via the local Win10 host system using the FLAT (management) network – 172.16.1.0/24. To refresh your memory, this management network is accessed via VIRL server's Eth1 interface (172.16.1.250) to access all running simulation nodes. Up to this point we were able to access these nodes because we configured a network card – on our Win10 workstation – to be on the same L2 network. But what if you're now remote – across the country – and need some kind of transport to once again access your running lab's nodes? To accomplish this we'll use the OpenVPN feature of VIRL server. OpenVPN will create a tunnel directly into your VIRL server allowing you direct access to the FLAT network. Let me show you how this is done…

Note: while this section shows how to directly connect "inside" of your lab, keep in mind that if you desire connectivity "outside" of the lab (i.e., directly to the host) in order to accomplish other types of configurations, you should use a 3rd party remote access application (i.e., TeamViewer) to accomplish this.

Login to the UWM interface – http://192.168.1.197/login/ with credentials: uwmadmin | password.

In the left-side pane, click VIRL Server | System Configuration.

Click *OpenVPN* and…

- **Enable OpenVPN Server:** choose *Yes* to enable the process.
- Use TCP Connections:
    - Choose *Yes* to enable OpenVPN to listen over TCP.
    - Choose *No* to instead use UDP. Since UDP's overhead is substantially less than TCP it should provide faster response; but since most open hotspot environments that you may be using nearly always allows TCP port 443 (or

HTTPS) out; your chances of connecting back to your system is greater increased.

- **Port Number:** whether using TCP or UDP, click the  and it will choose port 443 for TCP or port 1194 for UDP by default.
- **Shared Network**
    - FLAT (default) terminates your VPN connection on the built-in (172.16.1.0/24) management network that all nodes will be on.
    - FLAT1 - if you'd rather connect to an external L2 connection that you have to a physical environment, as mentioned in *Chapter 9: FLAT1 (L2) External Access*, choose *FLAT1*.
- **Client IP Range:** set the beginning and ending addresses to offer to remote VPN connections.
- **Enable routes to shared networks:** choose *Yes* if you wanted both the FLAT (172.16.1.0/24) and FLAT1 (172.16.2.0/24) networks to be advertised to your VPN clients. Enable this if indeed you wanted to access both networks. The VIRL server's NIC address, on each of these subnets, will be used as the gateway for access.

I've configured my OpenVPN as follows, then I clicked *Apply Changes*.

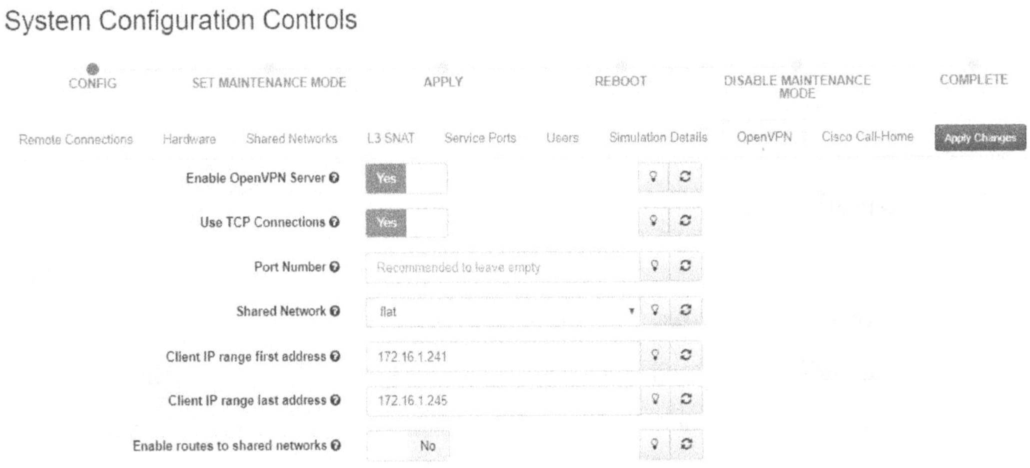

System Configuration Controls

CONFIG SET MAINTENANCE MODE APPLY REBOOT DISABLE MAINTENANCE MODE COMPLETE

Remote Connections Hardware Shared Networks L3 SNAT Service Ports Users Simulation Details OpenVPN Cisco Call-Home Apply Changes

Enable OpenVPN Server	Yes
Use TCP Connections	Yes
Port Number	Recommended to leave empty
Shared Network	flat
Client IP range first address	172.16.1.241
Client IP range last address	172.16.1.245
Enable routes to shared networks	No

We must make this change – or any major changes to the VIRL VM – while in "maintenance mode" so click Apply Changes, then Enable maintenance mode, next Enable and lastly ✔ Apply Changes.

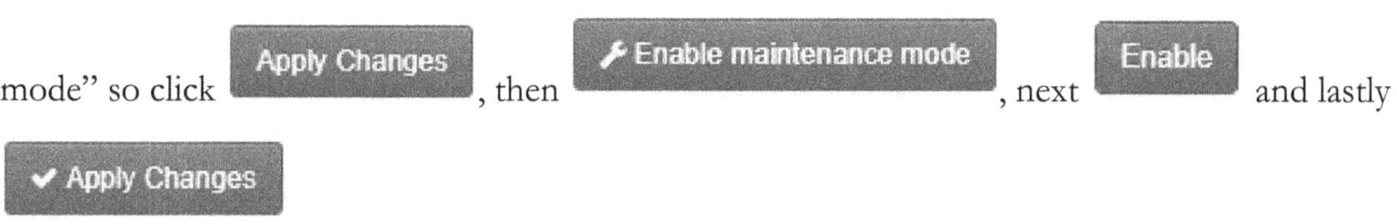

You will see a screen similar to this – Jobs in Progress…

Jobs in progress

Job	Status	Last update	Runtime	Success	Options
state.sls virl.vinstall	scheduled	2018-09-03 17:32:09	—	? N/A	Cancel
vinstall salt	scheduled	2018-09-03 17:32:09	—	? N/A	Cancel
state.sls virl.openvpn.setup	scheduled	2018-09-03 17:32:09	—	? N/A	Cancel

Refresh

Please wait until the above jobs are finished ...

Although your browser window may automatically refresh the status, you can also click

until the status column for all jobs shows **finished**.

Jobs in progress

Job	Status	Last update	Runtime	Success	Options
state.sls virl.vinstall	finished	2018-09-03 17:34:31	9s	✔ (2 out of 2)	
vinstall salt	finished	2018-09-03 17:34:31	5s	✔ (0 out of 0)	
state.sls virl.openvpn.setup	finished	2018-09-03 17:34:31	1m 46s	✔ (22 out of 22)	

Note: If you did not receive (x out of x) successes then something went wrong and OpenVPN may not function as expected. Click the *state.sls.virl.openvpn.setup* link to view additional logs and the potential error – under the job column.

Now click Disable maintenance mode, then Disable and lastly, OK. All configuration controls are now grayed out showing you are out of maintenance mode.

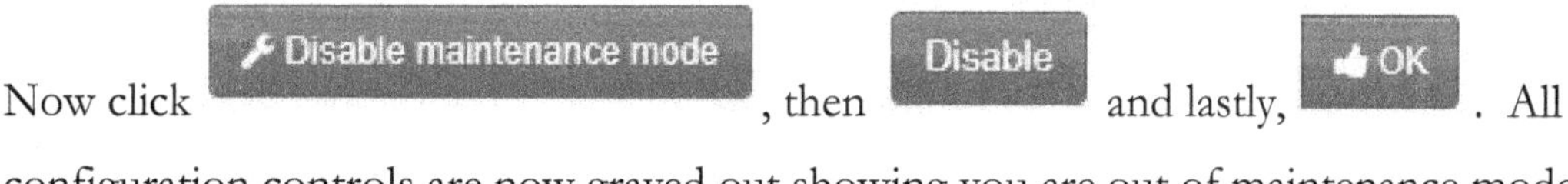

Note: During the previous reconfiguration, the VIRL server was configured as a CA server. As such it created a certificate and the OpenVPN configuration that will be used by all users to connect. There are no individual configuration files.

Now let's download the certificate and configuration file that will be used by our OpenVPN client.

On the upper right side of the browser you see the following:

Click on *uwmadmin*. Scroll down and click on:

OpenVPN

Download OpenVPN client configuration file

Save the *client.ovpn* file somewhere for now.

From your VPN Client: proceed to https://openvpn.net/index.php/open-source/downloads.html and download your OpenVPN client software. Since my VPN client is a Win10 host, I chose to download *openvpn-install-2.4.6-I602.exe.* I chose all the default options during the installation.

With the OpenVPN client software installed, I copied the *client.ovpn* file to my system's C:\Program Files\OpenVPN\config directory.

<u>For initial testing only</u>: With my Win10 VPN laptop client currently on the same internal WiFi network as my VIRL server's Win10 host machine – I double-clicked the *OpenVPN GUI* icon on my VPN client's desktop, then from the tray icon I right-clicked on the icon and chose *Connect.*

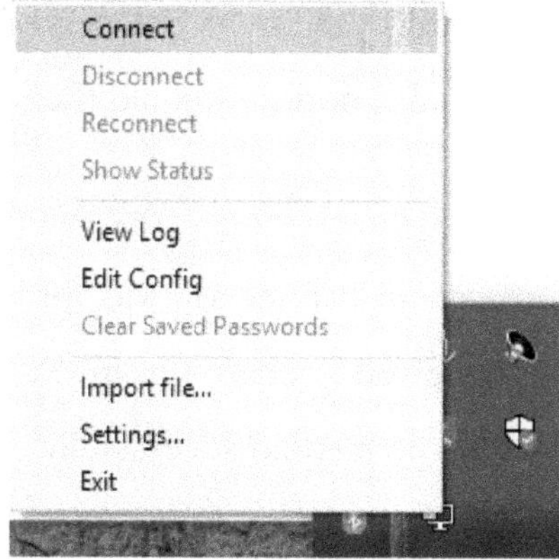

I was presented the following connection messages:

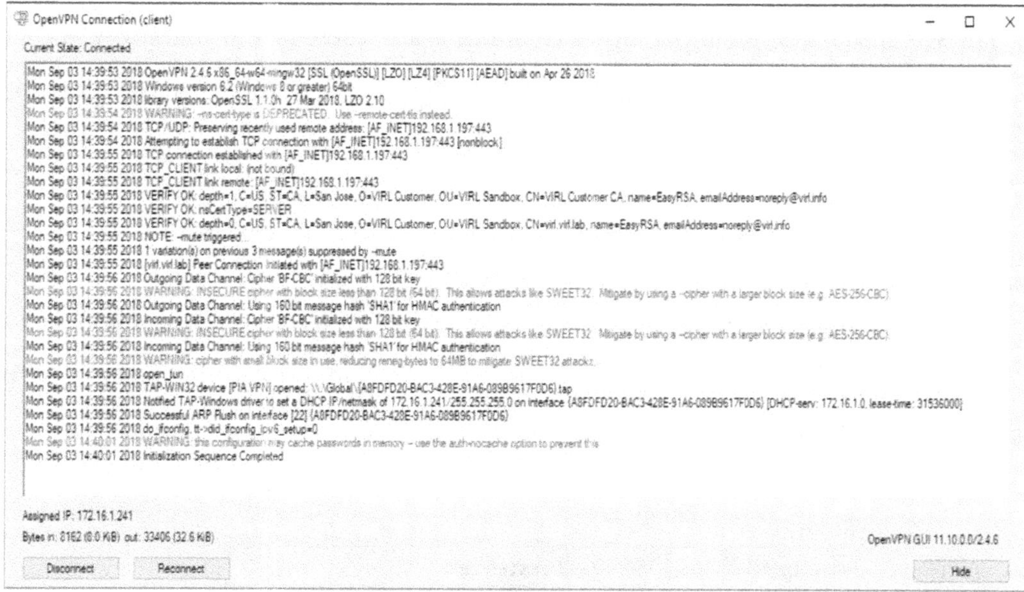

I see that I was assigned (172.16.1.241) the first IP address in my *Client IP range* during the OpenVPN configuration.

Then was presented with:

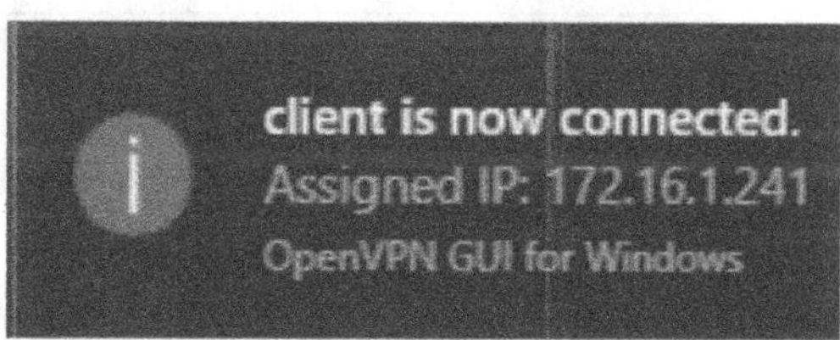

At this point I was now able to successfully ping my VIRL server's Eth1 (management) NIC – 172.16.1.250 – as well as any/all of my lab's nodes. I could then telnet to any of the lab's nodes also.

As I previously mentioned, the above client connection was for initial testing only because my Win10 VPN laptop client is on the same WiFi network as my Win10 VM host machine. This merely showed me that the OpenVPN client could successfully connect while inside my environment.

To now make this work over the Internet, you must allow *Port Forwarding* on your Internet facing router/gateway. Allow TCP port 443 to come inbound – from the Internet – to your VIRL server. The screenshot below simply shows you once again where in VM Maestro you can find your VIRL server's IP - mine being 192.168.1.197. I allowed any IP (host) to TCP port 443 to my inside 192.168.1.197 host on my ISP's gateway.

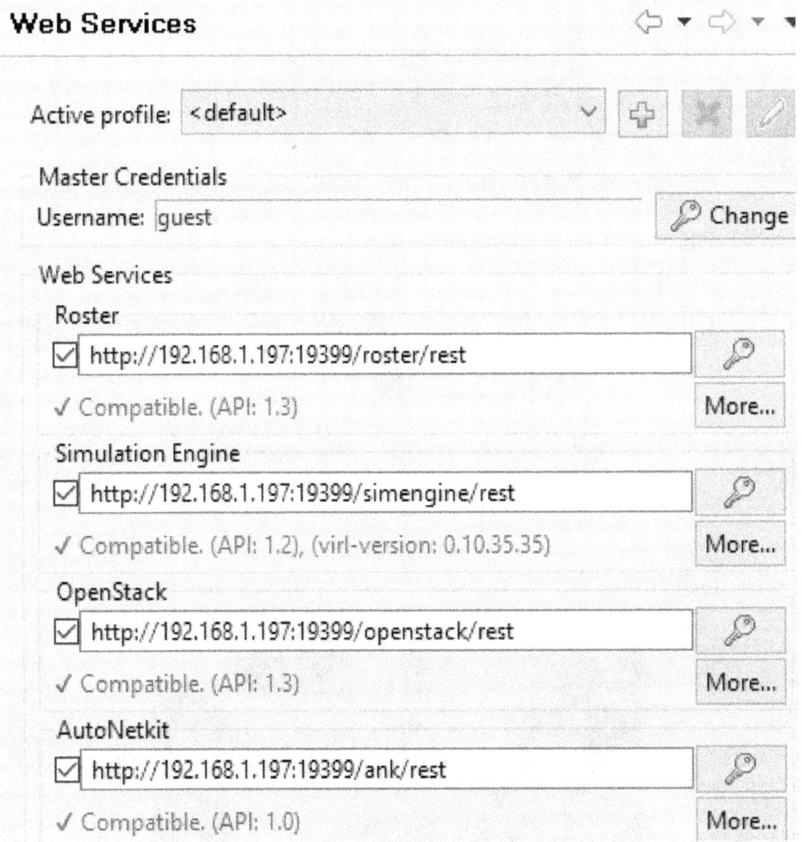

Next, I modified the *client.ovpn* file. In it you'll see an entry similar to this:

remote 192.168.1.197<ca>

I replaced my VIRL server's internal IP address with my Internet router's public IP address. Actually, if you subscribe to a dynamic DNS service (https://dyn.com) you can replace the IP address with the actual hostname you've configured under this service – that way you never have to worry about the IP address changing. If you actually enter your public hostname into the client.ovpn file, don't be alarmed when you connect and your hostname doesn't show up in the OpenVPN log because that name will be resolved to the public IP address.

Congratulations! You've now VPNed into your VIRL lab.

CHAPTER 11: Extra, Extra…Read All About It!

Having the ability to look at actual packets traversing a "true" physical network is easy because there's real end-user data as well as L2 traffic (i.e., CDP, VTP, STP), L3 traffic (i.e., EIGRP, OSPF, HSRP) and so forth constantly moving back and forth. Having this with a simulated environment can be a bit challenging. Luckily for you there are add-on features that allow you to: send traffic, capture traffic, inject routes, and perform speed tests; as well built-in features that allow: altering latency/jitter/packet loss and virtually tracking a packet's path. Let's learn more about each one.

Ostinato v0.8 (Traffic Generator)

Ostinato is an open source network traffic generator and analyzer tool we'll be using to generate some network traffic in a topology. With this product you can send several streams of data packets using different protocols…at different rates…and to different destinations. Although I suggest you visit their website for more in-depth knowledge of the product I will briefly demonstrate it.

Download and then unzip the Win32 product, from http://ostinato.org to a directory of your choice.

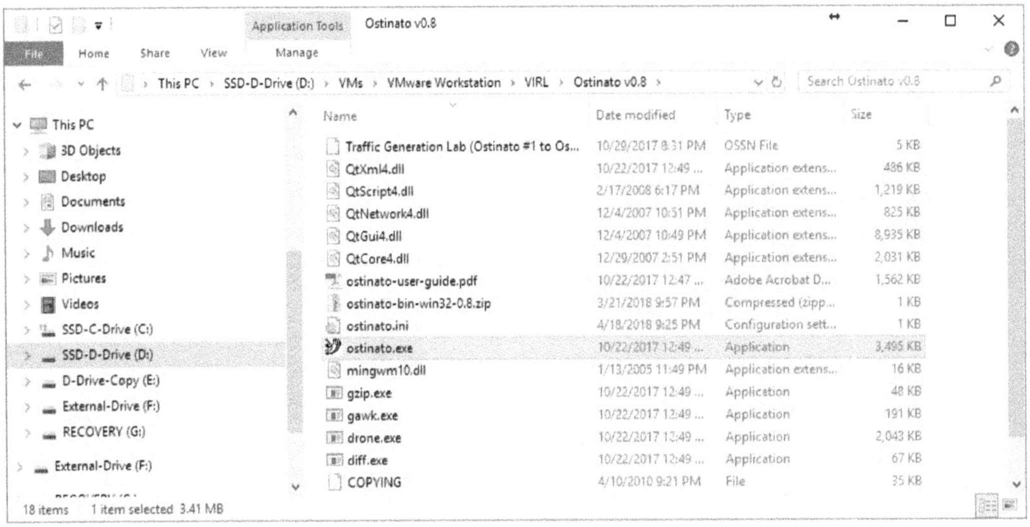

At this point you should drag the *ostinato.exe* program to your desktop in order to create a shortcut. This will make it easier for you to run the program later.

I've created the following lab (next screenshot). Notice the Ostinato lightweight LXC containers that VIRL supplies. These are the backend (drone) nodes that we'll use. One will send traffic and one will receive traffic; while my Win10 workstation will use the frontend (GUI) application to configure the data stream for the "send" drone. As you may know SSH runs over TCP port 22, so what we'll do is create an ACL on *iosv-1* that will verify this traffic. For simplicity sake this simulation will make use of the **Shared Flat Network** (so that my Win10 workstation can use the Ostinato frontend GUI and directly communicate to all nodes via their management interfaces); as well as using **AutoNetkit** (so that the configuration is automated).

Note: All the nodes use the credentials: cisco / cisco.

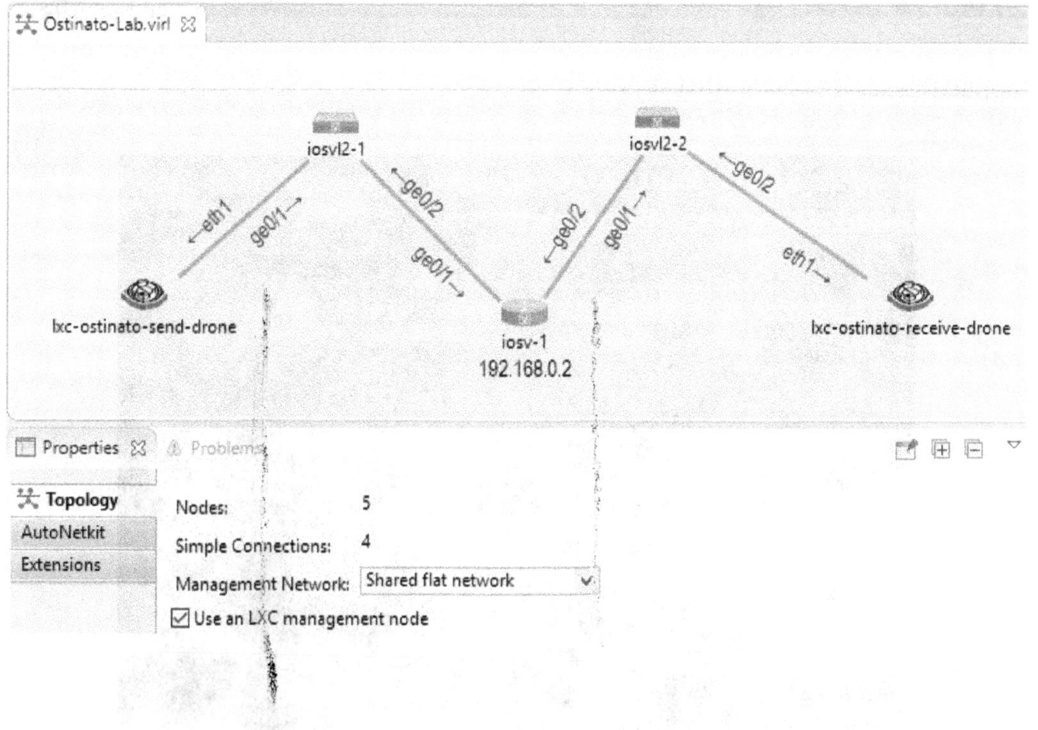

My nodes were auto configured as such:

Lxc-ostinato-send-drone

- Eth0 (mgmt): 172.16.1.67
- Eth1 (network): 10.0.0.6 (MAC fa:16:3e:2c:46:1f)

Lxc-ostinato-receive-drone

- Eth0 (mgmt): 172.16.1.66
- Eth1 (network): 10.0.0.10

Iosv-1:

- Gi0/1 (MAC: fa16.3eee.eef9)

Here is my access control list:

```
iosv-1#sh access-list
Extended IP access list AllowedTraffic
    10 permit tcp host 10.0.0.6 host 10.0.0.10 eq 22 log
    20 permit icmp host 10.0.0.6 host 10.0.0.10 echo log
    30 deny ip any any log
```

I then applied the access-list to **iosv-1 Gi0/1** interface:

```
iosv-1#sh run int gi0/1
Building configuration...

Current configuration : 189 bytes
!
interface GigabitEthernet0/1
 description to iosvl2-1
 ip address 10.0.0.5 255.255.255.252
 ip access-group AllowTraffic in
 ip ospf cost 1
 duplex full
 speed auto
 media-type rj45
```

From the “send-drone” I pinged the “receive-drone” to make sure they could communicate.

```
cisco@lxc-ostinato-send-drone$ ping -c 5 10.0.0.10
PING 10.0.0.10 (10.0.0.10) 56(84) bytes of data.
64 bytes from 10.0.0.10: icmp_seq=1 ttl=63 time=3.30 ms
64 bytes from 10.0.0.10: icmp_seq=2 ttl=63 time=5.14 ms
64 bytes from 10.0.0.10: icmp_seq=3 ttl=63 time=2.71 ms
64 bytes from 10.0.0.10: icmp_seq=4 ttl=63 time=3.71 ms
64 bytes from 10.0.0.10: icmp_seq=5 ttl=63 time=4.54 ms

--- 10.0.0.10 ping statistics ---
5 packets transmitted, 5 received, 0% packet loss, time 4005ms
rtt min/avg/max/mdev = 2.718/3.886/5.143/0.868 ms
```

The ACL verified the 5 ping packets.

```
iosv-1#sh access-list AllowTraffic
Extended IP access list AllowTraffic
    10 permit tcp host 10.0.0.6 host 10.0.0.10 eq 22 log
    20 permit icmp host 10.0.0.6 host 10.0.0.10 echo log (5 matches)
    30 deny ip any any log
```

The logging doubly verified the packets.

```
iosv-1#sh log | inc icmp
*Apr 22 19:06:52.451: %SEC-6-IPACCESSLOGDP: list AllowTraffic permitted icmp 10.0.0.6 -> 10.0.0.10
(8/0), 1 packet
```

Now let's prove that TCP port 22 (SSH) traffic gets through via Ostinato. Open the Ostinato shortcut you created earlier.

By default all of your Win10 workstation's interfaces will be displayed.

```
Port Group 0: [127.0.0.1]:7878 (4)
    Port 0: if0 (TeamViewerVPN Adapter)
    Port 1: if1 (TAP-Windows Adapter V9)
    Port 2: if2 (VMware Virtual Ethernet Adapter)
    Port 3: if3 (Realtek PCIe GBE Family Controller)
```

Right-click whatever your port group is called and select *Delete Port Group.*

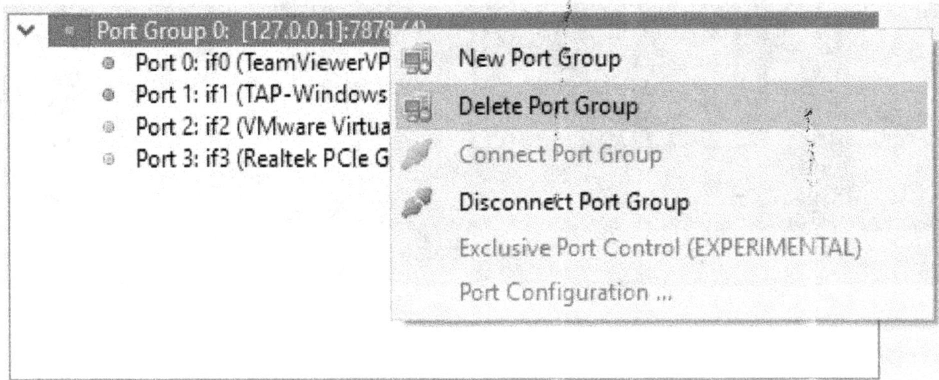

We'll now add each Ostinato node's management IP addresses and append 7878 to them. TCP Port 7878 is what the Ostinato GUI uses to communicate to each VIRL drone. Right-click in that upper box and choose *New Port Group.* Enter: *172.16.1.67:7878* (or whatever your sending drone's management IP address is).

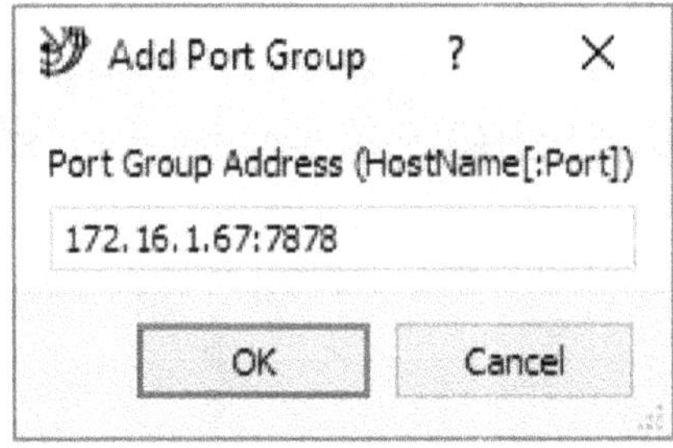

Now repeat this step using the receiving drone's management IP address.

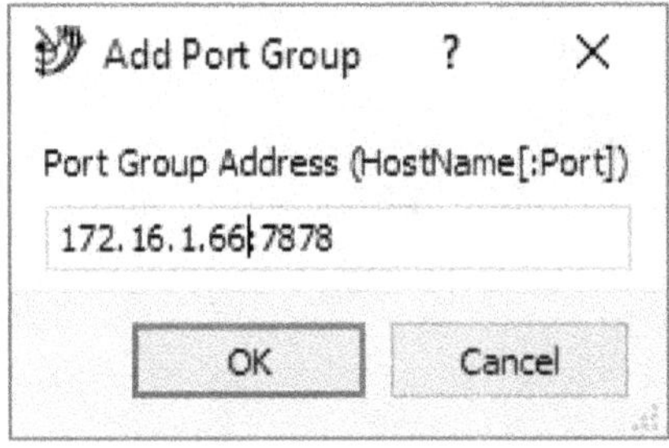

After expanding each Port Group, each interface's Port0 (eth0) and Port1 (eth1) should show up with a green status. These are the only ones we're concerned with.

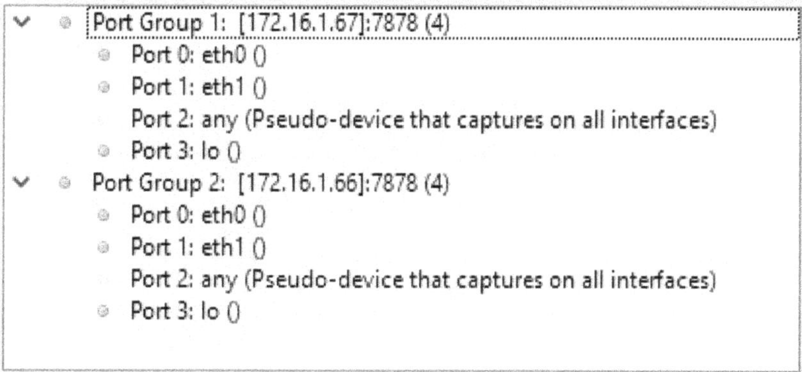

Highlight *Port 1: eth1* on your "sending" node. Mine is 172.16.1.67. Right-click on an empty area in the "Streams" window and choose *New Stream.*

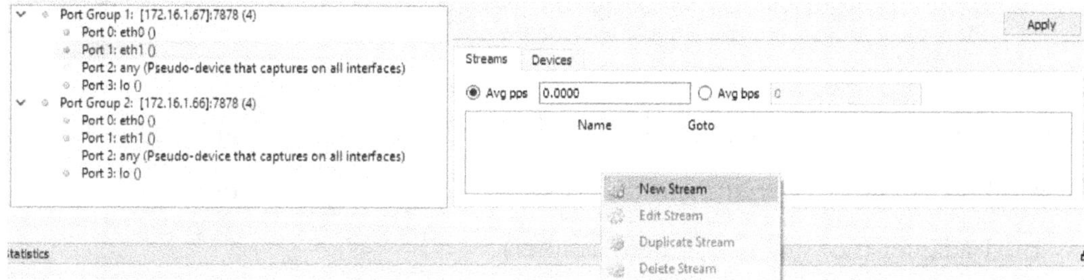

With entry #1 now created, double-click under the "Name" field and put in whatever name you wish. Double-click under the "Goto" field and change it to *Stop*. I chose *stop* because I wanted Ostinato to stop sending any more data after this was complete. This isn't really necessary but it shows you that if you had multiple streams, and if this was the last of several streams configured, the program would stop after it completed this stream.

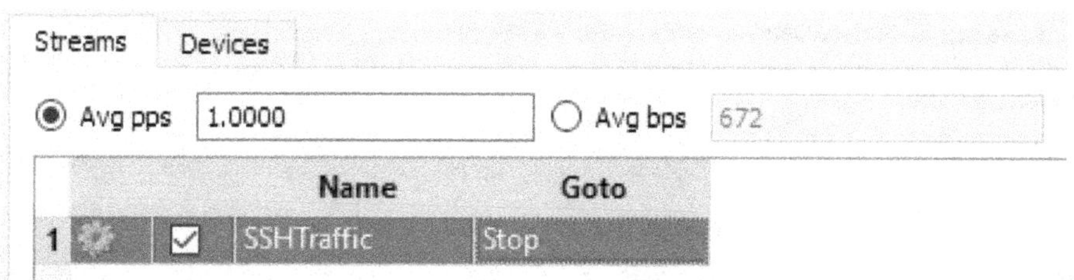

Double-click the so that we can edit the stream and set it exactly how I show below. Here we're enabling TCP v4 traffic.

Edit Stream ?

Protocol Selection | Protocol Data | Variable Fields | Stream Control | Packet View

Frame Length (including FCS)

Fixed Min 64

64 Max 1518

Simple

L1: None, Mac, Other

L2: None, Ethernet II, 802.3 Raw, 802.3 LLC, 802.3 LLC SNAP, Other

L3: None, ARP, IPv4, IPv6, IP 6over4, IP 4over6, IP 4over4, IP 6over6, Other

L5: None, Text, Other

VLAN: Untagged, Tagged, Stacked

L4: None, ICMP, IGMP, MLD, TCP, UDP, Other

Payload: None, Pattern, Hex Dump, Other

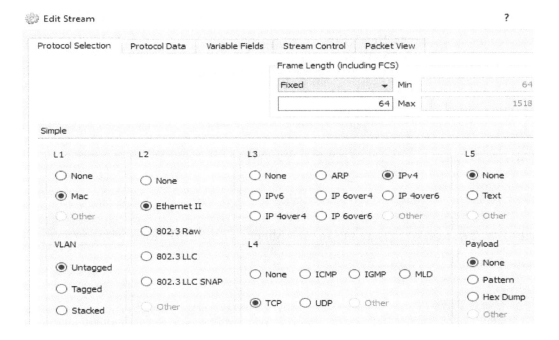

Under the "Protocol Data | Media Access Protocol" tab, the "Destination" field is the MAC address of IOSv-1's Gi0/1 interface and the "Source" field is the MAC address of the "send-drone's" Eth1 adapter (not its management adapter).

Note: Keep in mind that when Ostinato drones are separated by a L3 device the "Destination" field's MAC address is <u>always</u> the router's interface on the side of the "sending" drone. If Ostinato drones are separated by a L2 device the "Destination" and "Source" field's MAC addresses are of the "receiving-drone" and "sending-drone" respectively.

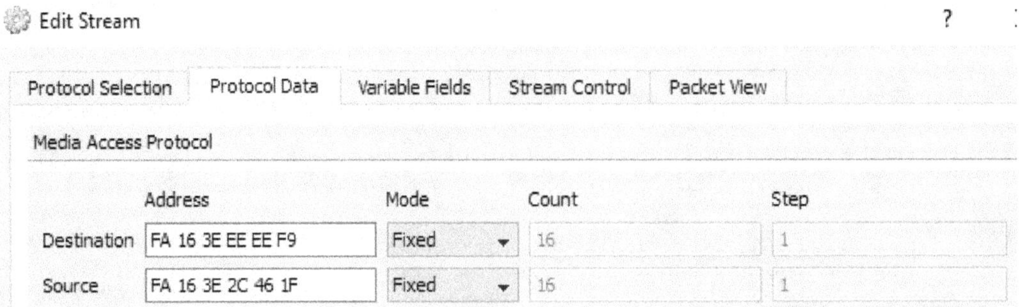

Under the "Protocol Data | Internet Protocol ver 4" tab, the "Source" field is the "send-drone's" Eth1 adapter IP address (not its management adapter's IP) and the "Destination" field is the "receive-drone's" Eth1 adapter IP address (not its management adapter's IP).

Edit Stream ?

Protocol Selection | Protocol Data | Variable Fields | Stream Control | Packet View

Media Access Protocol

Ethernet II

Internet Protocol ver 4

☐ Override Version 4 Fragment Offset (x8) 0

☐ Override Header Length (x4) 5 ☐ Don't Fragment ☐ More Fragments

TOS/DSCP 00 Time To Live (TTL) 127

☐ Override Length 46 ☐ Override Protocol 06

Identification 04 D2 ☐ Override Checksum 36 F9

		Mode	Count	Mask
Source	10 .0 .0 .6	Fixed	16	255.255.255.0
Destination	10 .0 .0 .10	Fixed	16	255.255.255.0

Under the "Protocol Data | Transmission Control Protocol" tab, we override the source port (10233) and destination port (22). This specifically configures Ostinato to only send packets from and to specific ports.

Edit Stream ?

Protocol Selection | Protocol Data | Variable Fields | Stream Control | Packet View

Media Access Protocol

Ethernet II

Internet Protocol ver 4

Transmission Control Protocol

☑ Override Source Port 10233
☑ Override Destination Port 22
Sequence Number 129018
Acknowledgement Number 0
☐ Override Header Length (x4) 5
Window 1024
☐ Override Checksum B3 E9
Urgent Pointer 0
Flags
☐ URG ☐ ACK ☐ PSH
☐ RST ☐ SYN ☐ FIN

Lastly, under the "Stream Control" tab, we'll send 20 total packets with each packet being sent every 2 seconds and once the stream is done, just stop. Click *OK* when done.

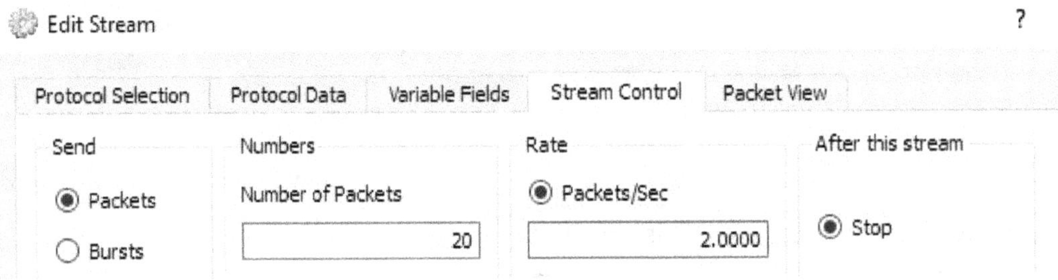

Now you're back at the Ostinato home screen, click the Apply button to save your changes. Whenever you add, delete or change a stream of data in this program, you must <u>always</u> remember to click this button.

You may have noticed that there are many ports showing in the lower half of the window.

	Port 1-0	Port 1-1	Port 1-2	Port 1-3	Port 2-0	Port 2-1	Port 2-2	Port 2-3
Link State	Up	Up	Unknown	Up	Up	Up	Unknown	Up
Transmit State	Off	Off	Off	Off	Off	Off	Off	Off
Capture State	Off	Off	Off	Off	Off	Off	Off	Off
Frames Received	862	219	0	0	865	221	0	0
Frames Sent	476	0	0	0	478	0	0	0
Frame Send Rate (fps)	4	0	0	0	1	0	0	0
Frame Receive Rate (fps)	5	1	0	0	2	1	0	0
Bytes Received	67497	16056	0	0	67503	16477	0	0
Bytes Sent	102755	0	0	0	102899	0	0	0
Byte Send Rate (Bps)	554	0	0	0	261	0	0	0
Byte Receive Rate (Bps)	426	60	0	0	132	60	0	0
Receive Drops	0	0	0	0	0	0	0	0

To allow us to only focus on the traffic leaving and entering interfaces we want to look at, click (at the right lower half window) and move all ports, except Port 1-1 and Port 2-1, to the left window.

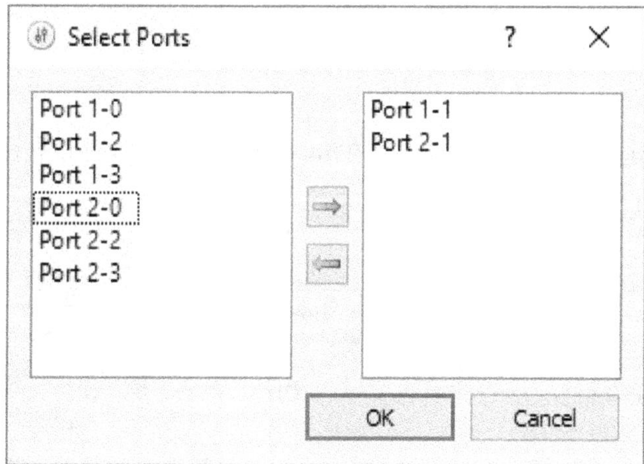

Start by clearing the statistics for ports 1-1 and 2-1. Click at the top of each column (holding down the Ctrl-key), then click either button. This will temporarily clear out all statistics. The row we're really concerned with is the **Frames Sent** under **Port 1-1** (our "sending" node).

Statistics

	Port 1-1	Port 2-1
Link State	Up	Up
Transmit State	Off	Off
Capture State	Off	Off
Frames Received	0	0
Frames Sent	0	0
Frame Send Rate (fps)	0	0
Frame Receive Rate (fps)	1	0
Bytes Received	0	0
Bytes Sent	0	0
Byte Send Rate (Bps)	0	0
Byte Receive Rate (Bps)	60	0
Receive Drops	0	0

Now with both ports highlighted, click . This will start the Ostinato traffic. Notice how mine shows the 20 packets I told it to send.

	Port 1-1	Port 2-1
Link State	Up	Up
Transmit State	Off	Off
Capture State	Off	Off
Frames Received	166	186
Frames Sent	20	0

And we've also verified the traffic via our access-list and the log on **iosv-1**.

```
iosv-1#sh access-list
Extended IP access list AllowTraffic
    10 permit tcp host 10.0.0.6 host 10.0.0.10 eq 22 log (20 matches)
    20 permit icmp host 10.0.0.6 host 10.0.0.10 echo log
    30 deny ip any any log
iosv-1#
iosv-1#sh log | inc permitted
*Apr 22 21:36:25.353: %SEC-6-IPACCESSLOGP: list AllowTraffic permitted tcp 10.0.0.6(10233) -> 10.0.0.10
(22), 1 packet
```

Before exiting out of Ostinato, you can save the session by clicking *File* | *Save Session* for later use.

```
@echo off
TITLE VIRL Live PCap
MODE con:cols=80 lines=12
COLOR 1F
set NETCAT_PATH=D:\VMs\VMware Workstation\VIRL\nc.exe
set WIRESHARK_PATH=C:\Program Files\Wireshark\Wireshark.exe
echo.
echo Make sure the capture is already running in the Simulation window (GUI)
echo and make sure you know the port number.
echo.
set /P VIRL_HOST="VIRL Host IP: "
set /P PCAP_PORT="Enter Live Port: "
echo.
echo Reading live pCap from port %PCAP_PORT%.
echo Close this window to stop capture!
echo.
"D:\VMs\VMware Workstation\VIRL\nc.exe" %VIRL_HOST%
%PCAP_PORT% | "C:\Program Files\Wireshark\wireshark.exe" -k -i -
```

Live PCap (Live Packet Capturing

Note: We will continue to use the Ostinato lab topology here.

For this lab I'm using Wireshark v2.4.1 and NetCat v1.11. You can obtain Wireshark from https://www.wireshark.org and NetCat from https://eternallybored.org/misc/netcat/

Being able to view live packets flowing across a topology is something VIRL can do natively, but with the assistance of 3rd party products: wireshark and nc.exe (NetCat). This feature allows you to view packets flowing in and out of a node's interface. We open a listening port on the VIRL server and "pipe" the traffic to the 3rd party (i.e., Wireshark) sniffer application in order to display the packets in real-time. No information is stored on the VIRL server – it is viewed on your Win10 workstation.

First and foremost, create the following script, taking into account where you've installed Wireshark and stored the nc.exe file from the NetCat download. Create a shortcut to this file on your desktop. I named my file: live_pcap_gui.cmd.

Test the script by opening it. It should look like this:

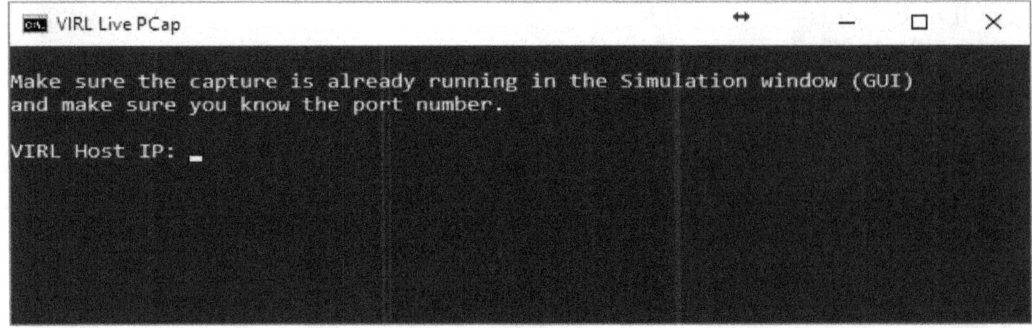

Login to VIRL's UWM interface as guest | guest.

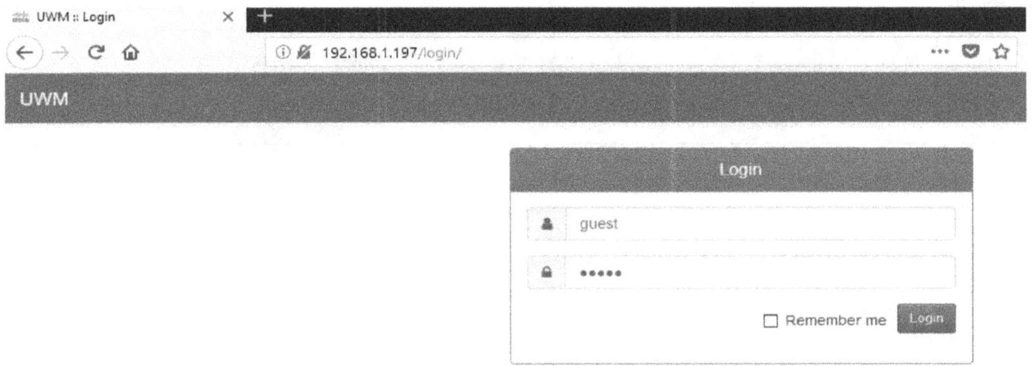

On the left side pane, click *My simulations.* Then click on your simulation's link. Mine is **Ostinato-Lab-TI6UJI**.

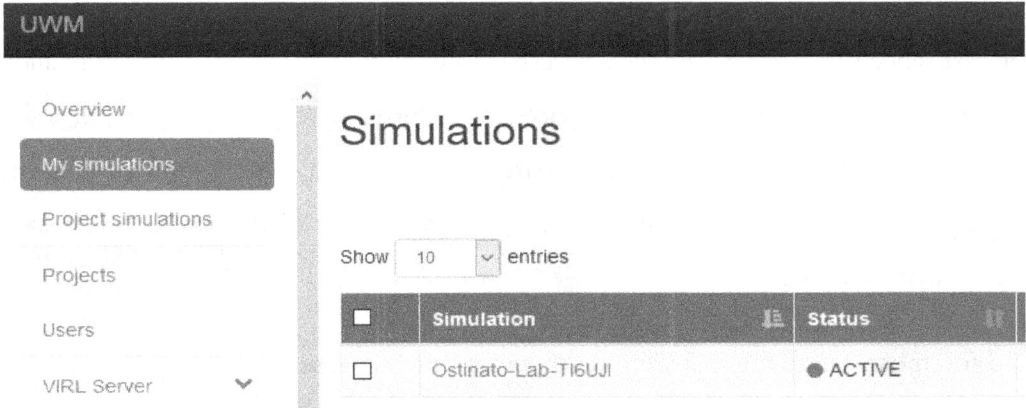

Once open, your simulation's details are displayed. Scroll down to the **Interfaces** section and check the interface you want to capture traffic from. Here I've chosen **IOSv-1's Gi0/1** interface. To recall, this is the interface that the "sending" Ostinato drone's traffic has to traverse to reach the "receiving" Ostinato drone.

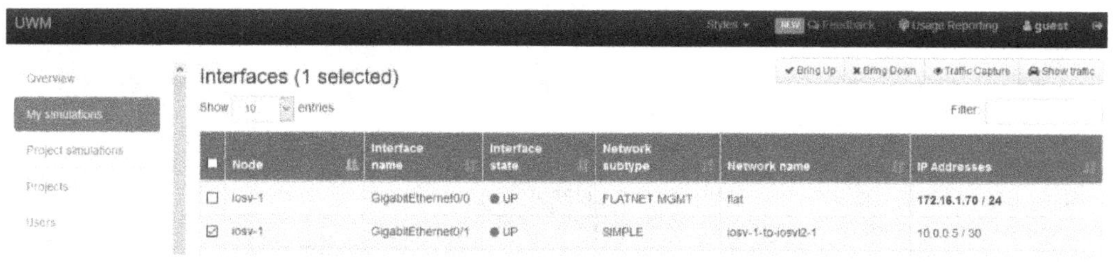

Click **Traffic Capture** and the following screen will be displayed.

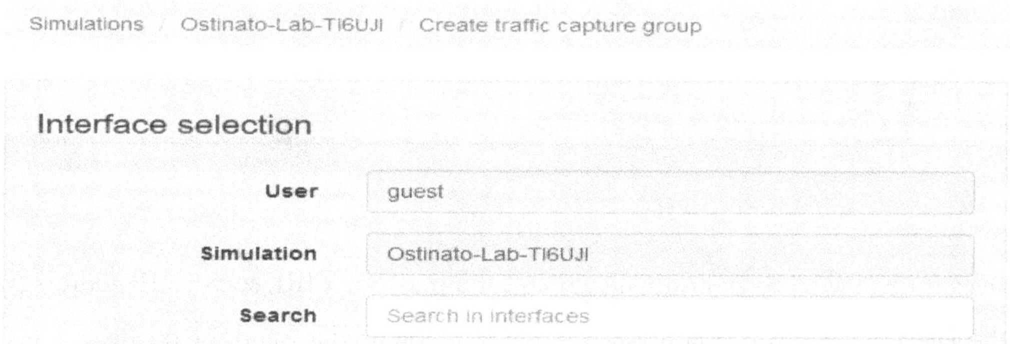

Scroll down to the **General Settings** section, click *Live capture on TCP port*, then input a number between 10000 and 17000. This is the port number the VIRL server will use to send the live capture. I used 12345 in my example. Also notice that I've left **Start capture immediately** checked. This starts the capture as soon as I click ✔ Create. So please click ✔ Create now.

General Settings

Capture group name iosv-1_GigabitEthernet0-1_iosv-1-to-iosvl2-1_un

Capture mode ○ **Offline capture to file**
◉ **Live capture on TCP port**

Live port 12345

Filter packets on the interface, e.g. "icmp or arp", "host 1.2.3.4", "tcp port 123". See syntax reference.

PCAP filter unfiltered

☑ **Start capture immediately**

You can now see under the **Traffic captures** section, our capture.

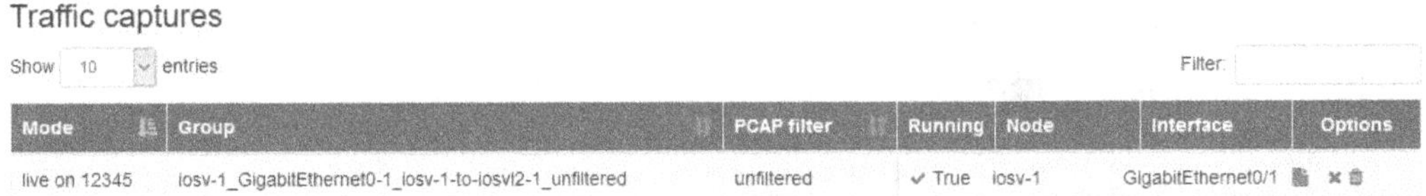

Traffic captures

Show 10 entries Filter:

Mode	Group	PCAP filter	Running	Node	Interface	Options
live on 12345	iosv-1_GigabitEthernet0-1_iosv-1-to-iosvl2-1_unfiltered	unfiltered	✓ True	iosv-1	GigabitEthernet0/1	

With the capture now setup and running, you must input your VIRL server's IP address (which is also displayed in the VMware console) and the port you used to send the traffic.

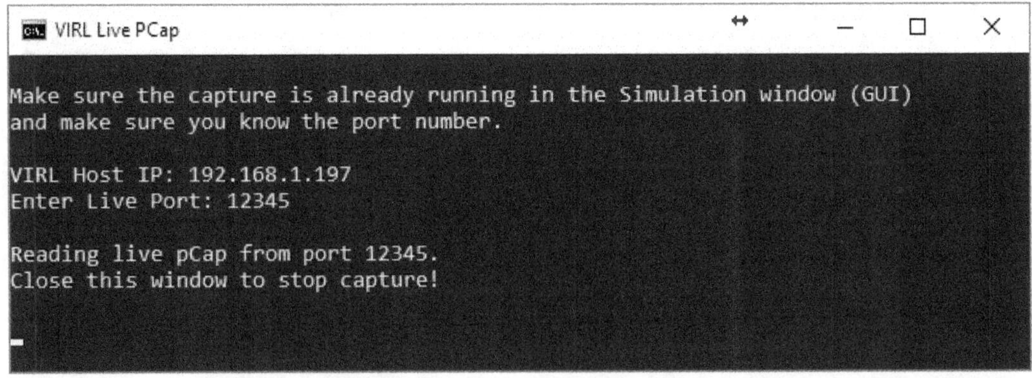

Hit <*enter*> and WireShark should automatically open.

Capturing from Standard input

File Edit View Go Capture Analyze Statistics Telephony Wireless Tools Help

Apply a display filter … <Ctrl-/>

No.	Time	Source	Destination	Protocol	Length	Info
1	0.000000	fa:16:3e:65:98:ce	Spanning-tree-(for-…	STP	60	Conf. Root = 32768/2/5e:00:00:01:00:00 Cost = 0 Port = 0x8003
2	[illegible]	[illegible]	[illegible]	[illegible]	[illegible]	[illegible]
3	3.063630	10.0.0.5	224.0.0.5	OSPF	90	Hello Packet
4	[illegible]	[illegible]	[illegible]	[illegible]	[illegible]	[illegible]
5	[illegible]	[illegible]	[illegible]	[illegible]	[illegible]	[illegible]
6	6.801217	fa:16:3e:53:59:9b	fa:16:3e:53:59:9b	LOOP	60	Reply

At this point I opened an SSH session to the "sending" Ostinato drone and continuously pinged the "receiving" Ostinato drone.

```
cisco@lxc-ostinato-send-drone$ ping 10.0.0.10
PING 10.0.0.10 (10.0.0.10) 56(84) bytes of data.
64 bytes from 10.0.0.10: icmp_seq=1 ttl=63 time=4.01 ms
64 bytes from 10.0.0.10: icmp_seq=2 ttl=63 time=3.89 ms
64 bytes from 10.0.0.10: icmp_seq=3 ttl=63 time=4.18 ms
64 bytes from 10.0.0.10: icmp_seq=4 ttl=63 time=3.55 ms
64 bytes from 10.0.0.10: icmp_seq=5 ttl=63 time=3.53 ms
64 bytes from 10.0.0.10: icmp_seq=6 ttl=63 time=6.76 ms
64 bytes from 10.0.0.10: icmp_seq=7 ttl=63 time=4.12 ms
```

As you can see, Wireshark displays the ICMP packets as they are happening.

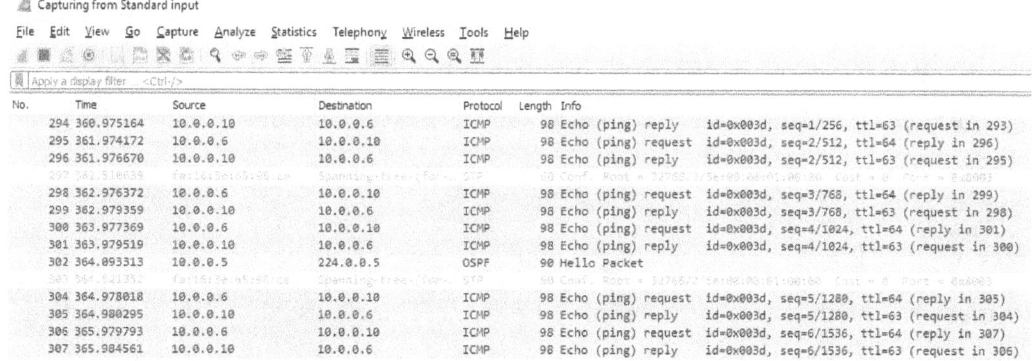

Capturing from Standard input

File Edit View Go Capture Analyze Statistics Telephony Wireless Tools Help

Apply a display filter … <Ctrl-/>

No.	Time	Source	Destination	Protocol	Length	Info
294	360.975164	10.0.0.10	10.0.0.6	ICMP	98	Echo (ping) reply id=0x003d, seq=1/256, ttl=63 (request in 293)
295	361.974172	10.0.0.6	10.0.0.10	ICMP	98	Echo (ping) request id=0x003d, seq=2/512, ttl=64 (reply in 296)
296	361.976670	10.0.0.10	10.0.0.6	ICMP	98	Echo (ping) reply id=0x003d, seq=2/512, ttl=63 (request in 295)
297	[illegible]	[illegible]	[illegible]	[illegible]	[illegible]	[illegible]
298	362.976372	10.0.0.6	10.0.0.10	ICMP	98	Echo (ping) request id=0x003d, seq=3/768, ttl=64 (reply in 299)
299	362.979359	10.0.0.10	10.0.0.6	ICMP	98	Echo (ping) reply id=0x003d, seq=3/768, ttl=63 (request in 298)
300	363.977369	10.0.0.6	10.0.0.10	ICMP	98	Echo (ping) request id=0x003d, seq=4/1024, ttl=64 (reply in 301)
301	363.979519	10.0.0.10	10.0.0.6	ICMP	98	Echo (ping) reply id=0x003d, seq=4/1024, ttl=63 (request in 300)
302	364.093313	10.0.0.5	224.0.0.5	OSPF	90	Hello Packet
303	[illegible]	[illegible]	[illegible]	[illegible]	[illegible]	[illegible]
304	364.978018	10.0.0.6	10.0.0.10	ICMP	98	Echo (ping) request id=0x003d, seq=5/1280, ttl=64 (reply in 305)
305	364.980295	10.0.0.10	10.0.0.6	ICMP	98	Echo (ping) reply id=0x003d, seq=5/1280, ttl=63 (request in 304)
306	365.979793	10.0.0.6	10.0.0.10	ICMP	98	Echo (ping) request id=0x003d, seq=6/1536, ttl=64 (reply in 307)
307	365.984561	10.0.0.10	10.0.0.6	ICMP	98	Echo (ping) reply id=0x003d, seq=6/1536, ttl=63 (request in 306)

After completing your capture simply close the script's window and in UWM, just click the **X** under the **Options** window.

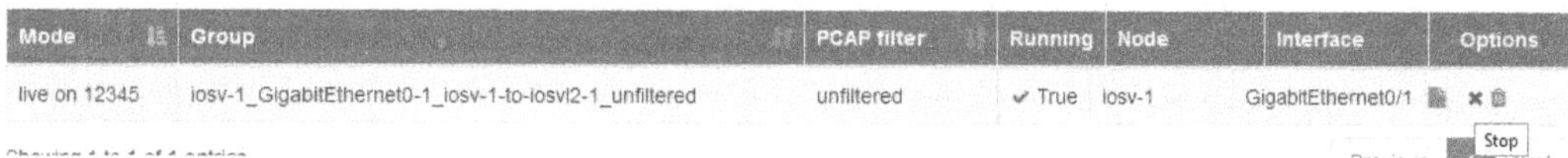

Mode	Group	PCAP filter	Running	Node	Interface	Options
live on 12345	iosv-1_GigabitEthernet0-1_iosv-1-to-iosvl2-1_unfiltered	unfiltered	✔ True	iosv-1	GigabitEthernet0/1	Stop

You'll see confirmation that the capture was stopped.

Capture group "**iosv-1_GigabitEthernet0-1_iosv-1-to-iosvl2-1_unfiltered**" was stopped

The capture will stay in place in case you'd like to run it again sometime in the future. If you want to edit or remove it, click one of the respective icons .

In conclusion, you can use this live packet capture feature for any type of traffic traversing any node in any topology. Where I find this tool very helpful is in watching OSPF (or any other routing protocol) conversations between routers.

RouteM (Injecting Routes)

So you've got a topology running and you want to experiment with a large number of routes coming into your environment (i.e., an ISP advertising routes to you, etc) so that you can learn how to filter them, perform summarization, etc. How do you accomplish this? You could create numerous loopback and/or SVI interfaces to accomplish this but this could be very time consuming. Instead, using VIRL's built-in **RouteM** feature is the preferred choice. This control-plane traffic generator works with routing protocols: RIP, OSPF, ISIS, and BGP; as well as ICMP, TCP, MSDP (Multicast Source Discovery Protocol), and SCTP (Stream Control Transmission Protocol).

Examples of using RouteM with each of the aforementioned protocols can be found in your VIRL server's UWM under Documentation | Routem. There's also an lxc-routem subtype node included that you'll need to add to your topology to make this happen – so let's learn how to use this feature.

First make sure that you can view the lxc-routem node in VM Maestro. If it doesn't appear in the node pane go under File | Preferences | Node Subtypes and verify that "true" is set under the lxc-routem's "Show in Palette" column. Don't forget to click *Apply* if you had to toggle this option to "true", then click *OK*.

I've created the following topology in order to act as an ISP who will advertise a handful of external subnets to a customer. I've configured this topology to use **Shared flat network** so that my Win10 workstation can directly access any of the nodes and although I'll utilize **AutoNetkit** to build the initial configurations, I made a few modifications myself.

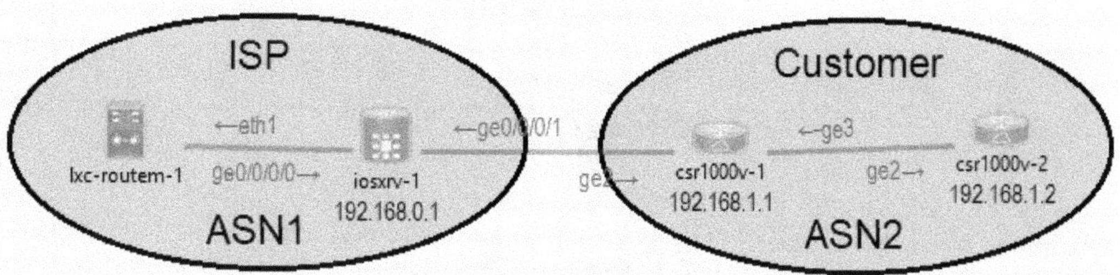

I clicked the iossrv-1 node and set the following:

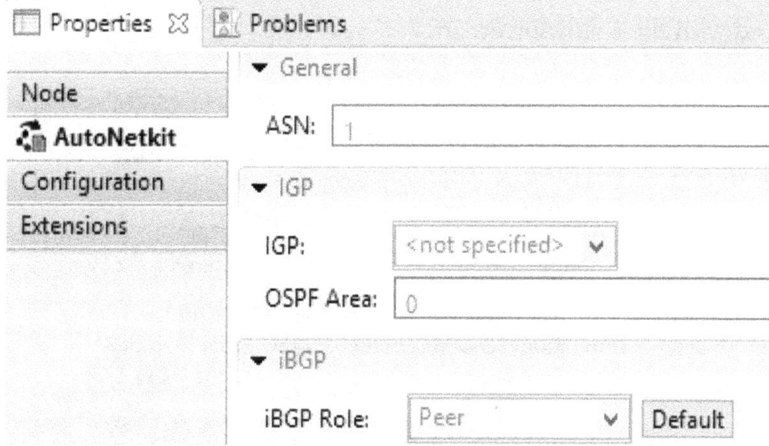

I then clicked on each csr100v node and set the following:

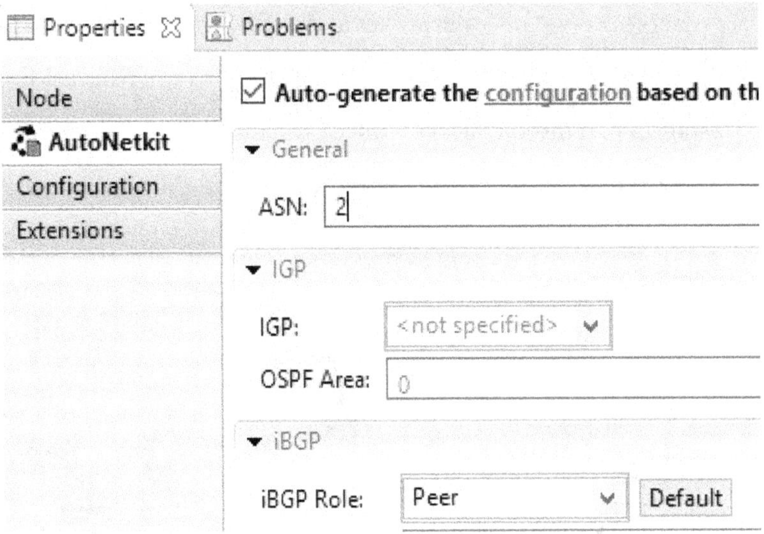

After clicking in order to save and name the lab: **routem-lab.virl**, I launched the simulation but was confronted with the following error:

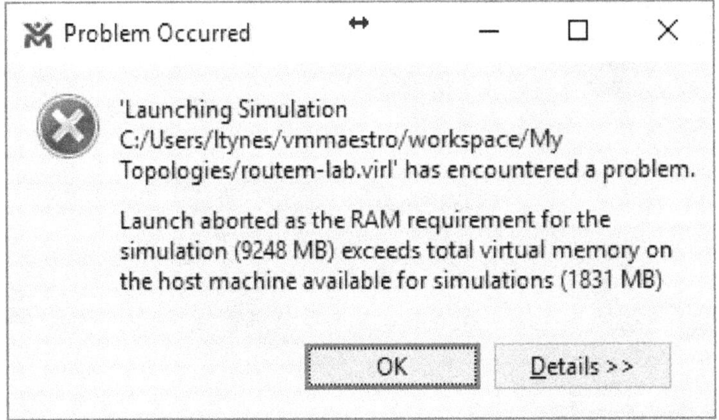

Actually, having this occur provides me the opportunity to show you how to remedy it in case it happens with any topology you might create.

Login to the UWM interface – http://192.168.1.197/login/ with credentials: uwmadmin / password.

In the left-side pane choose *VIRL Server* | *System Configuration* | *Hardware* and change **RAM Overcommit Multipler** from **2** to **4**. If you place your mouse of the **?** you'll see why we've changed this. Now click , , then click and then .

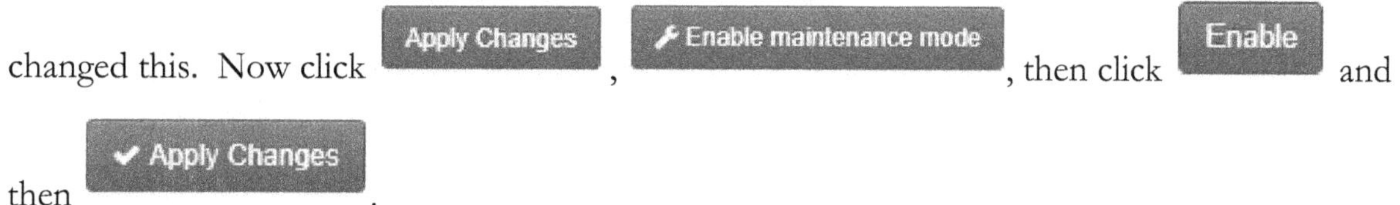

You will see a screen similar to this – Jobs in Progress…

Jobs in progress

Job	Status	Last update	Runtime	Success	Options
state.sls virl.vinstall	● finished	2018-04-15 00:49:33	6s	✔ (2 out of 2)	
vinstall salt	● finished	2018-04-15 00:49:33	10s	✔ (0 out of 0)	
state.sls openstack.neutron.config	● running	triggered at 2018-04-15 00:49:32	1s ..	? N/A	■ Cancel
state.sls openstack.neutron.recreate-basic	● scheduled	2018-04-15 00:49:02	—	? N/A	■ Cancel
state.sls virl.network.interfaces	● scheduled	2018-04-15 00:49:02	—	? N/A	■ Cancel
state.sls virl.openvpn.setup	● scheduled	2018-04-15 00:49:02	—	? N/A	■ Cancel

Refresh

Please wait until the above jobs are finished ...

Although your browser window may automatically refresh the status, you can also click

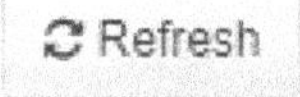

until the status column for all jobs shows **finished**.

Jobs in progress

Job	Status
state.sls virl.vinstall	● finished
vinstall salt	● finished
state.sls openstack.neutron.config	● finished
state.sls openstack.neutron.recreate-basic	● finished
state.sls virl.network.interfaces	● finished
state.sls virl.openvpn.setup	● finished

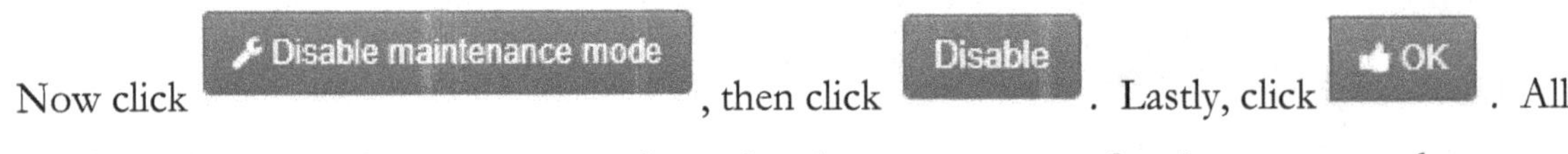

Now click [Disable maintenance mode], then click [Disable]. Lastly, click [OK]. All configuration controls are now grayed out showing you are out of maintenance mode.

System Configuration Controls

CONFIG SET MAINTENANCE MODE APPLY REBOOT DISABLE MAINTENANCE MODE COMPLETE

Now rerun the simulation. This fixed my issue, but if this doesn't fix yours, try slightly increasing the variable again. Also you may want to take into account (i.e., adjusting) the amount of virtual memory configured on your Win10 workstation.

Note: All nodes' credentials are: cisco / cisco.

First let's verify the subnets that **iosxrv-1** is aware of:

```
RP/0/0/CPU0:iosxrv-1#sh ip route
Sat Apr 28 23:17:48.996 UTC

Codes: C - connected, S - static, R - RIP, B - BGP, (>) - Diversion path
       D - EIGRP, EX - EIGRP external, O - OSPF, IA - OSPF inter area
       N1 - OSPF NSSA external type 1, N2 - OSPF NSSA external type 2
       E1 - OSPF external type 1, E2 - OSPF external type 2, E - EGP
       i - ISIS, L1 - IS-IS level-1, L2 - IS-IS level-2
       ia - IS-IS inter area, su - IS-IS summary null, * - candidate default
       U - per-user static route, o - ODR, L - local, G  - DAGR, l - LISP
       A - access/subscriber, a - Application route
       M - mobile route, r - RPL, (!) - FRR Backup path

Gateway of last resort is not set

C    10.0.0.4/30 is directly connected, 01:05:11, GigabitEthernet0/0/0/0
L    10.0.0.5/32 is directly connected, 01:05:11, GigabitEthernet0/0/0/0
C    10.0.0.8/30 is directly connected, 01:05:11, GigabitEthernet0/0/0/1
L    10.0.0.10/32 is directly connected, 01:05:11, GigabitEthernet0/0/0/1
B    10.0.0.12/30 [20/0] via 10.0.0.9, 01:04:57
L    192.168.0.1/32 is directly connected, 01:05:11, Loopback0
B    192.168.1.1/32 [20/0] via 10.0.0.9, 01:04:57
B    192.168.1.2/32 [20/0] via 10.0.0.9, 01:04:57
```

This also shows **iosxrv-1's** BGP neighbors. Here we see a neighbor peering with csr1000v-1 (10.0.0.9) only.

```
RP/0/0/CPU0:iosxrv-1#sh ip bgp summary
Sun Apr 29 01:30:30.261 UTC
BGP router identifier 192.168.0.1, local AS number 1
BGP generic scan interval 60 secs
Non-stop routing is enabled
BGP table state: Active
Table ID: 0xe0000000   RD version: 281
BGP main routing table version 281
BGP NSR Initial initsync version 9 (Reached)
BGP NSR/ISSU Sync-Group versions 0/0
BGP scan interval 60 secs

BGP is operating in STANDALONE mode.


Process       RcvTblVer   bRIB/RIB   LabelVer  ImportVer  SendTblVer  StandbyVer
Speaker             281        281        281        281         281           0

Neighbor        Spk    AS MsgRcvd MsgSent   TblVer  InQ OutQ  Up/Down  St/PfxRcd
10.0.0.9          0     2     222     206      281    0    0 03:17:46          3
```

Secondly let's verify the BGP routes currently being advertised from the ISP (ASN1) into the Customer (ASN2).

After SSHing into **csr100v-1** we see that it knows about **iosxrv-1's** 10.0.0.4 subnet (Gi0/0/0/0) as well as its Loopback0 address (192.168.0.1).

```
csr1000v-1#sh ip route bgp
Codes: L - local, C - connected, S - static, R - RIP, M - mobile, B - BGP
       D - EIGRP, EX - EIGRP external, O - OSPF, IA - OSPF inter area
       N1 - OSPF NSSA external type 1, N2 - OSPF NSSA external type 2
       E1 - OSPF external type 1, E2 - OSPF external type 2
       i - IS-IS, su - IS-IS summary, L1 - IS-IS level-1, L2 - IS-IS level-2
       ia - IS-IS inter area, * - candidate default, U - per-user static route
       o - ODR, P - periodic downloaded static route, H - NHRP, l - LISP
       a - application route
       + - replicated route, % - next hop override, p - overrides from PfR

Gateway of last resort is not set

      10.0.0.0/8 is variably subnetted, 5 subnets, 2 masks
B        10.0.0.4/30 [20/0] via 10.0.0.10, 00:33:24
      192.168.0.0/32 is subnetted, 1 subnets
B        192.168.0.1 [20/0] via 10.0.0.10, 00:33:24
```

After SSHing into **csr100v-2** we see that it also knows about **iosxrv-1's** 10.0.0.4 subnet and its Loopback0 address (192.168.0.1); as well as its neighbor, **csr1000v-1's** 10.0.0.8 subnet.

```
csr1000v-2#sh ip route bgp
Codes: L - local, C - connected, S - static, R - RIP, M - mobile, B - BGP
       D - EIGRP, EX - EIGRP external, O - OSPF, IA - OSPF inter area
       N1 - OSPF NSSA external type 1, N2 - OSPF NSSA external type 2
       E1 - OSPF external type 1, E2 - OSPF external type 2
       i - IS-IS, su - IS-IS summary, L1 - IS-IS level-1, L2 - IS-IS level-2
       ia - IS-IS inter area, * - candidate default, U - per-user static route
       o - ODR, P - periodic downloaded static route, H - NHRP, l - LISP
       a - application route
       + - replicated route, % - next hop override, p - overrides from PfR

Gateway of last resort is not set

      10.0.0.0/8 is variably subnetted, 4 subnets, 2 masks
B        10.0.0.4/30 [200/0] via 192.168.1.1, 00:32:02
B        10.0.0.8/30 [200/0] via 192.168.1.1, 00:32:02
      192.168.0.0/32 is subnetted, 1 subnets
B        192.168.0.1 [200/0] via 192.168.1.1, 00:32:02
```

Using Notepad, create the following script and then copy it into your system's buffer (Ctrl-C). You will have to adjust this script to fit your particular topology's configuration. I also discuss what each line does.

router bgp 1
neighbor 10.0.0.5 remote-as 1
neighbor 10.0.0.5 update-source 10.0.0.6
network 1 172.16.1.0/24 15
aspath 1 random 10
network 2 192.168.2.0/24 30
aspath 1 random 10
sendall

Line 1: (router bgp 1) - the BGP process you'll be running
Line 2: (neighbor 10.0.0.5 remote-as 2) – refers to **iosxvr-1's** Gi0/0/0/0 interface (it's connected to **lxc-routem-1's** Eth1 interface) as well as the ASN number to use
Line 3: (neighbor 10.0.0.5 update-source 10.0.0.6) - refers to **iosxvr-1's** Gi0/0/0/0 interface and the interface (10.0.0.6) that **lxc-routem-1** will use to communicate the routes to **iosxvr-1**
Line 4: (network 1 172.16.1.0/24 15) – refers to how many 172.16./24 networks to advertise. In this case we'll be advertising 15 subnets: 172.16.1. – 172.16.16.
Line 5: (aspath 1 random 10) – refers to how many random AS path numbers are used when advertising a route (subnet)
Line 6: (network 2 192.168.2.0/24 30) – refers to how many 192.168./24 networks to advertise. In this case we'll be advertising 30 subnets: 192.168.2. – 192.168.31.
Line 7: (aspath 1 random 10) - refers to how many random AS path numbers are used when advertising a route (subnet)
Line 8: (sendall) – sends all prefixes

SSH into the **lxc-routem** node. Execute the command: ***vi routem.conf***, type ***i*** (for insert) then right-click. The script's commands are now pasted into your **routem.conf** configuration file.

```
172.16.1.86 - PuTTY
router bgp 1
neighbor 10.0.0.5 remote-as 1
neighbor 10.0.0.5 update-source 10.0.0.6
network 1 172.16.1.0/24 15
aspath 1 random 10
network 2 192.168.2.0/24 30
aspath 1 random 10
sendall

~
~
~
~
"routem.conf" 9 lines, 187 characters
```

Save the file by pressing the <Esc> key then typing: ***:wq!***

Now let's run the program. Type: ***routem -f routem.conf***. If successful you should be presented with a similar screen as I have. This **routem** host is now prepped and waiting to begin communication to **iosxvr-1**.

```
cisco@lxc-routem-1$ routem -f routem.conf
Version 2.1(8)(routem_august21.2015) by khphan on Fri Aug 21 15:52:13 PDT 2015
Copyright (c) 1998-1999, 2002-2003, 2007-2009, 2014 by cisco Systems, Inc.
All rights reserved.
ROUTEM:start reading config file  :Sat Apr 28 23:56:59 2018
(bgp:1 bmp:0 ospf:0 isis:0 bfd:0 tcp:0 msdp:0 traff:0)
ROUTEM:finish reading config file :Sat Apr 28 23:56:59 2018
```

Now we must configure **iosxvr-1** to peer with **lxc-routem-1** and get the routes from the **routem.conf** file.

Using Notepad, create the following script and then copy it into your system's buffer (Ctrl-C). You will have to adjust this script to fit your particular topology's configuration. I also discuss what each line does.

```
router bgp 1
 neighbor 10.0.0.6
 remote-as 1
 update-source GigabitEthernet0/0/0/0
 address-family ipv4 unicast
  route-policy bgp_in in
  route-policy bgp_out out
  commit
```

Line 1: (router bgp 1) - the BGP process you're running
Line 2: (neighbor 10.0.0.6) – **lxc-routem-1's** Eth1 interface we want to peer with
Line 3: (remote-as 1) – the Autonomous System Number **lxc-routem-1** is in
Line 4: (update-source GigabitEthernet0/0/0/0)- the specific interface that **iosxvr-1** will use when exchanging BGP updates with **lxc-routem-1**
Line 5: (address-family ipv4 unicast) - places the router in IP version 4 family configuration mode
Line 6: (route-policy bgp_in in) – IOSXRV routers create this route policy by default; thus it allows all BGP routes in.
Line 7: (route-policy bgp_out out) - IOSXRV routers create this route policy by default; thus it allows all BGP routes out.
Line 8: (commit) – IOSXRV routers use this command to commit (save) changes – rather than the changes occurring immediately.

Next we see that **iosxrv-1** has peered with **lxc-routem-1** and obtained 45 routes.

```
RP/0/0/CPU0:iosxrv-1#sh ip bgp summary
Sun Apr 29 01:36:48.085 UTC
BGP router identifier 192.168.0.1, local AS number 1
BGP generic scan interval 60 secs
Non-stop routing is enabled
BGP table state: Active
Table ID: 0xe0000000   RD version: 326
BGP main routing table version 326
BGP NSR Initial initsync version 9 (Reached)
BGP NSR/ISSU Sync-Group versions 0/0
BGP scan interval 60 secs

BGP is operating in STANDALONE mode.


Process       RcvTblVer   bRIB/RIB   LabelVer  ImportVer  SendTblVer  StandbyVer
Speaker             326        326        326        326         326           0

Neighbor        Spk    AS MsgRcvd MsgSent   TblVer  InQ OutQ  Up/Down  St/PfxRcd
10.0.0.6          0     1       6       7      326    0    0 00:01:10         45
10.0.0.9          0     2     229     213      326    0    0 03:24:04          3
```

This screenshot displays some of those routes.

172.16.1.85 - PuTTY

```
RP/0/0/CPU0:iosxrv-1#sh ip route bgp
Sun Apr 29 01:55:57.066 UTC

B    10.0.0.12/30 [20/0] via 10.0.0.9, 03:43:05
B    172.16.1.0/24 [200/0] via 10.0.0.6, 00:01:24
B    172.16.2.0/24 [200/0] via 10.0.0.6, 00:01:24
B    172.16.3.0/24 [200/0] via 10.0.0.6, 00:01:24
B    172.16.4.0/24 [200/0] via 10.0.0.6, 00:01:24
B    172.16.5.0/24 [200/0] via 10.0.0.6, 00:01:24
B    172.16.6.0/24 [200/0] via 10.0.0.6, 00:01:24
B    172.16.7.0/24 [200/0] via 10.0.0.6, 00:01:24
B    172.16.8.0/24 [200/0] via 10.0.0.6, 00:01:24
B    172.16.9.0/24 [200/0] via 10.0.0.6, 00:01:24
B    172.16.10.0/24 [200/0] via 10.0.0.6, 00:01:24
B    172.16.11.0/24 [200/0] via 10.0.0.6, 00:01:24
B    172.16.12.0/24 [200/0] via 10.0.0.6, 00:01:24
B    172.16.13.0/24 [200/0] via 10.0.0.6, 00:01:24
B    172.16.14.0/24 [200/0] via 10.0.0.6, 00:01:24
B    172.16.15.0/24 [200/0] via 10.0.0.6, 00:01:24
B    192.168.1.1/32 [20/0] via 10.0.0.9, 03:43:05
B    192.168.1.2/32 [20/0] via 10.0.0.9, 03:43:05
B    192.168.2.0/24 [200/0] via 10.0.0.6, 00:01:24
B    192.168.3.0/24 [200/0] via 10.0.0.6, 00:01:24
B    192.168.4.0/24 [200/0] via 10.0.0.6, 00:01:24
```

Lastly, we see a sampling of some of the 192.168. and 172.16 routes that have propagated into the Customer's routers.

```
csr1000v-1#sh ip route bgp | inc 192.168.
      192.168.0.0/32 is subnetted, 1 subnets
B        192.168.0.1 [20/0] via 10.0.0.10, 03:47:38
B     192.168.2.0/24 [20/0] via 10.0.0.10, 00:05:24
B     192.168.3.0/24 [20/0] via 10.0.0.10, 00:05:24
B     192.168.4.0/24 [20/0] via 10.0.0.10, 00:05:24
B     192.168.5.0/24 [20/0] via 10.0.0.10, 00:05:24
B     192.168.6.0/24 [20/0] via 10.0.0.10, 00:05:24
B     192.168.7.0/24 [20/0] via 10.0.0.10, 00:05:24
```

```
csr1000v-2#sh ip route bgp | inc 172.16.
      172.16.0.0/24 is subnetted, 15 subnets
B        172.16.1.0 [200/0] via 192.168.1.1, 00:08:01
B        172.16.2.0 [200/0] via 192.168.1.1, 00:08:01
B        172.16.3.0 [200/0] via 192.168.1.1, 00:08:01
B        172.16.4.0 [200/0] via 192.168.1.1, 00:08:01
B        172.16.5.0 [200/0] via 192.168.1.1, 00:08:01
B        172.16.6.0 [200/0] via 192.168.1.1, 00:08:01
B        172.16.7.0 [200/0] via 192.168.1.1, 00:08:01
B        172.16.8.0 [200/0] via 192.168.1.1, 00:08:01
B        172.16.9.0 [200/0] via 192.168.1.1, 00:08:01
B        172.16.10.0 [200/0] via 192.168.1.1, 00:08:01
B        172.16.11.0 [200/0] via 192.168.1.1, 00:08:01
```

Iperf Performance Test

As I mentioned back in Chapter 4, VIRL's simulated topologies should not be looked upon in terms of actual speed/performance; but instead as a functional, Proof of Concept, environment. With that said, iperf is an open-source, client and server, network performance measuring tool that can be used to send TCP or UDP data streams end-to-end to measure the amount of data transferred and the throughput achieved.

I created the following topology letting AutoNetkit configure the nodes. I configured the management network interfaces to use *Shared flat network* (so that I could directly SSH to the nodes from my Win10 workstation). I used iperf's default TCP, 10-second test, with the default window size for our test.

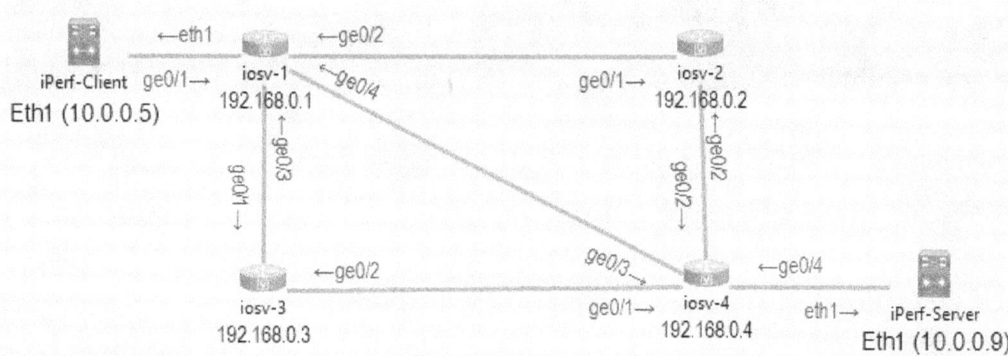

Using credentials: cisco / cisco, I SSHed into the iperf server and configured the program to bind to the server's Eth1 (10.0.0.9) interface.

172.16.1.126 - PuTTY

```
cisco@iPerf-Server$ iperf -s --bind 10.0.0.9
bind failed: Address already in use
------------------------------------------------------------
Server listening on TCP port 5001
Binding to local address 10.0.0.9
TCP window size: 85.3 KByte (default)
------------------------------------------------------------
```

I then SSHed into the iperf client and configured the program to connect to the server's Eth1 (10.0.0.9) interface.

172.16.1.133 - PuTTY

```
cisco@iPerf-Client$ iperf -c 10.0.0.9
------------------------------------------------------------
Client connecting to 10.0.0.9, TCP port 5001
TCP window size: 85.0 KByte (default)
------------------------------------------------------------
[  3] local 10.0.0.5 port 53936 connected with 10.0.0.9 port 5001
[  3]  0.0-10.4 sec  2.95 MBytes  2.38 Mbits/sec
cisco@iPerf-Client$
```

The program sent 2.95MB of data during that 10 seconds – of which it calculated the average speed to reach the iperf server to be 2.38Mb/sec.

The iperf client used the following path to reach the iperf server:

iperf Client ←→ iosv-1 (Gi0/4) ←→ iosv-4 (Gi0/3) ←→ iperf Server

172.16.1.133 - PuTTY

```
cisco@iPerf-Client$ traceroute 10.0.0.9
traceroute to 10.0.0.9 (10.0.0.9), 30 hops max, 60 byte packets
 1  10.0.0.6 (10.0.0.6)  2.889 ms  5.462 ms  7.203 ms
 2  10.0.0.22 (10.0.0.22)  4.601 ms  6.447 ms  6.424 ms
 3  10.0.0.9 (10.0.0.9)  3.593 ms  3.600 ms  3.595 ms
cisco@iPerf-Client$
```

Iperf offers different scenario options. For example, instead of using TCP you could use UDP if you were experimenting with VoIP or video streaming data; changing the TCP window size; changing the MSS; and many others. As of this writing the latest version, iperf3, is what I use and can be obtained at https://iperf.fr/iperf-download.php.

UWM Virtual Traceroute

In the previous iperf test you saw that I ran a manual traceroute from the iperf client to the iperf server. In a real world this is what we do. VIRL also provides this functionality in the UWM – a graphical representation of the packet flow. Let's see how this works:

From VM Maestro – with my topology running – I right-clicked on an empty area in topology pane and chose *Launch Live Visualization.*

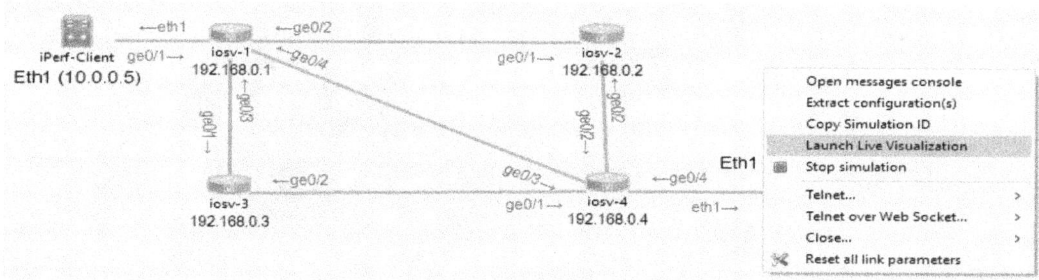

Enter credentials: guest / guest, when prompted. You'll then see your topology in UWM.

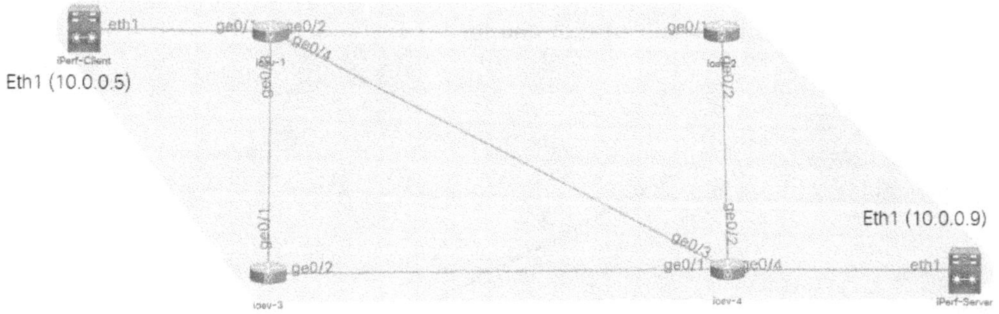

I left-clicked the first router and chose *Trace From.* You cannot trace from the iperf-client.

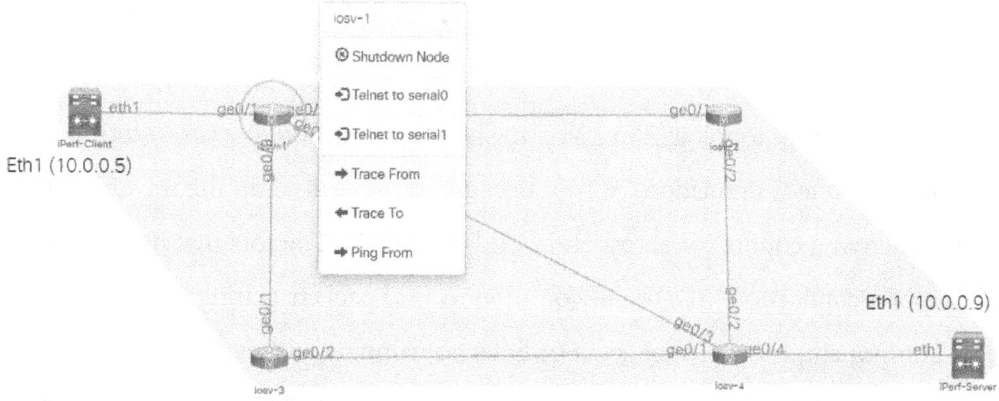

I then left-clicked the iperf-server and chose *Trace To.*

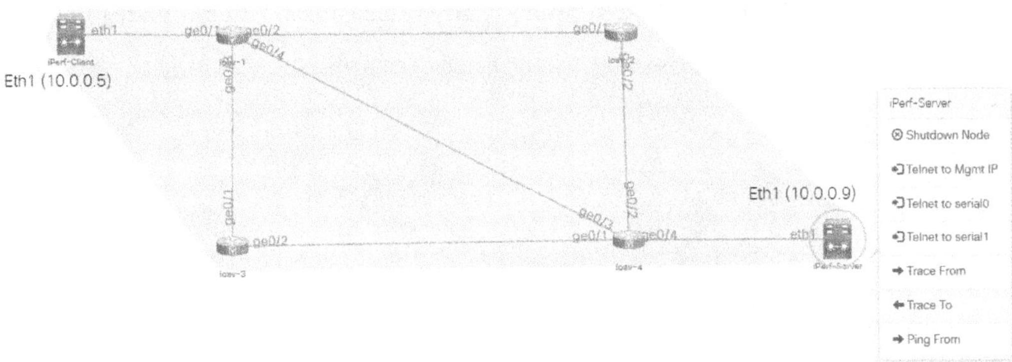

Now I've verified that the manual traceroute process I ran earlier coincides with UWM's visual traceroute. Nice tool huh? UWM's Live Visualization has many features of which I discuss in *Getting to Know* UWM. You can also think about using this tool after you make modifications to a topology and want to test the result of that change.

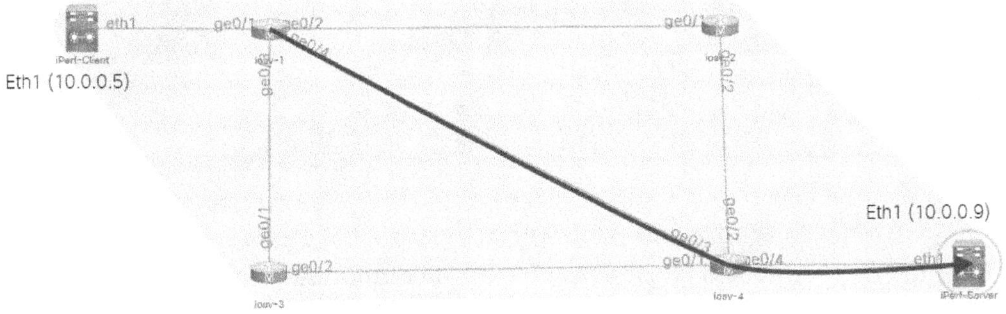

Latency, Jitter and Packet Loss Tools

Keeping with our current topology I'm going to show you 3 different ways to introduce latency, jitter or packet loss into a simulation. Why? Because in the real-world the traversal of packets across a state, across a country or across the world are constant factors that determine the performance of a connection. It's not uncommon to find packets getting lost (i.e., due to a failing link component, route change, etc.) or links not running at speeds they were intended to (i.e., policing, misconfiguration, etc.). Learning to incorporate these features into a topology are helpful when working with routing protocols since their metrics (path determination) is predicated on such factors as bandwidth speed, delay and reliability.

Note: Introducing latency, jitter or packet loss into a running simulation only lasts until the simulation is stopped. These settings are not, and cannot, be saved as part of the topology.

Via VM Maestro

Let's first test the response time between **iperf-client** and **iperf-server** and I, once again, show the path the packets are taking.

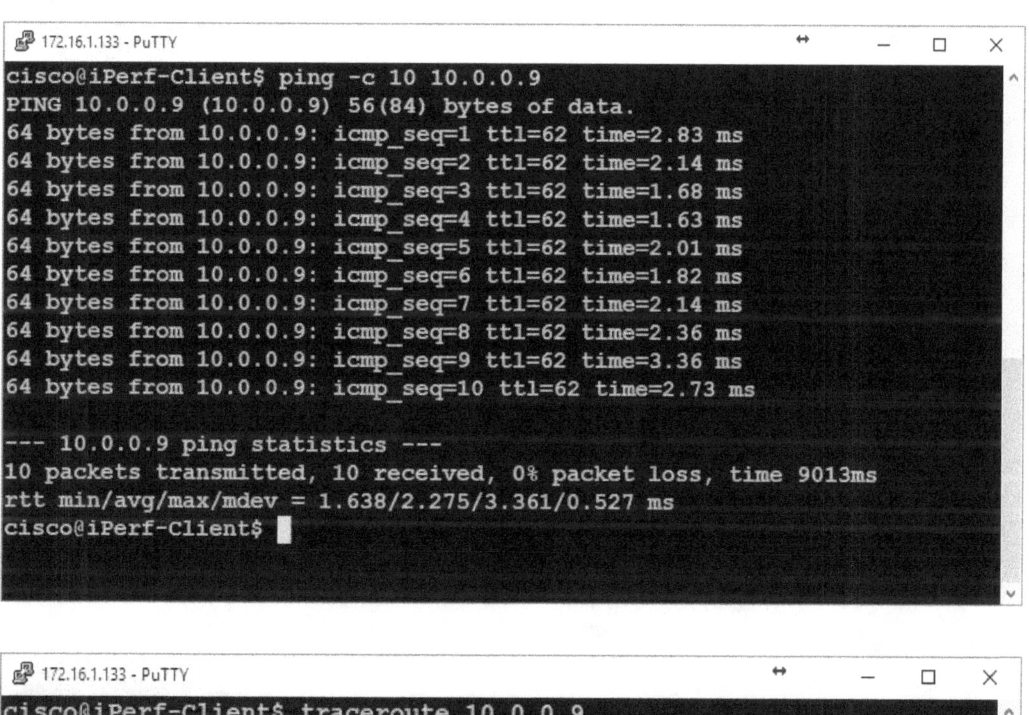

172.16.1.133 - PuTTY

```
cisco@iPerf-Client$ ping -c 10 10.0.0.9
PING 10.0.0.9 (10.0.0.9) 56(84) bytes of data.
64 bytes from 10.0.0.9: icmp_seq=1 ttl=62 time=2.83 ms
64 bytes from 10.0.0.9: icmp_seq=2 ttl=62 time=2.14 ms
64 bytes from 10.0.0.9: icmp_seq=3 ttl=62 time=1.68 ms
64 bytes from 10.0.0.9: icmp_seq=4 ttl=62 time=1.63 ms
64 bytes from 10.0.0.9: icmp_seq=5 ttl=62 time=2.01 ms
64 bytes from 10.0.0.9: icmp_seq=6 ttl=62 time=1.82 ms
64 bytes from 10.0.0.9: icmp_seq=7 ttl=62 time=2.14 ms
64 bytes from 10.0.0.9: icmp_seq=8 ttl=62 time=2.36 ms
64 bytes from 10.0.0.9: icmp_seq=9 ttl=62 time=3.36 ms
64 bytes from 10.0.0.9: icmp_seq=10 ttl=62 time=2.73 ms

--- 10.0.0.9 ping statistics ---
10 packets transmitted, 10 received, 0% packet loss, time 9013ms
rtt min/avg/max/mdev = 1.638/2.275/3.361/0.527 ms
cisco@iPerf-Client$
```

172.16.1.133 - PuTTY

```
cisco@iPerf-Client$ traceroute 10.0.0.9
traceroute to 10.0.0.9 (10.0.0.9), 30 hops max, 60 byte packets
 1  10.0.0.6 (10.0.0.6)  2.889 ms  5.462 ms  7.203 ms
 2  10.0.0.22 (10.0.0.22)  4.601 ms  6.447 ms  6.424 ms
 3  10.0.0.9 (10.0.0.9)  3.593 ms  3.600 ms  3.595 ms
cisco@iPerf-Client$
```

Now right-click the link between **iosv-1** and **iosv-4** and choose *Modify link parameters…*

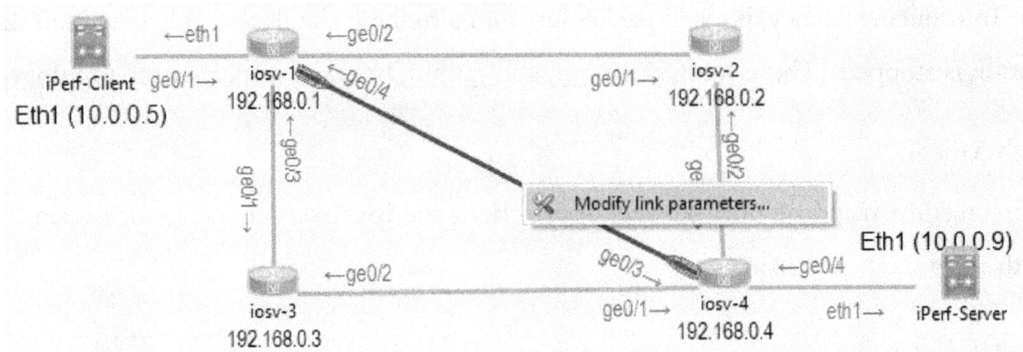

I've changed the "latency" to 500ms (5 seconds), "jitter" to 150ms and "packet loss" to 10% and clicked *OK.*

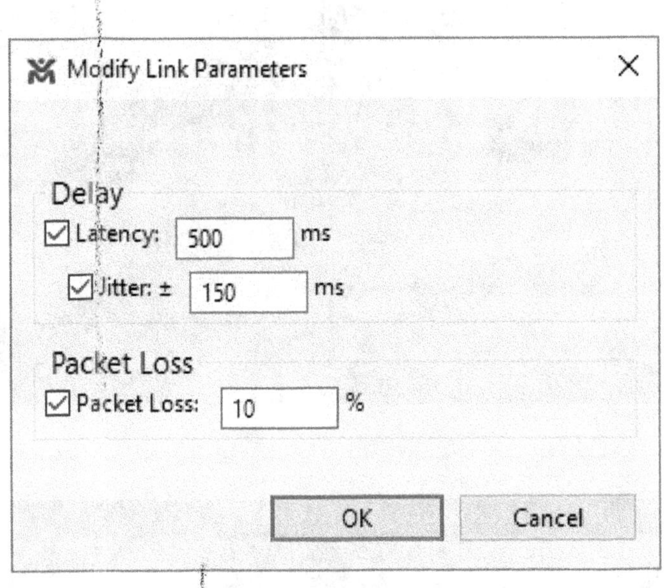

Notice how the link has the following icon displayed on it – indicating that a change has been made to it.

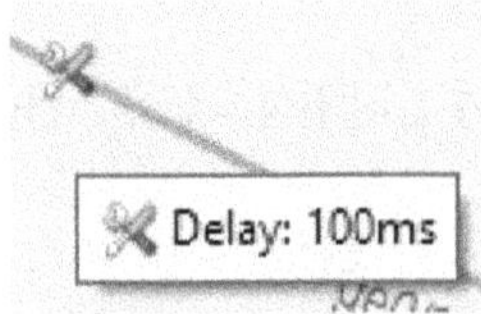

Notice the results after running the ping and traceroute tests again. The ICMP packets took an average time of 967ms, as opposed to 2ms, before we degraded the link.

Notice anything else? The same path was still chosen, even though it was degraded. So why didn't OSPF (auto configured by AutoNetkit) choose a different route since there are multiple routes to the same destination? Answer: because OSPF was only concerned with the "cost" of the link, not the degradation of it. Even if I had shut down **iosv-4**'s Gi0/3 interface, allowing OSPF to reconverge and advertise dual paths to **iperf-server**, via **iosv-2** and **iosv-3**, then degraded the link between **iosv-3** and **iosv-4**, OSPF would <u>not</u> have chosen the **iosv-2** to **iosv-4** link instead. I bring this to your attention so that you're aware that using these features don't change routing path – it only degrades the path.

```
172.16.1.133 - PuTTY
cisco@iPerf-Client$ ping -c 10 10.0.0.9
PING 10.0.0.9 (10.0.0.9) 56(84) bytes of data.
64 bytes from 10.0.0.9: icmp_seq=1 ttl=62 time=829 ms
64 bytes from 10.0.0.9: icmp_seq=2 ttl=62 time=973 ms
64 bytes from 10.0.0.9: icmp_seq=3 ttl=62 time=793 ms
64 bytes from 10.0.0.9: icmp_seq=4 ttl=62 time=1103 ms
64 bytes from 10.0.0.9: icmp_seq=5 ttl=62 time=871 ms
64 bytes from 10.0.0.9: icmp_seq=7 ttl=62 time=1140 ms
64 bytes from 10.0.0.9: icmp_seq=8 ttl=62 time=1116 ms
64 bytes from 10.0.0.9: icmp_seq=9 ttl=62 time=913 ms

--- 10.0.0.9 ping statistics ---
10 packets transmitted, 8 received, 20% packet loss, time 9023ms
rtt min/avg/max/mdev = 793.486/967.845/1140.693/128.580 ms, pipe 2
cisco@iPerf-Client$
```

```
172.16.1.133 - PuTTY
cisco@iPerf-Client$ traceroute 10.0.0.9
traceroute to 10.0.0.9 (10.0.0.9), 30 hops max, 60 byte packets
 1  10.0.0.6 (10.0.0.6)  1.618 ms  3.641 ms  5.110 ms
 2  10.0.0.22 (10.0.0.22)  1151.943 ms  1236.472 ms  1029.037 ms
 3  * * 10.0.0.9 (10.0.0.9)  1065.134 ms
cisco@iPerf-Client$
```

Via UWM

Performing the same previous test, we once again view the response time between **iperf-client** and **iperf-server** and the path the packets are taking between them.

172.16.1.133 - PuTTY

```
cisco@iPerf-Client$ ping -c 10 10.0.0.9
PING 10.0.0.9 (10.0.0.9) 56(84) bytes of data.
64 bytes from 10.0.0.9: icmp_seq=1 ttl=62 time=2.83 ms
64 bytes from 10.0.0.9: icmp_seq=2 ttl=62 time=2.14 ms
64 bytes from 10.0.0.9: icmp_seq=3 ttl=62 time=1.68 ms
64 bytes from 10.0.0.9: icmp_seq=4 ttl=62 time=1.63 ms
64 bytes from 10.0.0.9: icmp_seq=5 ttl=62 time=2.01 ms
64 bytes from 10.0.0.9: icmp_seq=6 ttl=62 time=1.82 ms
64 bytes from 10.0.0.9: icmp_seq=7 ttl=62 time=2.14 ms
64 bytes from 10.0.0.9: icmp_seq=8 ttl=62 time=2.36 ms
64 bytes from 10.0.0.9: icmp_seq=9 ttl=62 time=3.36 ms
64 bytes from 10.0.0.9: icmp_seq=10 ttl=62 time=2.73 ms

--- 10.0.0.9 ping statistics ---
10 packets transmitted, 10 received, 0% packet loss, time 9013ms
rtt min/avg/max/mdev = 1.638/2.275/3.361/0.527 ms
cisco@iPerf-Client$
```

172.16.1.133 - PuTTY

```
cisco@iPerf-Client$ traceroute 10.0.0.9
traceroute to 10.0.0.9 (10.0.0.9), 30 hops max, 60 byte packets
 1  10.0.0.6 (10.0.0.6)  2.889 ms  5.462 ms  7.203 ms
 2  10.0.0.22 (10.0.0.22)  4.601 ms  6.447 ms  6.424 ms
 3  10.0.0.9 (10.0.0.9)  3.593 ms  3.600 ms  3.595 ms
cisco@iPerf-Client$
```

Note: If you haven't already done so, remove the icon (link modifications) from the link in VM Maestro.

Login into UWM (https://192.168.1.197/admin) using credentials: guest / guest.

Click on *My simulations* in the left-hand pane. Here I see my simulation:

Click the hyperlink – in my case: *iPerf-2DEODT* – and details about the simulation are displayed.

Scroll down to the **Links** section and click under the **Options** column. Mine happens to be "Link_5".

Just as in VM Maestro, I've modified the link's characteristics, clicked *Apply*, then was shown that the parameter settings were successful.

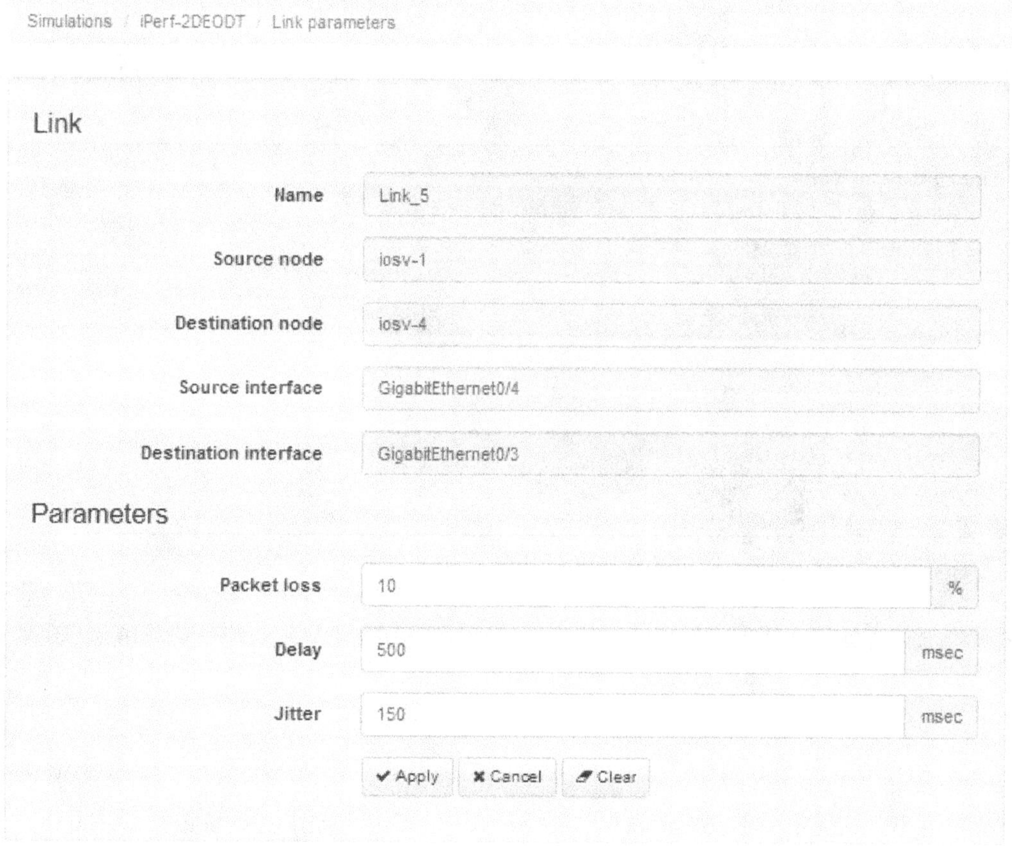

Link_5 link parameters were successfully set

Notice under the **Links** section that "Link_5" displays my modifications.

Link_5	iosv-1	GigabitEthernet0/4	iosv-4	GigabitEthernet0/3	10	500	150

Notice the results after running the ping and traceroute tests again. The ICMP packets took an average time of 981ms, nearly identical to performing the same tests in VM Maestro.

```
172.16.1.133 - PuTTY
cisco@iPerf-Client$ ping -c 10 10.0.0.9
PING 10.0.0.9 (10.0.0.9) 56(84) bytes of data.
64 bytes from 10.0.0.9: icmp_seq=2 ttl=62 time=1047 ms
64 bytes from 10.0.0.9: icmp_seq=3 ttl=62 time=1039 ms
64 bytes from 10.0.0.9: icmp_seq=4 ttl=62 time=994 ms
64 bytes from 10.0.0.9: icmp_seq=5 ttl=62 time=857 ms
64 bytes from 10.0.0.9: icmp_seq=6 ttl=62 time=1002 ms
64 bytes from 10.0.0.9: icmp_seq=7 ttl=62 time=1045 ms
64 bytes from 10.0.0.9: icmp_seq=8 ttl=62 time=921 ms
64 bytes from 10.0.0.9: icmp_seq=9 ttl=62 time=1032 ms
64 bytes from 10.0.0.9: icmp_seq=10 ttl=62 time=891 ms

--- 10.0.0.9 ping statistics ---
10 packets transmitted, 9 received, 10% packet loss, time 9011ms
rtt min/avg/max/mdev = 857.200/981.364/1047.189/68.356 ms, pipe 2
cisco@iPerf-Client$
```

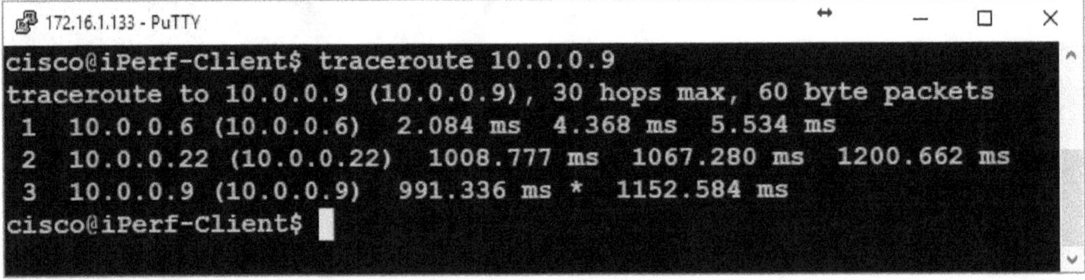

```
172.16.1.133 - PuTTY
cisco@iPerf-Client$ traceroute 10.0.0.9
traceroute to 10.0.0.9 (10.0.0.9), 30 hops max, 60 byte packets
 1  10.0.0.6 (10.0.0.6)  2.084 ms  4.368 ms  5.534 ms
 2  10.0.0.22 (10.0.0.22)  1008.777 ms  1067.280 ms  1200.662 ms
 3  10.0.0.9 (10.0.0.9)  991.336 ms *  1152.584 ms
cisco@iPerf-Client$
```

Via Live Visualization

Once again, performing the same tests in VM Maestro and UWM, we once again view the response time between **iperf-client** and **iperf-server** and the path the packets are taking between them.

```
172.16.1.133 - PuTTY
cisco@iPerf-Client$ ping -c 10 10.0.0.9
PING 10.0.0.9 (10.0.0.9) 56(84) bytes of data.
64 bytes from 10.0.0.9: icmp_seq=1 ttl=62 time=2.83 ms
64 bytes from 10.0.0.9: icmp_seq=2 ttl=62 time=2.14 ms
64 bytes from 10.0.0.9: icmp_seq=3 ttl=62 time=1.68 ms
64 bytes from 10.0.0.9: icmp_seq=4 ttl=62 time=1.63 ms
64 bytes from 10.0.0.9: icmp_seq=5 ttl=62 time=2.01 ms
64 bytes from 10.0.0.9: icmp_seq=6 ttl=62 time=1.82 ms
64 bytes from 10.0.0.9: icmp_seq=7 ttl=62 time=2.14 ms
64 bytes from 10.0.0.9: icmp_seq=8 ttl=62 time=2.36 ms
64 bytes from 10.0.0.9: icmp_seq=9 ttl=62 time=3.36 ms
64 bytes from 10.0.0.9: icmp_seq=10 ttl=62 time=2.73 ms

--- 10.0.0.9 ping statistics ---
10 packets transmitted, 10 received, 0% packet loss, time 9013ms
rtt min/avg/max/mdev = 1.638/2.275/3.361/0.527 ms
cisco@iPerf-Client$
```

```
172.16.1.133 - PuTTY
cisco@iPerf-Client$ traceroute 10.0.0.9
traceroute to 10.0.0.9 (10.0.0.9), 30 hops max, 60 byte packets
 1  10.0.0.6 (10.0.0.6)  2.889 ms  5.462 ms  7.203 ms
 2  10.0.0.22 (10.0.0.22)  4.601 ms  6.447 ms  6.424 ms
 3  10.0.0.9 (10.0.0.9)  3.593 ms  3.600 ms  3.595 ms
cisco@iPerf-Client$
```

Note: If you haven't already done so, click the under the **Links** section | **Options** column and remove your link modifications by clicking the Clear, the clicking *Apply.*

You should see: Link_5 link parameters were successfully set and you can also verify the parameters are gone by looking at the link under the **Links** section.

Now there are several ways we can launch the *Live Visualization*, so we'll do it as we have before.

From VM Maestro – with my topology running – I right-clicked on an empty area in topology pane and chose *Launch Live Visualization.*

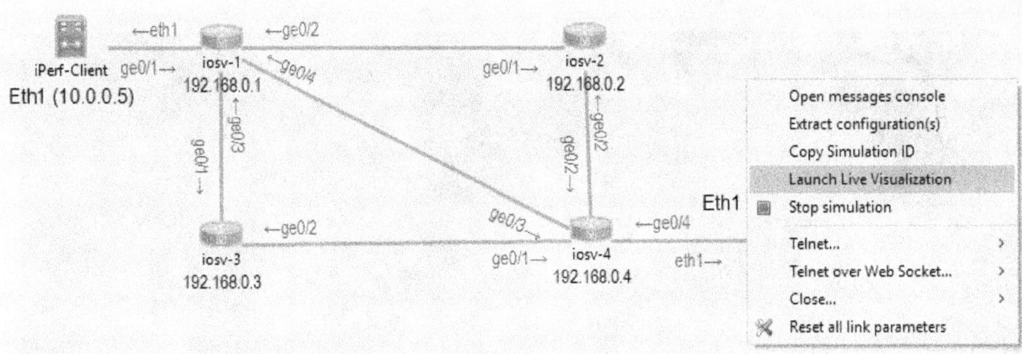

If needed, enter credentials: guest / guest, when prompted. You'll then see your topology in UWM.

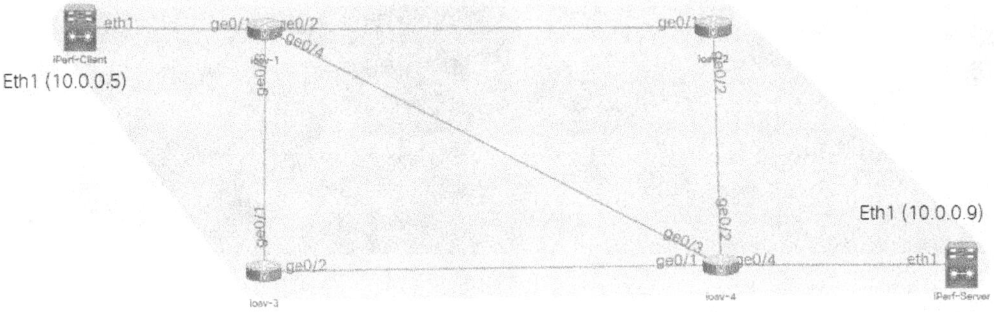

Left-click on the link, add the same modifications and click *Submit.*

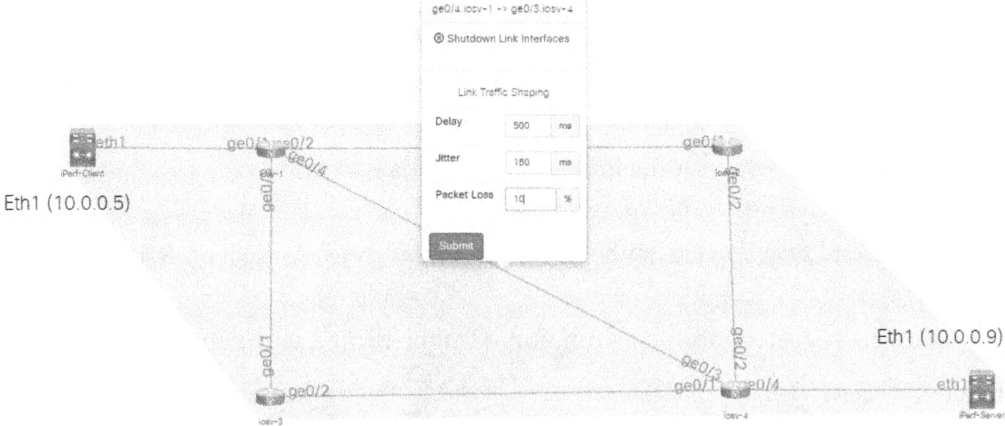

You'll see messages similar to these:

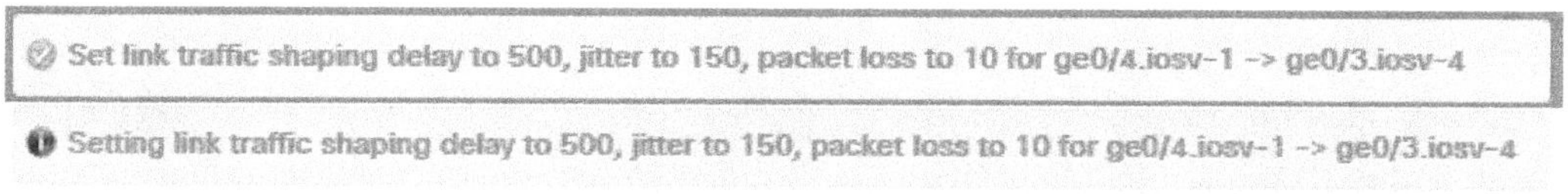

Set link traffic shaping delay to 500, jitter to 150, packet loss to 10 for ge0/4.iosv-1 -> ge0/3.iosv-4

Setting link traffic shaping delay to 500, jitter to 150, packet loss to 10 for ge0/4.iosv-1 -> ge0/3.iosv-4

Notice the results after running the ping and traceroute tests again. The ICMP packets took an average time of 1002ms – a bit longer than previously – but nevertheless nearly identical to performing the same tests in UWM and VM Maestro.

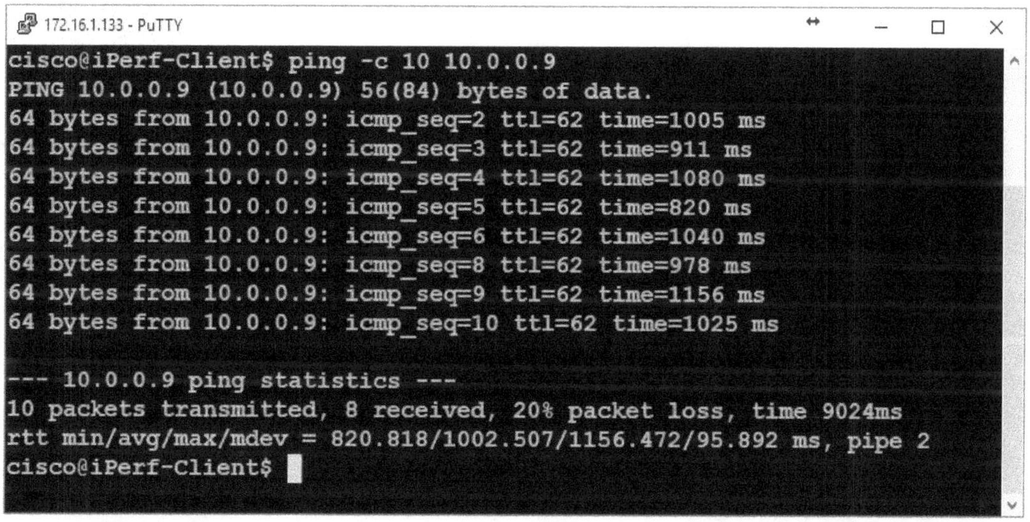

172.16.1.133 - PuTTY

```
cisco@iPerf-Client$ ping -c 10 10.0.0.9
PING 10.0.0.9 (10.0.0.9) 56(84) bytes of data.
64 bytes from 10.0.0.9: icmp_seq=2 ttl=62 time=1005 ms
64 bytes from 10.0.0.9: icmp_seq=3 ttl=62 time=911 ms
64 bytes from 10.0.0.9: icmp_seq=4 ttl=62 time=1080 ms
64 bytes from 10.0.0.9: icmp_seq=5 ttl=62 time=820 ms
64 bytes from 10.0.0.9: icmp_seq=6 ttl=62 time=1040 ms
64 bytes from 10.0.0.9: icmp_seq=8 ttl=62 time=978 ms
64 bytes from 10.0.0.9: icmp_seq=9 ttl=62 time=1156 ms
64 bytes from 10.0.0.9: icmp_seq=10 ttl=62 time=1025 ms

--- 10.0.0.9 ping statistics ---
10 packets transmitted, 8 received, 20% packet loss, time 9024ms
rtt min/avg/max/mdev = 820.818/1002.507/1156.472/95.892 ms, pipe 2
cisco@iPerf-Client$
```

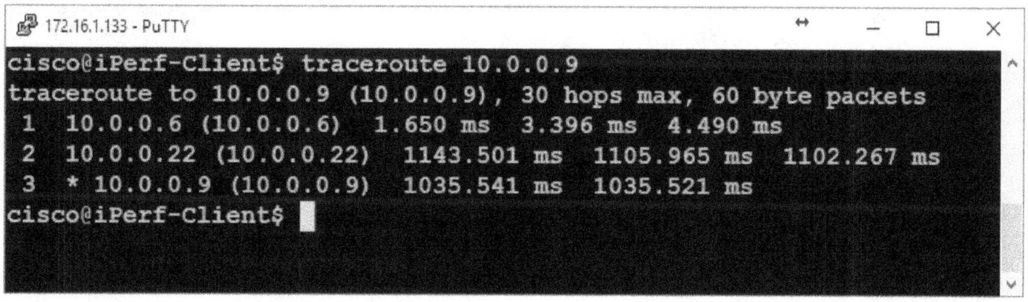

172.16.1.133 - PuTTY

```
cisco@iPerf-Client$ traceroute 10.0.0.9
traceroute to 10.0.0.9 (10.0.0.9), 30 hops max, 60 byte packets
 1  10.0.0.6 (10.0.0.6)  1.650 ms  3.396 ms  4.490 ms
 2  10.0.0.22 (10.0.0.22)  1143.501 ms  1105.965 ms  1102.267 ms
 3  * 10.0.0.9 (10.0.0.9)  1035.541 ms  1035.521 ms
cisco@iPerf-Client$
```

3rd Party VM – Palo Alto

You'll need to establish an account at https://paloaltonetworks.com in order to obtain the VM image. My account was established through my company since we have these Palo Alto firewalls under support. You can inquire about an account here:

https://live.paloaltonetworks.com/t5/Support-Articles/How-to-Create-Your-User-Account/ta-p/57494

Once you've logged into https://support.paloaltonetworks.com/Support/Index, navigate to *Software Updates* under *Tools* and look for images whose names are PA-VM-KVM-<version>.qcow2. I downloaded the one shown. The PDF is useful to learn about changes and features introduced in this version.

PAN-OS for VM-Series KVM Base Images

8.1.0 03/03/2018 PAN-OS_8.1.0_RN.pdf PA-VM-KVM-8.1.0.qcow2 2.1 GB Checksum

Put the image to the side for a moment.

Login to VIRL's UWM (http://192.168.1.197/login/) with credentials: uwmadmin / password

and navigate in the left pane to *Node resources* | *Subtypes*. Click  Import dynamic subtypes and type the following text into the import pane window:

```
{
 "dynamic-subtypes": [
 {
 "hw_vcpus": 2,
 "plugin_desc": "Palo Alto Firewall",
 "cli_serial": 1,
 "plugin_name": "Palo_Alto",
 "gui_visible": true,
 "interface_range": 24,
 "interface_pattern": "Ethernet1/{0}",
 "hw_disk_bus": "virtio",
 "baseline_flavor": "",
 "hw_vm_extra": "",
 "hw_ram": 4096,
 "gui_icon": "firewall",
 "interface_first": 1,
 "config_file": "/bootstrap-networkconfig.xml",
 "hw_vif_model": "virtio",
 "interface_management": "mgt",
 "baseline_image": "",
 "plugin_base": "generic"
 }
 ]
}
```

Now Click ✔ Import dynamic subtypes. You should see:

Subtype "Palo_Alto" successfully imported ×

Followed by the newly created Palo_Alto entry:

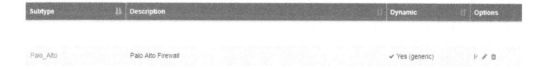

Under the **Options** column click the (modify) link and change the following:

- Change Protocol for network CLI to *ssh*.
- Check the **Require HW acceleration in kvm** box. This helps to speed up the boot process of the VM since a Palo VM can take some time to come up.

Scroll to the bottom of the screen and click *Save*. This allows us the ability to directly open a terminal (PuTTY) session from our Win10 workstation to this node.

Now import the actual image by navigating to *Node resources* | *Images* and click Add in the "Images" section. If you downloaded the same image that I did, fill out the version and release fields as I have – if not, put in your version number – also modify the source of your image file.

Owning project uwmadmin

Project specific

Subtype Palo_Alto

Name/Version Palo_Alto- 8.1.0

Release 8.1.0

Source
File on server
URL
Local image file

Image File Browse... No file selected.

The required default values will be supplied by the subtype. Please, DO NOT edit Properties, unless you know that the image does not match known defaults.

Meaningful properties to define here are *hw_vif_model* and *hw_disk_bus*
hw_vif_model: VM image property for compute's VIF configuration
hw_disk_bus: VM image property for compute's disks handling

Properties hw_vif_model = e1000

Click *Browse…* and navigate to where you stored the Palo Alto VM image. Select it then click *Open*.

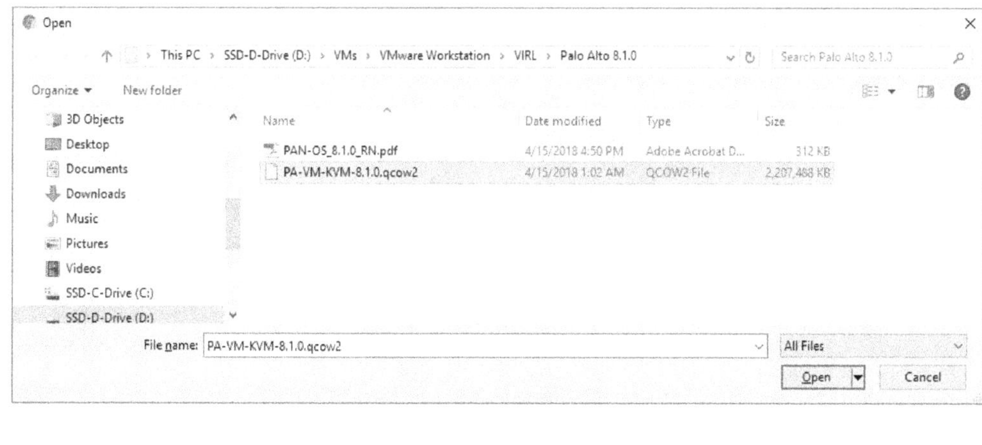

Click ✔ Create.

After about 1 ½ minutes the image was imported and created.

Open VM Maestro and navigate to *File | Preferences | Node Subtypes.* Scroll down to the bottom of this subtype list and click *Fetch from Server*, then click *OK*. Congratulations, you should now see your Palo_Alto subtype. Click *Apply*, then *OK*.

You may want to re-click on some or all subtype entries due to the fact that some – under the *Show in Palette* column – had their entry changed back to **false**. If you don't they won't continue to show up in VM Maestro's Nodes pane. Then click *Apply* and *OK*.

Now put a single Palo Alto node into the Topology Editor pane. Click on any empty area within this window and under the **Properties** tab, choose ***Shared flat network***. I did this so that my Windows 10 workstation can directly ping and/or SSH into the Palo Alto (see the FLAT OOB Management Access section).

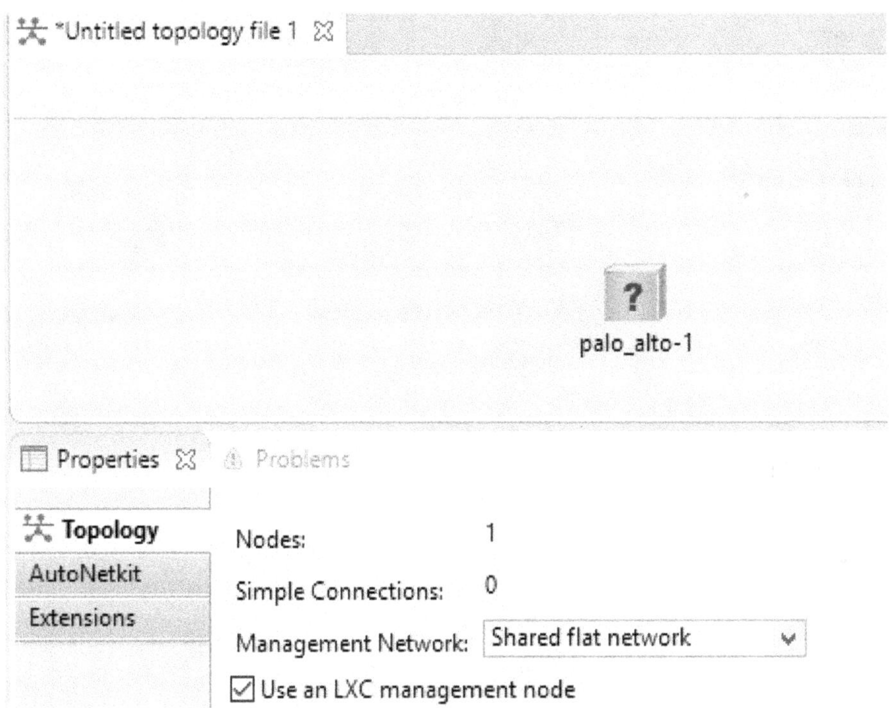

Now click on the **palo_alto-1** node and under its **Properties | Node** tab you will fill in the *VM Image* and *VM Flavor* fields by clicking the respective *Browse…* buttons and choosing the **Palo_Alto-8.1.0** selection we created earlier.

VM Image: Palo_Alto-8.1.0 [279b9a6b-7b24-460e-8e06-3e5b0f951e77] Browse...

VM Flavor: Palo_Alto [eae308e5-b378-4ae8-b68d-b9b8da0a6967] Browse...

By the way, notice that the **VM Image's** number [in brackets] corresponds to the **OpenStack ID** number, shown earlier when we created the image. Since there is only 1 image per subtype, this number never changes unless you remove it and reinstall/import same. The **VM Flavor's** number [in brackets] corresponds to the **OpenStack ID** number shown under *Node resources | Flavors | Palo Alto.*

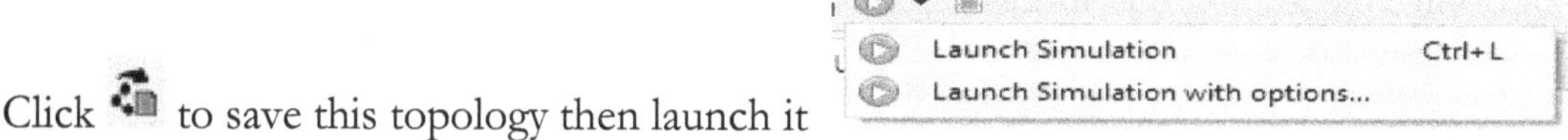

Click to save this topology then launch it

Once the node shows that it's reachable, console into it.

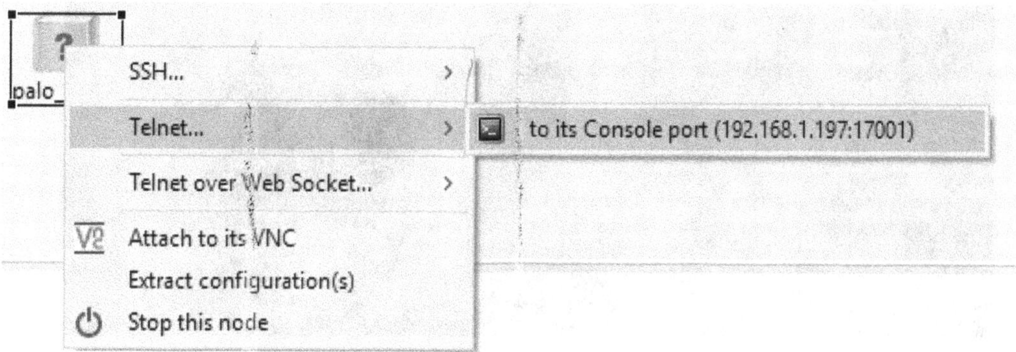

If you're presented with the **"PA-HDF login:"** prompt you need to close the console session and try again because the image is still booting. When the prompt displays **"PA-VM login:"** you're ready to login with credentials: admin / admin.

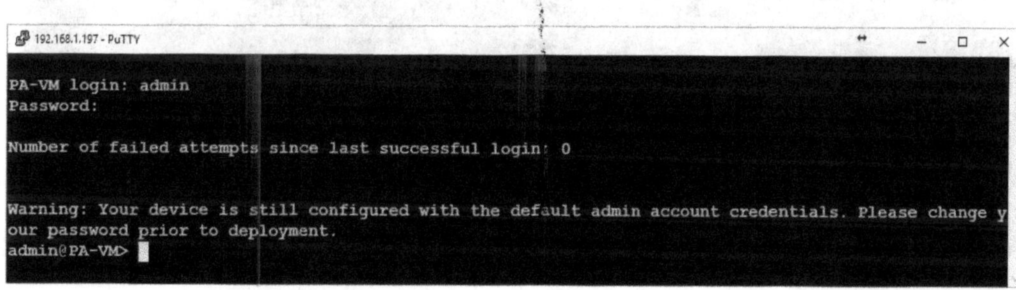

Here I verified what my Palo Alto's management IP address is.

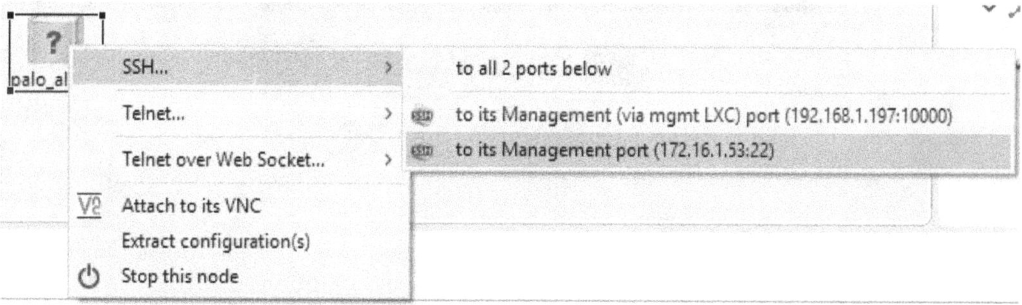

I was not only able to ping this address…

```
Command Prompt

C:\>ping 172.16.1.53

Pinging 172.16.1.53 with 32 bytes of data:
Reply from 172.16.1.53: bytes=32 time<1ms TTL=64
Reply from 172.16.1.53: bytes=32 time<1ms TTL=64
Reply from 172.16.1.53: bytes=32 time<1ms TTL=64
Reply from 172.16.1.53: bytes=32 time<1ms TTL=64

Ping statistics for 172.16.1.53:
    Packets: Sent = 4, Received = 4, Lost = 0 (0% loss),
Approximate round trip times in milli-seconds:
    Minimum = 0ms, Maximum = 0ms, Average = 0ms

C:\>
```

I was also able to SSH into as well.

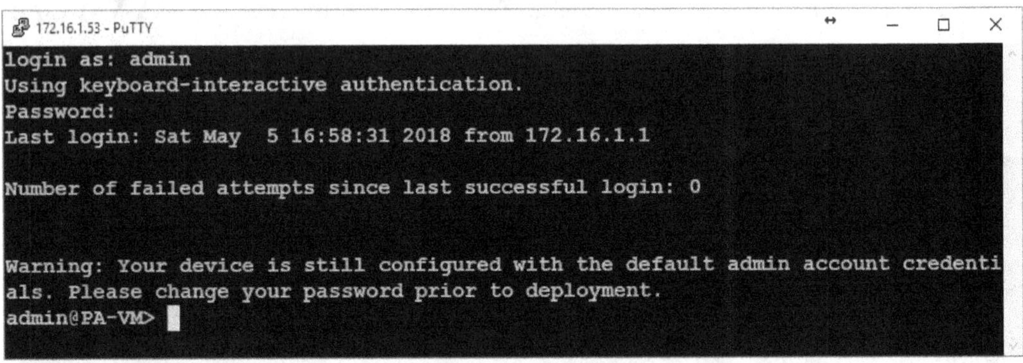

And lastly, I connected to the Palo's GUI.

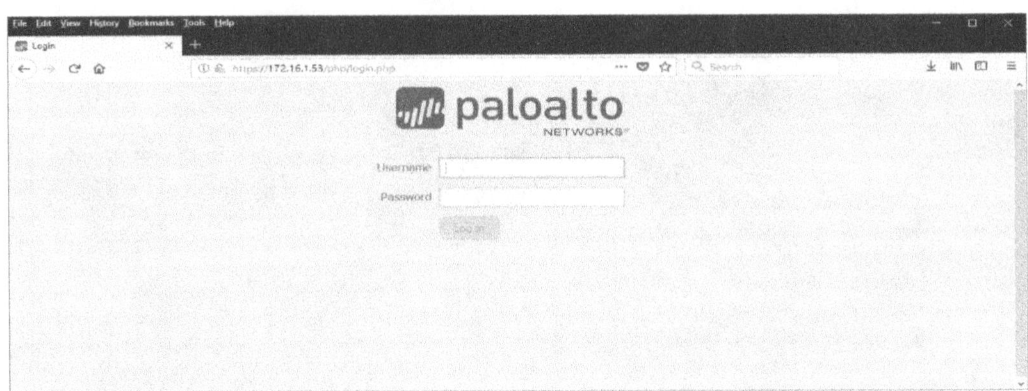

CHAPTER 12: Best Practices

All-in-all I created small labs to demonstrate various features available in VM Maestro, UWM and the add-on software and although there are many more features in this software suite that I haven't covered; let me assure you that the ones referenced are the most useful and widely used. So instead of ending this guide with a grandioso lab encompassing every feature detailed thus far; let me instead remind you of some of the best practices in using this software.

Increasing Memory for Large Simulations

You attempt to run a simulation and are presented with the following error message: Launch aborted as the RAM requirement for the simulation (xxxx MB) exceeds total virtual memory on the host machine available for simulations (xxxx MB). To remedy this, login to UWM as uwmadmin, click VIRL Server | System Configuration | Hardware and increase the RAM Overcommit Multiplier by multiples of 2 until the error is no longer presented.

External Connectivity Recommendation

Use separate, additional NICs for FLAT1 or SNAT connectivity: you can then use your VMware host's primary NIC for Internet access or to access this host via an OpenVPN connection.

Manual vs Automatic Network Configuration

Use AutoNetkit (see Chapter 7): at least initially to build your topology's L3 configuration until you're more comfortable doing it yourself. It does save you a lot of time in getting a topology up and running quickly.

Verifying Backend Services Running

Every time you open VM Maestro check the backend connection services: *File* | *Preferences* | *Web Services* - see Chapter 7.

Making Subtypes Available

If/When you upgrade your VIRL image, re-download the subtypes available: *File* | *Preferences* | *Node Subtypes* – see Chapter 7.

Saving Your Work

There are several ways to save your topology; depending on the context you're in.

During the design phase (before the simulation is started)

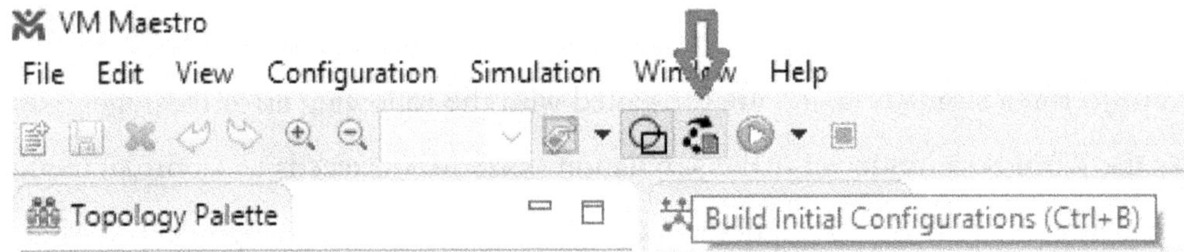

- During a live simulation by right clicking a node. You can do this for each node.

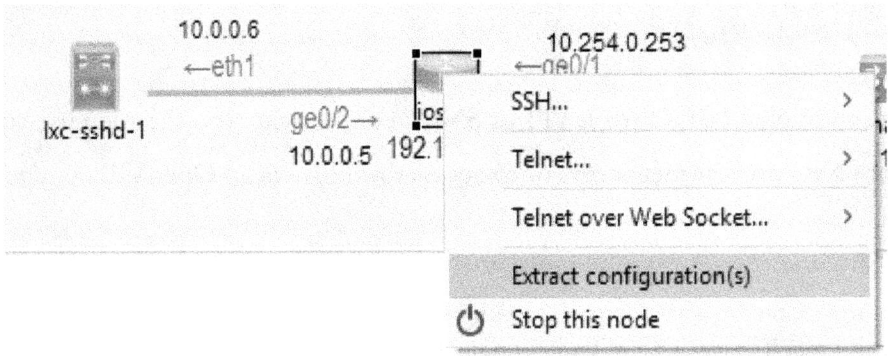

  - When shutting down a simulation, you choose to extra the configurations as shown:

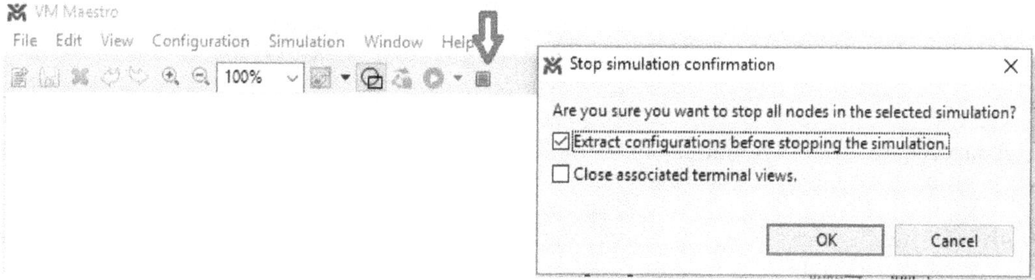

Internal vs External Terminal Session

Use an external terminal emulator (i.e., PuTTY) – as mentioned in Chapter 6. This provides more flexibility connecting to nodes rather than having to depend on using VM Maestro and its built-in terminal.

Don't have a QCOW2, man?!

Some vendors (i.e., https://www.arista.com/en/) do not have .qcow2 VIRL images for their products; as such you cannot add them as a subtype node inside of VIRL. An alternative is to use their VM image that works directly with VMware Workstation. Simply click *edit virtual machine settings* and choose the network adapter that's on the same L2 adjacent network as your simulation. For example, in our *FLAT1 (L2) External Access* section I showed you how to connect physical external devices to your lab. Here you're doing the same thing except you're connecting a logical L2 device to your VIRL simulation by use of VMware's VMnet2 interface.

Appendix A: Subtype Definitions

ASAv: Adaptive Security Appliance (firewall).

CSR1000v: (Cloud Services Router) heavyweight IOS-XE WAN router similar to CSR1000 with Cloud services.

CoreOS: actually part of the Docker support feature

Docker: a tool designed to make it easier to create, deploy, and run applications by using containers. A good example is from a previous webinar: Docker on VIRL - Integrated Docker containers into your VIRL topologies - YouTube in which Docker CoreOS Apache servers are used as part of the network simulation, allowing the user to simulate "wget" functions.

Generic: Windows XP image (https://ciscoskills.net/2017/01/07/cisco-virl-and-windows-vms/)

IOL: IOS on Linux

IOL-L2: L2 switch similar to a Catalyst 2950 or 2960.

IOS XRv: Service Provider, high-end grade, IOS-XR router similar to the 12000 or ASR9000. Supports MPLS features (L2VPN, L3VPN, mGRE, Traffic Engineering).

IOS XRv 9000: 9000 series of IOS XRv.

IOS XRv64: 64-bit successor of the 32-bit IOS XRv.

IOSv: lightweight IOS router

IOSvL2: lightweight IOS L2 switch

Kali: a tool set for advanced penetration testing and finding vulnerabilities in network systems.

Lxc: lightweight Linux container.

Lxc-iperf: Linux container that has iPerf baked in.

Lxc-ostinato-drone: Linux container with packet traffic generation baked in.

Lxc-routem: Linux container with route injection baked in.

Lxc-sshd: Lightweight Linux container SSH server.

NX-OSv: Nexus data center switch that supports L2 and L3 Nexus specific features; as well as MDS-series Fiber Channel SAN switch features.

NX-OSv 9000: similar to NX-OSv but with more advanced features.

Security-onion: for intrusion detection, network security monitoring, and log management.

Server: Ubuntu VM, replaced with LXC.

Server_unmanaged: standard VM, replaced with LXC.

StarOS: Cisco's dCloud, Evolved Packet Core network, providing MME, SGSN, SGW, PGW and GGSN functionality.

Unmanaged Switch: virtual switch similar to GNS3's virtual switch. Just provides connections between devices.

VPP: an open-source project installed as part of the VM creation

VSRX: Juniper JunOS image

Vyatta: a 3rd party VM Router

Appendix B: URL Resources

- Cisco's VIRL YouTube Channel: https://www.youtube.com/CiscoVIRL
- 3rd Party VMs for VIRL: https://learningnetwork.cisco.com/docs/DOC-30476
- Cisco Lab External Connectivity: https://www.cisco.com/c/en/us/td/docs/cloud_services/cisco_modeling_labs/v100/configuration/guide/b_cml_user_guide/b_cml_user_guide_chapter_0111.pdf
- Cisco IOS XRv 9000 Router Data Sheet: https://www.cisco.com/c/en/us/products/collateral/routers/asr-9000-series-aggregation-services-routers/datasheet-c78-734034.html
- Cisco VIRL Clustering: http://get.virl.info/pre.req.cluster.php
- Cisco VIRL Features: https://learningnetworkstore.cisco.com/virlfaq/features
- Docker: https://coreos.com/os/docs/latest/getting-started-with-docker.html
- Docker on VIRL: https://www.youtube.com/watch?v=ZhzQSSdAuUE&feature=youtu.be&a=
- Docker Hub Repository: https://hub.docker.com/
- Kali Linux in VIRL: https://learningnetwork.cisco.com/docs/DOC-30427
- MPLS OAM: https://www.cisco.com/c/en/us/td/docs/routers/asr9000/software/asr9k_r4-2/mpls/configuration/guide/b_mpls_cg42asr9k/b_mpls_cg42asr9k_chapter_0101.html
- Ostinato (Network Traffic Generator and Analyzer): https://ostinato.org/
- Security Onion on VIRL: https://learningnetwork.cisco.com/docs/DOC-30431
- User Workspace Management (UWM) Interface: http://192.168.1.197/doc/uwm_server.html?highlight=uwm#

www.ingramcontent.com/pod-product-compliance
Lightning Source LLC
Chambersburg PA
CBHW080555060326
40689CB00021B/4858

9780692105887